## *Economic Ideas in Political Time*

Over the past century, the rise and fall of economic policy orders have been shaped by a paradox, as intellectual and institutional stability have repeatedly caused market instability and crisis. To highlight such dynamics, this volume offers a theory of *Economic Ideas in Political Time*. The author counters paradigmatic and institutionalist views of ideas as enabling self-reinforcing path dependencies, offering an alternative social psychological argument that ideas which *initially* reduce uncertainty can *subsequently* fuel misplaced certainty and crises. Historically, the book then traces the development and decline of the Progressive, Keynesian, and Neoliberal orders, arguing that each order's principled foundations were gradually displaced by macroeconomic models that obscured new causes of the Great Depression, Great Stagflation, and Global Financial Crisis. Finally, in policy terms, Widmaier stresses the costs of intellectual autonomy, as efforts to "prevent the last crisis" have repeatedly obscured new causes of crises.

WESLEY W. WIDMAIER is an associate professor of Political Science at Griffith University, in Brisbane, Australia, where he has advanced parallel research agendas into the construction of economic crises and wars as mechanisms which drive large-scale change. Over the past decade, his research has been published in such journals as *International Studies Quarterly, Review of International Political Economy, New Political Economy, Review of International Studies*, and *the European Journal of International Relations*. Dr. Widmaier served as 2014 Program Chair and 2015 Section Chair of the International Political Economy Section of the International Studies Association, and is Lead Editor of *Review of International Political Economy*.

**Advance Praise for *Economic Ideas in Political Time***

"One of the rediscovered wisdoms of the financial crisis was Hyman Minsky's line that 'stability breeds instability.' The line was good, but the puzzle was why that should be the case? Minsky's answer was the growth of Ponzi finance. Wes Widmaier gives us another: that periods of institutional construction marked by a politics of principle inevitably give way to a politics of technocratic maintenance that mistakes stability in models for stability in the world. These disjunctures in political time, between models and the world, generate regime-changing crises. Minsky has just been given political microfoundations."

Mark Blyth, Eastman Professor of Political Economy, Brown University

# Economic Ideas in Political Time

The Rise and Fall of Economic Orders from the Progressive Era to the Global Financial Crisis

WESLEY W. WIDMAIER

*Griffith University, Queensland*

# CAMBRIDGE
UNIVERSITY PRESS

University Printing House, Cambridge CB2 8BS, United Kingdom

Cambridge University Press is part of the University of Cambridge.

It furthers the University's mission by disseminating knowledge in the pursuit of education, learning, and research at the highest international levels of excellence.

www.cambridge.org
Information on this title: www.cambridge.org/9781316604571

© Wesley W. Widmaier, 2016

This publication is in copyright. Subject to statutory exception and to the provisions of relevant collective licensing agreements, no reproduction of any part may take place without the written permission of Cambridge University Press.

First published 2016

*A catalogue record for this publication is available from the British Library.*

Library of Congress Cataloging-in-Publication Data
Names: Widmaier, Wesley, author.
Title: Economic ideas in political time: the rise and fall of economic orders from the progressive era to the global financial crisis / Wesley W. Widmaier.
Description: New York: Cambridge University Press, 2016. |
Includes bibliographical references and index.
Identifiers: LCCN 2016010904 | ISBN 9781107150317 (hardback) |
ISBN 9781316604571 (paperback)
Subjects: LCSH: Economic history. | Economic policy. |
Economic development. | Global Financial Crisis, 2008–2009. |
BISAC: POLITICAL SCIENCE / Economic Conditions.
Classification: LCC HC21.W53 2016 | DDC 330.1–dc23
LC record available at https://lccn.loc.gov/2016010904

ISBN 978-1-107-15031-7 Hardback
ISBN 978-1-316-60457-1 Paperback

Cambridge University Press has no responsibility for the persistence or accuracy of URLs for external or third-party Internet Web sites referred to in this publication and does not guarantee that any content on such Web sites is, or will remain, accurate or appropriate.

# Contents

| | |
|---|---|
| Preface | *page* vii |
| Acknowledgments | xi |

### Part I  Theoretical and Historical Foundations

| | | |
|---|---|---|
| 1 | Economic Ideas in Political Time: Construction, Conversion, and Crisis | 3 |
| 2 | The Construction, Conversion, and Collapse of the Progressive Order | 29 |

### Part II  The Construction, Conversion, and Collapse of the Keynesian Order

| | | |
|---|---|---|
| 3 | Constructing the Keynesian Order: Breaking Finance and Boosting Labor | 51 |
| 4 | Converting the Keynesian Order: Toward the Neoclassical Synthesis | 77 |
| 5 | Constructing the Great Stagflation: From Accommodation to Transformation | 109 |

### Part III  The Construction, Conversion, and Crisis of the Neoliberal Order

| | | |
|---|---|---|
| 6 | Constructing the Neoliberal Order: Breaking Labor and Boosting Finance | 135 |
| 7 | Converting the Neoliberal Order: Toward the New Keynesianism | 157 |

| 8 | Constructing the Global Financial Crisis: From Accommodation to Iteration | 179 |

**Part IV  Conclusions**

| 9 | Theoretical, Historical, and Policy Implications | 205 |

| *Bibliography* | 213 |
| *Index* | 241 |

# *Preface*

Just as generals are often criticized for "fighting the last war," economic policymakers often remain focused on "preventing the last crisis." Consider that in June 2008, just three months before the collapse of Lehman Brothers and onset of the Global Financial Crisis, Federal Reserve Chairman Ben Bernanke raised alarms regarding a possible revival of 1970s-styled stagflation – in which rising oil prices could fuel a renewed wage-price spiral. Testifying before the Senate Committee on Banking, Housing, and Urban Affairs, Bernanke warned of an "increase in upside inflation risk" and expressed concerns that "inflationary impulses from commodity prices are becoming embedded in the domestic wage- and price-setting process."[1] Such concerns for wage-price pressures reflected the Federal Reserve's continued reliance on models that stressed the interplay of unemployment and inflation, while obscuring the concentrations of financial market power and speculative dynamics that would bring on the Global Financial Crisis.[2] Nevertheless, Bernanke would later argue that nothing had been wrong with prevailing models – they simply had not been designed to prevent financial crises. Looking back, Bernanke would concede that "standard macroeconomic models ... did not predict the

---

[1] Bernanke (2008b).
[2] Echoing the 1960s Phillips curve, which charts an unemployment-inflation trade-off, the 1990s witnessed the rise of a Taylor rule, which balanced concerns for growth and inflation in devising a rule governing interest rate targets. On the Phillips curve, see Samuelson and Solow (1960); on the Taylor rule, see Taylor (1993; 2009); on links between the Phillips curve and Taylor rule, see Koenig, Leeson, and Kahn (2012); and on the policy relevance of the Taylor rule, see Greenspan (2004a) and Yellen (1996; 2012). For an analysis that stresses the need to apply the rule with discretion, see Bernanke (2015). Significantly, just ten days after Bernanke's July 2008 testimony, Federal Open Market Committee (FOMC) (2008a, 111) deliberations would see Taylor rule arguments used by FOMC member Janet Yellen as a justification for considering a shift toward raising interest rates.

crisis, nor did they incorporate very easily the effects of financial instability." Indeed, posing the question of whether "these failures of standard macroeconomic models mean that they are irrelevant or at least significantly flawed," Bernanke offered "a qualified no," arguing that

> economic models are useful only in the context for which they are designed. Most of the time, including during recessions, serious financial instability is not an issue. The standard models were designed for these non-crisis periods, and they have proven quite useful in that context.

Despite their flaws, Bernanke accordingly lauded such models for having "helped deliver low inflation and macroeconomic stability ... during the two decades that began in the mid-1980s."[3]

In advancing such claims, Bernanke can be seen as evincing the main argument of this book – that ideas which *initially* reduce uncertainty and enable stability can *subsequently* fuel misplaced certainty, instability, and renewed crisis. In the case of the Global Financial Crisis, ideas stressing the potential reemergence of the long-vanquished wage-price spirals of the 1970s obscured the asset-price instability that had brought the economy to the brink of collapse. Yet, such dysfunctional dynamics have been obscured where Political Economy debates have been premised on rationalist assumptions that agents use information efficiently – in ways that have led scholars to overrate the scope for self-sustaining stability and to underrate the inefficiencies that can fuel self-reinforcing instability and crisis.[4]

In this volume, I redress such oversights by offering a "social psychological institutionalist" model, one which assumes that even as economic ideas can initially limit uncertainty and enhance stability, agents

---

[3] Speaking to this stress on macroeconomic variables, George W. Bush (2010, 453) would recall being "surprised by the sudden crisis. My focus had been kitchen-table economic issues like jobs and inflation. I assumed any major credit troubles would have been flagged by the regulators or rating agencies." Echoing Bernanke in heralding prevailing models, Paul Krugman would laud an "MIT style" that entails the "use of small models applied to real problems, blending real-world observation and a little mathematics to cut through to the core of the issue" (Miller and Ryan, 2012). Put simply, one might argue that Bernanke and Krugman effectively reduce the scope for economic policy debate to what can be fit within macroeconomic models. Quote in text from Bernanke (2010c).

[4] On policy orders – broadly defined as sets of ideas, institutions, and interests – see Skowronek (1993; 2011); on rationalist assumptions regarding efficiency in the use of information, see Fearon and Wendt (2002).

can also refine such ideas in ways that engender a misplaced certainty, instability, and renewed crises.[5] Developing a staged model, I argue first that the *principled construction* of economic policy orders often sees interpretive leaders issue value-laden appeals for regulatory restraints on market power and speculative abuses. Second, I argue that where these efforts succeed, the resulting stability can ironically enable the *intellectual conversion* of principled restraints into Bernanke-styled "standard models" that guide fiscal or monetary fine-tuning. Finally, I argue that as such refined models fuel *misplaced certainty* regarding policy effectiveness, they can obscure new sources of market power and speculative excess that culminate in crises. Having developed this approach, I apply it to offer insight into economic policy development over the past century – distinguishing Progressive, Keynesian, and Neoliberal orders, as each saw stability yield to instability in ways that brought on the Great Depression, Great Stagflation, and Global Financial Crisis. The result is to highlight a recurring paradox, as stability causes instability – and efforts at "preventing the last crisis" help to bring on the next one.

---

[5] On constructivism, see Best (2005; 2008) and Blyth (2002); on discursive institutionalism, see Schmidt (2008; 2010); for social psychological insights into fast and slow thinking across time, see Kahneman (2011).

# Acknowledgments

No book is truly a solo project, and I owe a range of intellectual debts to colleagues who have provided key insights. These include David V. Edwards, James Galbraith, Alexander Wendt, Jacqueline Best, Andrew Baker, Mlada Bukovansky, Rawi Abdelal, Jeff Chwieroth, Colin Hay, Rodney Bruce Hall, Eric Helleiner, David Andrews, Vivien Schmidt, John Ravenhill, Juliet Johnson, Cornell Ban, Ben Clift, Andrew Ross, Oddny Helgadottir, Robert H. Cox, Martin Carstensen, Daniel Mügge, Matthias Matthijs, Manuela Moschella, Orfeo Fioretos, Kate Weaver, Susan Park, Charlotte Epstein, Jason Sharman, Jarrod Hayes, Ian Hall, Renee Jeffrey, Juan Wang, Luke Glanville, Sara Davies, Jacquie True, Juanita Elias, Stephen Bell, Steven Feng, Frank Smith, Dennis Grube, Alex Bellamy, Patrick Weller, Haig Patapan, Giorel Curran, Elizabeth Van Acker, John Kane, Cosmo Howard, Yi-Chong Xu, John Parkinson, Shannon Brincat, Duncan McDonnell, Luis Cabrera, and Andrew O'Neil, as well as participants in seminars at the Griffith Asia Institute and Griffith Centre for Governance and Public Policy. One of the earliest iterations of this project came in a seminar through the "Warwick Manuscript Development" (WMD) initiative led by Leonard Seabrooke – who offered feedback on the entire manuscript. For their insights at this WMD seminar, I also owe thanks to James Brassett, Lorraine Elliott, Lena Rethel, and Eleni Tsingou. Finally, like anyone working in the field of Political Economy, I owe thanks to Mark Blyth – for having advanced debate and for his insights regarding this project. For financial support, I owe thanks to the Griffith Asia Institute and the Griffith Centre for Governance and Public Policy, as well as the John F. Kennedy and Lyndon B. Johnson Presidential libraries, and the Australian Research Council for ARC Discovery Project grant DP130104088, with Dr. Richard Eccleston and ARC Future Fellowship FT100100833. Finally, I owe a huge debt of gratitude to John Haslam, Carrie Parkinson, and Ian McIver, my editors at Cambridge, whose support and insights have been crucial to the development of this project.

On a personal note, I owe some special expressions of love and gratitude: first, to Declan and Daisy, and Henrietta, Abbey, Gigi, and Maynard – two dogs and four cats – Michelle and I miss you all. Second, I could not have written this book without the love and motivation of my three beautiful daughters, Chloe, Brynn, and Scarlett – and I now look forward to spending much more time with each of them. Finally, I owe my greatest thanks and love to my wife, Michelle, who followed me half way around the world. Without her love and support, I could not have finished this book, and so I dedicate it to her – as I have been, and always shall be, hers.

# PART I

*Theoretical and Historical Foundations*

# 1 Economic Ideas in Political Time: Construction, Conversion, and Crisis

## 1.1 Introduction: The Problem and Argument

Economic policy is marked by a recurring paradox: stability and order often lead to instability and crisis. Consider the United States over the past century, as it has been marked by shifts from the recurring construction of economic policy orders – or sets of ideas, institutions, and interests – to their collapse in moments of instability and crisis.[1] Over the foundational Progressive era, through the rise of mid-century Keynesianism, and to the more recent Neoliberal era, regulatory frameworks that initially restrained abuses of market power and speculative excesses have repeatedly eroded, as deregulation and overconfidence in macroeconomic fine-tuning have enabled the reemergence of market power, speculation, and crises. First, while the Progressive order enabled the construction of basic macroeconomic institutions such as the Federal Reserve, it would collapse as overconfidence in monetary fine-tuning fueled the bull market of the 1920s, the Great Crash, and the Great Depression. Similarly, while the Keynesian order that emerged from the 1930s initially enabled postwar stability, overconfidence in the fiscal fine-tuning of the 1960s eventually led to the emergence of the wage-price spirals and Great Stagflations of the 1970s. Finally, even as the Neoliberal order that emerged in the early 1980s set the stage for the Federal Reserve's monetary fine-tuning of the 1990s, overconfidence in a Greenspan-era "Great Moderation" would see the subprime bubble collapse in the Global Financial Crisis. Over each era, stability has fueled instability, spanning shifts from order construction to crisis in "political time."[2]

---

[1] On a similar view of orders as ideas and interests embedded in institutions, see Skowronek (1993; 2011).
[2] On political time, defined with respect to the stages of a political order, see Skowronek (1993; 2011).

What explains the rise and fall of such orders, and to what extent has stability itself caused instability and crisis? In recent decades, economists have widely stressed the innate instability of markets, casting them as prone to waves of psychological overreactions and self-reinforcing collapse. In the tradition of scholars such as John Maynard Keynes, John Kenneth Galbraith, and Hyman Minsky, these analyses have held that "stability breeds instability," as fading memories of risks eventually prompt revived risk taking.[3] For example, writing from a historical perspective, Carmen Reinhart and Kenneth Rogoff have stressed the importance of recurring enthusiasms for new technologies and production possibilities, while behavioral economists such as George Akerlof and Robert Shiller have focused on the psychological bases of Keynesian-styled "animal spirits."[4] In policy debates, such views have been espoused even by market enthusiasts such as former Federal Reserve Chairman Alan Greenspan and Treasury Secretary Timothy Geithner. For example, Greenspan argued that where "a surge of exuberance ... causes people to reach beyond the possible," market bubbles ensue – at least until "reality strikes home" and exuberance "turns to fear," which precipitates "a severe falloff of economic activity."[5] Similarly, addressing the Global Financial Crisis, Geithner argued that "stability can produce excessive confidence, which produces the seeds of future instability."[6]

Yet, even as such economic analyses offer useful insights, they are limited where they obscure shifts in *political* orders, as ideas and institutions that initially restrain market power and stabilize expectations come to obscure new sources of market power and speculative excess. To highlight such overlooked political dynamics, I integrate in this book insights from constructivist and discursive institutionalist perspectives, offering a *social psychological institutionalism*. This approach moves beyond a rationalist stress on the construction and institutionalization of policy orders to emphasize the sources of their diminishing stability, as agents *repress* shifting types of information in

---

[3] Galbraith (1954); Keynes (1936a; 1937); Minsky (1986; 1992); see also MacKay (1841).
[4] Akerlof and Shiller (2010); Reinhart and Rogoff (2009).
[5] Greenspan (2007, 17, 466).
[6] Geithner (2014, 67–69, 392); see also Yellen (2009; 2014) on Minsky, risk and crisis.

ways that see stability yield to instability.[7] Formalizing these insights, I offer a staged model of the social construction of policy orders, their intellectual conversion, and the onset of misplaced certainty and crisis. First, addressing the *principled construction* of such orders, I stress the role of interpretive leaders in establishing the value-laden bases of regulatory restraints on market power and speculative excesses.[8] Second, shifting to their *intellectual conversion*, I argue that subsequent economic stability can enable intellectual and institutional agents to exclude principled ideas from debate, refining instead macroeconomic models that guide fiscal or monetary fine-tuning. These include the Phillips curve trade-off – which guided the postwar use of fiscal policy to strike a balance between inflation and unemployment – and the more recent Taylor rule – which weighs concerns for growth and inflation in setting interest rates.[9] Finally, I argue that as such models blind policymakers to new sources of market power and speculation, *misplaced certainty* gives rise to renewed crisis.[10]

Having advanced this model, I offer a history tracing the development of US economic policy over three stages, as the Progressive, Keynesian, and Neoliberal orders each underwent their construction, conversion, and crises. First, I address their principled construction, as Theodore Roosevelt, Franklin Roosevelt, and Ronald Reagan provided principled justifications for efforts to rebalance market power and restrain speculative expectations. Second, I address their intellectual conversion, as these principled justifications were reduced to macroeconomic models and regulatory restraints were displaced in favor of policy fine-tuning – in the Wilson-era establishment of the

---

[7] On constructivism, see Best (2005; 2008); Blyth (2002); Hay (1996); Ross (2006); Ruggie (1982); and Wendt (1999). On historical institutionalism, see Capoccia and Kelemen (2007); Mahoney and Thelen (2010); and Pierson (2000; 2004); on discursive institutionalism, see Schmidt (2008; 2010; 2013); on incremental change, see Baker (2013); Blyth (2013); Carstensen (2011); Helleiner (2010); Moschella and Tsingou (2013); Seabrooke (2006); and Tsingou (2014); on rationalism in materialist and constructivist approaches, see Fearon and Wendt (2002). On repression and its forms, see Kaplan (1957); Kahneman (2011)

[8] Following Keynes (1936a, 158), I use the term "speculation" to encompass monetary and financial trends driven by "the psychology of the market," as market expectations come to assume lives of their own.

[9] On the Phillips curve, see Samuelson and Solow (1960). On the Taylor rule, see Taylor (1993).

[10] On misplaced certainty, see Mitzen and Schweller (2011).

Federal Reserve, the Kennedy-era rise of the Council of Economic Advisers, and the Greenspan-era reemergence of the Federal Reserve. Finally, I trace the destabilization of orders as misplaced certainty in fine-tuning obscured the emergence of new imbalances of market power and speculative pressures, in ways that help explain the onset of the Great Depression, Great Stagflation, and Global Financial Crisis.

## 1.2 Theoretical Overview: Paradigmatic and Institutional Perspectives

Stability causes instability. Over time, ideas and institutions that initially enable policymakers to limit abuses of market power and speculative excess can evolve in ways that obscure new concentrations of market power and speculative excesses. Yet, in prevailing Political Economy debates, the notion that stability causes instability represents an "impossible" contradiction, obscured by rationalist assumptions that agents make efficient use of information.[11] More specifically, rationalist assumptions have shaped two sets of paradigmatic and institutionalist debates, leading scholars to overrate the scope for self-correcting stabilization and to obscure the sources of self-reinforcing instability. On the one hand, paradigmatic debates have seen realist, liberal, and constructivist perspectives cast crises as exogenous shocks to systemic, coalitional, or ideational structures, which then spur state, societal, and norm entrepreneurs to establish self-reinforcing orders.[12] On the other hand, in institutionalist debates, rational choice, sociological, and historical institutionalist approaches have stressed not only the importance of "critical junctures" that enable the construction of orders but also the subsequent roles of distributional incentives, norms, and organizational mechanisms that can enable their self-reinforcing institutionalization.[13] Taken together, even

---

[11] On rationalism, see Fearon and Wendt (2002); Finnemore and Sikkink (1998); and Muth (1961).

[12] On neorealism, see Gilpin (1981); on neoliberalism, see Gourevitch (1986); on constructivism, see Finnemore and Sikkink (1998) and Wendt (1999); on the limits to paradigmatic debates, see Jackson and Nexon (2013).

[13] On historical institutionalism, see Capoccia and Kelemen (2007) and Pierson (2000; 2004); on sociological institutionalism, see DiMaggio and Powell (1991); Dobbin (1994); and Kim and Sharman (2014); on rational choice institutionalism, see Shepsle (2006); for an overview, see Fioretos (2011) and Hall and Taylor (1996).

as these perspectives have offered insights into the development of policy orders, this has come at a cost where their rationalist foundations have obscured the sources of order dysfunction and decline.

In this theoretical introduction, I advance beyond these rationalist premises by arguing for a social psychological institutionalism, building on the above-discussed insights regarding the construction and institutionalization of orders, but also stressing the inefficiencies that can see agents repress shifting types of ideas in ways that cause renewed instability. First, engaging paradigmatic debates, I note the limits of materialist and constructivist emphases on the shifts in power and ideas that shape self-reinforcing orders, as each obscures the ways in which misplaced confidence in power *or* ideas can hasten self-reinforcing collapse. However, I also highlight recent constructivist innovations that redress these limitations by directing attention to the social tensions that can fuel policy pathologies and self-reinforcing instability.[14] Second, engaging institutionalist debates, I argue that approaches which cast incentives, norms, and organizational arrangements as sources of self-reinforcing stability can similarly obscure the potential for self-reinforcing crisis. Yet, I also suggest that recent institutionalist innovations can offset such limitations – as historical institutionalists have stressed the scope for incremental change, and discursive institutionalists have stressed the tensions between different types of principled and causal ideas that can fuel renewed instability.[15] Taken together, by moving beyond rationalist assumptions, these new constructivist and institutionalist insights can enable a more social psychological analysis, premised on assumptions that principled and causal ideas shape the interests of agents, but that agents, in turn, reinforce or repress them in ways that can fuel tensions over time. In a further refinement, to stress the temporal context of such shifts, I draw on Daniel Kahneman's social psychological insights regarding shifting interpretive biases – as "fast thinking" affective interpretations yield to "slow thinking" intellectual adjustments.[16] Over the following

---

[14] On tensions and pathologies, see Barnett and Finnemore (2004); Best (2005; 2008); Ross (2006); and Hopf (2010). Blyth (2002, 36n) foreshadows these possibilities, suggesting the need to stress "the underlying destabilization of institutions," pointing toward a "Keynes/Kalecki/Minsky model of this uncertainty."

[15] On incremental change, see Mahoney and Thelen (2010); on discursive tensions, see Schmidt (2008; 2010).

[16] Kahneman (2011).

sections, I develop these arguments, offering a social psychological institutionalist model of order construction, conversion, and crisis.

## Paradigmatic Turns: Material and Social Structures Lead to Self-Sustaining Interests

In recent decades, political economists have engaged in paradigmatic debates over the importance of systemic, coalitional, or ideational influences on state interests. While realists and liberals offer "first cut" insights into the effects of market power on interests, constructivists offer a broader recognition of the ideas that shape varying interpretations of power and interests. Yet, where realists, liberals, and constructivists alike have overrated the efficiency with which agents interpret material *or* ideational incentives, each risks obscuring the scope for self-reinforcing instability. Redressing such oversights requires building on more recent constructivist work emphasizing the inefficiencies that fuel instability and crisis.

### Realism and Liberalism: Interests as Given; Instability Obscured

Consider first realist perspectives. While stressing international rather than comparative dynamics, these place a foundational stress on the distribution of power, arguing that a hegemonic state is necessary to maintain a stable, open global economy. Such analyses stress the importance of US hegemony to the postwar Bretton Woods order – and conversely highlight the role of US decline over the 1960s and 1970s, as capital mobility impeded its ability to reconcile global growth and currency stability.[17] Nevertheless, despite their descriptive merit, they remain limited where they obscure not only the scope for variation in hegemonic interests but also the sources of hegemonic decline and crisis. First, hegemonic interests can vary – as even hegemons must interpret their interests. For example, while the British hegemony of the nineteenth century promoted a deflationary gold standard, the US hegemony of the twentieth century favored an inflationary gold-exchange standard. Second, to the extent that hegemonic stability theorists have employed rationalist assumptions, this has obscured the inefficiencies

---

[17] See Gilpin (1981) and Keohane (1984) on hegemony; Andrews (1994) on capital mobility.

that can fuel overconfidence and instability over time, forcing reliance on ad hoc exogenous shocks to explain change. This obscures the ways in which hegemonic states may overrate their ability to fine-tune the global economy, as when the diminishing effectiveness of US efforts to contain the interrelated wage, price, and currency instability of the 1960s and 1970s contributed to the collapse of the Keynesian order. Similarly, US officials overrated their abilities to contain the subprime bubble of the 2000s, in ways that presaged the Global Financial Crisis. In this light, realist analyses obscure the scope for variation in state interests and the ways in which hegemonic stability can cause instability and crises of hegemonic orders.

Offering one alternative, liberal perspectives acknowledge the scope for variation in state interests, but shift their focus to intervening domestic struggles to explain such variation. Stressing the ways in which "policy requires politics," scholars such as Peter Gourevitch and Barry Eichengreen emphasize the effects of "major downturn(s)" in the business cycle on the relative power of capital or labor, in ways that drive subsequent policy realignments.[18] From this perspective, while the Great Depression weakened the position of capital, it enabled labor support for a greater stress on wage growth and the use of Keynesian macroeconomic policy to sustain demand. Likewise, while the Great Stagflation of the 1970s weakened labor, it enabled the reemergence of capital and liberalization of financial markets. Yet, liberal approaches still remain limited in key ways. First, just as hegemonic states must interpret their interests, coalitional agents can interpret market incentives in varied ways. Consider that postwar business often *favored* wage-price regulation as it held down labor costs, while labor often *opposed* controls as impediments to collective bargaining. Second, just as realists underestimate the scope for hegemonic hubris, liberals obscure the scope for domestic overconfidence – as societal agents overrated the ability of policymakers to contain the wage-price spirals of the 1970s and the asset-price bubbles of the 2000s. In sum, liberal analyses obscure the scope for variation in societal interests and the ways in which coalitional stability can cause instability and crises of coalitional orders.

---

[18] Eichengreen (1992; 1996); Gourevitch (1986, 17, 20).

### Constructivism: Interests as Variable; Instability Unexplained

In contrast to realist and liberal approaches, constructivist perspectives highlight the ideas that shape state and societal interests, on grounds that material incentives must always be interpreted in social contexts – which in turn shape agents' interests. To be sure, constructivists do not suggest that material incentives do not exist – only that they do not "speak for themselves" and so can be interpreted in a range of fashions. Indeed, as Alexander Wendt argues, ideas *are* interests, or "beliefs about how to meet needs."[19] From this perspective, what matters most in explaining the rise and fall of economic policy orders are not simply material shifts, but rather changes in the ideas that give them meaning.[20] For example, addressing the postwar order, John Gerard Ruggie and Mark Blyth argue across international and comparative settings that "embedded liberal" ideas shaped US views of hegemonic purposes, leading it to construct a Keynesian order that limited pressures for austerity and promoted full employment.[21] Characterizing the emergence of such ideas, constructivists highlight their self-sustaining nature, as they acquire "lives of their own" that enable a self-reinforcing stability. For example, Martha Finnemore and Kathryn Sikkink model a "norm life cycle" in which norm entrepreneurs persuade leaders to accept new "standards of behavior." In turn, as leaders succeed in convincing broader audiences of their merit, this can set off "norm cascades" in which norms or ideas are internalized, acquiring a "taken-for-granted quality."[22] Similarly stressing self-reinforcing possibilities, Blyth casts crises as giving rise to "Knightian" uncertainty, in which "unique events" leave agents "unsure as to what their interests actually are." In such settings, agents use ideas "to reduce uncertainty, redefine their

---

[19] Wendt (1992; 1999, 130); see also Blyth (2002, 29–30).
[20] In economic policy terms, constructivists have the advantage of highlighting the socially constructed bases of policy orders, highlighting a wider array of policy possibilities. For example, constructivist analyses call into question notions of macroeconomic trade-offs – like the systemic "impossible trinity" of capital mobility, full employment, and monetary stability or the domestic Phillips curve trade-off between employment and inflation. Instead, constructivists counter that such trade-offs are always based in ideas which can either highlight impediments to cooperation or enable agents to recognize possibilities for shared efforts to stabilize currencies, wage-price expectations, or speculative dynamics. Widmaier (2004).
[21] Blyth (2002); Ruggie (1982).
[22] Finnemore and Sikkink (1998, 895).

*Economic Ideas in Political Time* 11

interests, and contest and replace institutions" and so "make stability possible over time." In short, Blyth argues that "ideas reduce uncertainty while institutions promote stability."[23]

Yet, even as constructivists recognize a wider range of possibilities, they share with realists and liberals a difficulty in explaining the *inefficiencies* that can see agents undermine their own goals, fueling self-reinforcing instability and crisis. This has reflected the continued influence of rationalist premises, as constructivists assume that agents make efficient use of information in interpreting the shared ideas that reduce uncertainty and stabilize interests. This obscures the ways in which the ideas that *initially* reduce uncertainty can be reinterpreted with diminishing efficiency across time. However, moving to correct for such oversights, some constructivists have recently countered rationalist assumptions by emphasizing the inherent ambiguity of ideas and the scope for interpretive tensions. Perhaps most prominently, Jacqueline Best stresses the ambiguity of both material and ideational structures, arguing that efforts to stabilize shared expectations can lead agents to converge on interpretations in ways that impede efficiency in the use of information, fueling policy or market "manias" that eventually collapse.[24] Similarly, Michael Barnett and Martha Finnemore direct attention to the organizational pathologies that can see institutional agents insulate themselves from unwanted information, in ways that eventually subvert institutional purposes.[25] In economic terms, such approaches provide key insight into ways in which, for example, the Keynesian ideas which enabled postwar stability were reshaped into the Neoclassical Synthesis of the 1960s, fueling misplaced policy confidence in the scope for restraining wage-price pressures.[26] Given such

---

[23] Blyth (2002, 9, 37, 44).
[24] Mahoney and Thelen (2010) view ideas as ambiguous, but do not see material structures or coalitional interests as subject to interpretation. In contrast, Best (2005) sees material and social structures as equally ambiguous.
[25] Finnemore and Sikkink (1999) assume that norm life cycles are self-sustaining, but Barnett and Finnemore (2004) call this assumption into question, highlighting the need for a more "general theory" of development *and* decline. Likewise, Blyth (2002, 36n) highlights the ways in which ideas reduce uncertainty and stabilize institutions, but also offers insights into the psychological dynamics that can spur institutional instabilities. In each case, space remains for integrating stabilizing and destabilizing views of ideational and institutional processes.
[26] On the Neoclassical synthesis, see Samuelson and Solow (1960); Sobel (1980).

dynamics, however, the challenge is to further situate ideas in political time, moving from a stress on their construction to their dysfunctional institutionalization and potential demise.

## *Institutional Turns: From Efficient Time to Ideational Tensions*

If the paradigmatic turn in recent debates has been marked by a greater stress on discrete moments of choice, an institutionalist turn has manifested a greater concern for continuous processes of development. Characterizing such perspectives, Orfeo Fioretos argues that historical institutionalist approaches in particular "share a substantive focus on long temporal processes" and stress "the ways in which varied patterns of incremental adaptation shape institutions over time."[27] Moreover, Paul Pierson notes, such analyses are not tied to any specific theoretical stance, as a "pluralistic" historical institutionalism can encompass both materialist and constructivist paradigmatic views over "a wide range of theoretical traditions."[28] Building on this pluralism, I first engage the materialist "power-distributional" historical institutionalism of James Mahoney and Kathleen Thelen, arguing that while they stress the potential for incremental adjustment, they also overrate its rational, order-sustaining character. To provide insight into order-subverting change, I then engage Vivien Schmidt's discursive institutionalism, which foregrounds the "value-distributional" tensions between principled and cognitive beliefs that can fuel instability. Taken together, these more recent historical and discursive institutionalisms each offer something the other lacks, suggesting the possibility that they might be integrated to support a more general analysis of incremental tensions *in* political time.

### Historical Institutionalism: Efficiencies "in Time"

Historical institutionalist debates have long been shaped by what Giovanni Capoccia and R. Daniel Kelemen term "dualist" models of self-sustaining orders. These juxtapose shifts from critical junctures marked by "rapid change" to the emergence of self-reinforcing effects that characterize "longer phases of relative stability."[29] Perhaps most

---

[27] Fioretos (2011, 370).
[28] Pierson (2004, 176).
[29] Capoccia and Keleman (2007, 344).

prominently, Pierson has advanced a view of such junctures as marked by the emergence of small advantages which generate increasing returns, as agents form "adaptive" expectations or "adapt their actions in ways that help make those expectations come true."[30] Yet, this stress on shifts from shocks to stability has had costs where it has obscured the subsequent scope for incremental adjustments. To redress such shortcomings, James Mahoney and Kathleen Thelen have argued for the need to advance beyond a "discontinuous model of change in which enduring historical pathways are periodically punctuated by moments of choice," positing instead that institutional orders are always "contested settlements." To this end, they advance a "power distributional" view of institutions "above all else as distributional instruments" in which agents can gradually reinterpret rules to adapt to new developments.[31] From this perspective, institutional stability "rests not just on the accumulation but also on the ongoing mobilization of resources," leaving "source[s] of change" to reside in "shifts in the [coalitional] balance of power."[32] Mahoney and Thelen further identify a number of mechanisms enabling adaptive but incremental responses – as "displacement" enables adjustment "when existing rules are replaced by new ones" or the "conversion" of rules occurs where they "remain formally the same but are interpreted and enacted in new ways."[33] Similarly, Stephen Bell argues for a more nuanced "agent-centered" historical institutionalism, stressing the ways in which agents are "shaped (though not wholly determined)" by institutional environments. Bell posits three routes to incremental adjustment – as agents reinterpret their environment or "construct the experience of their institutional situation," reinterpret rules by exploiting their "bounded discretion" within institutions, or redeploy resources in societal struggles.[34] Highlighting such dynamics, Bell credits the acumen of policymakers at the mid-1990s Reserve Bank of Australia (RBA), which resisted pressures for monetary restraint following the Asian crisis – demonstrating the scope for adaptive agency.

These analyses offer insights into possibilities for incremental adjustment. Yet, they also have limits where they treat institutional

---

[30] Pierson (2000, 251–254; 2004, 176).
[31] Mahoney and Thelen (2010, 7–8).
[32] Mahoney and Thelen (2010, 9).
[33] Mahoney and Thelen (2010, 16–17).
[34] Bell (2011, 890, 893–895).

ideas as exogenous to broader principled debates, and obscure the *inefficiencies* which can see incremental mechanisms promote the gradual repression of information in ways that lead to destabilizing, order-subverting changes. First, power-distributional institutionalisms obscure the dependence of institutional agents on principled contexts in defining their interests. These can vary from Keynes's egalitarian stress on the existence of a public interest in restraining wage, price, or asset instability, to Milton Friedman's libertarian views that no such interests in restraint exist, on the grounds that "the social responsibility of business is to increase its profits."[35] Second, power-distributional approaches underrate the scope for institutional *dysfunction*, as agents can advance incremental changes that undermine prevailing orders. For example, where Mahoney and Thelen stress the ability of institutional agents to adjust to the coalitional "balance of power," they obscure the ways in which – just as hubristic powers can exhibit "imperial overstretch" – institutional agents can overrate their own abilities. Consider the overconfidence of the Council of Economic Advisers in the 1970s in the use of "gradualist" fiscal fine-tuning to limit wage-push pressures. This obscured the increasing market power of labor as the crises of the 1970s eventually brought on the collapse of the Keynesian order and the institutional eclipse of the Council by the Federal Reserve. Likewise, with respect to Bell's Australian case, even as the RBA resisted imposing restraint during the Asian crisis, similar successes at the US Federal Reserve in dealing with the Asian crisis demonstrate the potential for the onset of overconfidence. Only a few years later, in the early 2000s, the Federal Reserve would resist pressures for monetary restraint in ways that accommodated not simply renewed growth but also helped inflate the subprime bubble. In sum, even where historical institutionalist approaches provide insights into self-correcting adjustments, they can obscure the ways in which institutional stability can yield to institutional crisis.

### Discursive Institutionalism: Tensions "Out of Time"

While such power-distributional institutionalisms offer an important contribution in identifying possibilities for incremental change, they are limited by where they see such change as order-sustaining or efficient – obscuring order-subverting inefficiencies. Providing a key step toward

---

[35] Friedman (1970) and Keynes (1936a).

an alternative, I draw on discursive institutionalist work by scholars such as Vivien Schmidt, which disaggregates the intersubjective context in ways that highlight the scope for ideational tensions and inefficiencies. Such analyses enable scholars to focus less on power distributional than "value-distributional" tensions – for example, across what Berger and Luckmann term a "social distribution of knowledge" between shared values shaped in universal "primary socialization" and specialized professional or institutional beliefs shaped in "secondary socialization."[36] More recently, highlighting the interplay of such influences, Andrew Ross has argued that shared values are "inspired and absorbed before being chosen" and "tinge our intellectual beliefs" in ways that shape institutions and interests.[37] From this vantage point, the tensions between basic, principled views and the more refined causal beliefs can impede collective efficiency in the use of information.

Highlighting these value-distribution tensions, Schmidt offers a discursive institutionalist perspective that examines not only the influence of ideas on interests, but also variation in *types* of ideas, as principled beliefs prefigure causal ideas. Refining these distinctions, Schmidt contrasts principled beliefs regarding "what's right" with causal beliefs regarding "what works." Regarding the former, Schmidt suggests that principled ideas identify "what one ought to do" as they "attach values to political action" and "resonate with a deeper core of ... norms of public life." Regarding the latter, cognitive or causal ideas "provide the recipes, guidelines, and maps for political action and serve to justify policies and programs by speaking to their interest-based logic and necessity," defining "what is and what to do."[38] In turn, in terms of agency, syntheses of each type of idea can be sustained in different rhetorical forms – as Schmidt distinguishes "communicative" from "coordinative" discourses. While the former involve "the presentation, deliberation, and legitimation of political ideas to the general public,"

---

[36] Berger and Luckmann (1966, 149–157).
[37] Ross (2006, 199–200). One might also highlight the importance of a "practice turn" in directing attention to the precognitive, intuitive impulses that shape more formal choices, as stressed in Pouliot (2010) and Neumann and Pouliot (2011). However, while such efforts usefully highlight precognitive dynamics, they tend to parallel earlier constructivist efforts in overrating the efficiency with which agents form intuitions. Providing a corrective, Hopf (2010) stresses the role of unthinking "habits" as precognitive impediments to the efficient use of information.
[38] Schmidt (2008, 306–308).

the latter entail more narrow deliberations among agents "at the center of policy construction" whose appeals are often characterized by a desire to limit the affective charge of debates.[39]

Taken together, each institutionalism offers something that the other lacks. Historical institutionalists such as Mahoney and Thelen stress the dynamics of political time, but obscure ideational tensions. In contrast, discursive institutionalists such as Schmidt foreground ideational tensions, but abstract away from political time. Space, therefore, remains for an integrated focus on "tensions in time," as order construction and institutionalization yield to instability and crisis.

## 1.3 Order and Crisis in Political Time: Construction, Conversion, and Crisis

Recasting constructivist and institutionalist insights, this social psychological institutionalist analysis is premised on assumptions that the principled and causal ideas that stabilize policy orders may in turn be repressed by agents in ways that cause instability across time.[40] To place these tensions in time, I draw on Daniel Kahneman's distinction between styles of initial "fast," affective thinking and subsequent "slow," cognitive reactions – arguing that these drive stages marked by the principled construction of economic policy orders, their intellectual conversion, and misplaced confidence that culminates in crisis.[41] First, in principled construction, interpretive leaders construct value-laden bases for regulatory or legal reforms that stabilize the balance of market power and restrain speculative expectations. Second, ensuing stability can fuel the intellectual conversion of orders, as intellectual and institutional agents reduce principled debates to utilitarian questions, employing models like the Phillips curve or Taylor rule to

---

[39] Schmidt (2008, 310).
[40] Where agents confront anxiety – defined as tensions between aspects of the psyche – they use defence mechanisms like repression to limit them. In an IR setting, Morton Kaplan (1957, 259–261) defined repression as entailing "the suppression of information" that could lead "internal conflict or disturbance [to] ... become manifest."
[41] Where each type of thinking has advantages, Kahneman (2011, 140–141) stresses the need to avoid favoring either. While conceding that experts are "superior in dealing with numbers and amounts," he also highlights the need for popular debate, as differences "between experts and the public" may reflect "a genuine conflict of values."

*Economic Ideas in Political Time*

Table 1.1. *Economic Ideas in Political Time*

|  | Construction | Conversion | Certainty and crisis |
|---|---|---|---|
| Stage in political time | Principled construction – Interpretive leaders shape principled bases of causal beliefs | Intellectual conversion – Policy elites convert principled beliefs to causal models | Misplaced certainty and crisis – Causal models obscure shifts in power and expectations |
| Economic policy mix | Reform– Restraints on market power and speculative expectations contain wage- or asset-spirals | Macroeconomic fine-tuning– Regulatory/ legal restraints are displaced as macroeconomic models guide fine-tuning of trade-offs | Policy accommodation– Policy accommodates market power and wage- or asset-spirals |

fine tune tensions between growth and inflation. Third, such conversion can in turn spark misplaced confidence, obscuring new sources of market power, speculative excess and renewed crisis. (See Table 1.1 for an overview.)

## Stage 1: Principled Construction: Interpretive Leadership and Reformist Restraints

First, I posit that the *principled construction* of orders, or sets of ideas and interests, occurs as interpretive leaders – spanning public intellectuals and political figures – interpret events as crises which justify new principled beliefs, causal ideas, and economic policy interests. To the extent that such early crises carry affective weight, they are marked by what Kahneman terms "fast thinking" reactions that have the effect of "effortlessly originating impressions and feelings" that then inform "explicit beliefs and deliberate choices."[42] In such

---
[42] Such influences can be literally precognitive where they activate reactions in the amygdala which bypass the cerebral cortex (Kahneman 2011, 21; 301).

contexts, interpretive leaders issue communicative appeals marked by the use of "affective heuristics" that substitute principled claims for utilitarian questions.[43] In issue-specific terms, at the highest level of abstraction, the most enduring principled distinctions divide libertarian values from egalitarian values, as economists recognize the need to limit abuses of market power and speculative excesses but disagree on the means to these ends. For example, from a more libertarian view, Friedrich Hayek stressed the need less for controls than legal measures to promote more perfect competition, arguing that in order to ensure that "competition should work beneficially," legal frameworks should prevent private efforts "to control prices."[44] In this light, while Hayek is often seen as an unqualified advocate of free markets, his concession to the potential for *private* price-fixing suggests that his ultimate concern was to limit "bigness" where it threatened abuses of power – a view that Milton Friedman would echo in opposing postwar official support for labor power.[45] In contrast, from a more egalitarian perspective, John Maynard Keynes cast the state as having an ethical role in assuming a "greater responsibility for directly organising investment" and urging controls to restrain both, the "animal spirits" that can drive self-reinforcing financial bubbles and the labor power that can likewise spur wage-price spirals.[46] While expressing the notion that "it is relatively easy to fix prices that are already fixed," John Kenneth Galbraith similarly stressed the need for regulatory efforts to stabilize the speculative sources of financial instability and the wage-price expectations that fuel inflation.[47]

Given the need to justify such principles, interpretive leaders holding positions of authority play a key role in "ratcheting together" shared principles with more refined policy ideas in ways that stabilize a balance of market power and restrain speculative expectations. For example, Franklin Roosevelt's egalitarian denunciations of "money changers" foreshadowed efforts to not only reshape institutions in

---

This is not meant to suggest that agents are "hardwired" to respond in specific ways, but rather to highlight the precognitive mechanisms that mediate interpretations of events.

[43] Kahneman (2011, 98) defines a heuristic as "a simple procedure that helps find adequate, though imperfect, answers to difficult questions."
[44] Hayek (1944, 37–41).
[45] Friedman (1966); Friedman and Heller (1969).
[46] Keynes (1936a, 164).
[47] Galbraith (1952, 17; 1954).

ways that would reduce the power of finance, but also strengthen the power of labor in countervailing fashion. Having promoted this new balance of power, Roosevelt would in turn seek to stabilize ascendant wage-price expectations through communicative appeals to a "common interest" in price controls. Similarly, where Ronald Reagan denounced striking air traffic controllers for being in "violation of the law," this libertarian stance enabled not only a shift in the balance of power back toward finance, but also accompanied an antitrust-styled move against labor that had an enduring impact on wage trends, as expectations of annual wage increases yielded to the acceptance of "givebacks." Taken as a whole, such efforts to reshape the sectoral balance of power and restrain speculative excess involve the repurposing of institutions and rhetorical efforts to reshape market expectations.

Such principled appeals can reshape causal relations between economic aggregates as they "feed back" on the social relations underpinning macroeconomic correlations, in ways that ease Philips curve or Taylor rule-styled "trade-offs" between nominal (e.g., monetary or financial) and real (e.g., growth or unemployment) variables. In such contexts, where regulatory or legal mechanisms contain market power and speculative expectations, policymakers can ideally achieve "better" trade-offs, for example, shifting the Phillips curve "downward" or "to the left," and so reducing the point at which full employment spills over into wage and price instability. For example, over the postwar Keynesian era, incomes policies – spanning the use of exhortation, guidelines, and controls – were widely seen as reducing the costs of lowering inflation in this very way, enabling officials to fix expectations without requiring the imposition of austerity. Prominent examples of the use of "universal" wage-price guidelines include the Roosevelt-era "General Maximum Price Regulation" and the Kennedy administration wage guideposts. In turn, beyond the potential for stabilizing aggregate expectations, principled appeals and policy rules can enable the more concentrated application of restraint in sectors characterized by the existence of market power – reducing the need to slow the entire economy through austerity. Indeed, this possibility has been rediscovered in post-Global Financial Crisis discussions of macroprudential regulation. Macroprudential measures enable authorities to directly limit excessive private risk taking and so tamp down on asset-price bubbles without disrupting the wider economy.[48] In short, where principled appeals make possible a wider array of legal, regulatory, and macroeconomic options, policy can be more effectively targeted – and rapid growth need not force policy trade-offs. Of course, such stability is not self-reinforcing, and where success in these efforts leads to principled disengagement by leaders and publics, it can ironically prove self-limiting.

## Stage 2: Intellectual Conversion, Displacement, and Diminishing Returns

Even as interpretive leaders play a key role in order construction, success in such efforts can ironically lead them to cede authority to intellectual and institutional agents possessing specialized knowledge. This can in turn advance the *intellectual conversion* of principled understandings into causal models, as these agents repress principled concerns from debate to reduce their emotional charge and make greater use of more refined causal models. Put differently, in such settings, Kahneman-styled slow policy coordination supplants fast communicative appeals, as agents refine cognitive heuristics like the Phillips curve or Taylor rule to guide the manipulation of macroeconomic incentives. Indeed, in intellectual settings, the appeal of such shifts often lies in the degree to which they are unencumbered by the value-laden biases of an egalitarian Keynes or libertarian Hayek.[49] For example, such tendencies could be seen in the early postwar years in Daniel Bell's calls for an "end of ideology" and in the 1990s claims of Francis Fukuyama for the "end of history."[50] Likewise, among economists, these inclinations could be seen in the 1960s displacement of Institutional Keynesians by a Neoclassical Synthesis and in the 1990s displacement of New Classical economists by New Keynesians. Regarding the former, postwar Institutionalist Keynesians such as Galbraith highlighted Keynes' deeper arguments regarding the nature of uncertainty as a constraint on market efficiency, justifying ongoing efforts to stabilize

---

[48] On macroprudential regulation as an alternative to macroeconomic restraint, see Baker (2013); Fischer (2014).
[49] Intellectual conversion can also be seen as embodying what Daniel Ellsberg (1961) termed "ambiguity aversion" – reflecting preferences for quantifiable risks over qualitative appeals. Given such biases, intellectual elites may discount principled concerns as illegitimate intrusions into debate.
[50] Bell (1960); Fukuyama (1991).

wage-price expectations. However, Neoclassical Keynesians such as Paul Samuelson and Robert Solow would succeed in pushing such principled beliefs aside, treating markets as efficient over the long run in a way that still justified the short-run fiscal fine-tuning of a Phillips curve inflation-unemployment trade-off.[51] Regarding the latter, even as the 1980s witnessed the rise of a libertarian-styled New Classical view which cast policy as ineffective in both the long *and* short run, this position would increasingly be seen by economists as ideologically extreme. New Classical ideas would accordingly be displaced by New Keynesian views which echoed the 1960s-era Neoclassical treatment of markets as efficient in the long run but not in the short run. Paralleling the Phillips curve, this approach manifested itself in the rise of a Taylor rule which offered a guide to fine-tuning interest rates in a way that balanced growth and inflation.[52]

In institutional terms, intellectual conversion is often paralleled by the displacement of interpretive leadership and regulatory possibilities by more macroeconomic instruments, which then suffer diminishing effectiveness. First, where interpretive leadership is displaced, this can impede the maintenance of common interests in wage-price or investment restraint, undermining earlier social or regulatory successes in limiting monetary or financial instability. In such settings, as utilitarian models obscure the scope for shared responsibility, agents may, as Alexander Wendt put it, become "desocialized" and more willing to employ market power to its fullest, in ways that cause growth to push against monetary or financial stability.[53] Second, where regulatory institutions are displaced, this can leave macroeconomic policy as the sole mechanism to address two opposing objectives – of promoting real growth *and* stabilizing nominal prices. Such trade-offs may be contained for a time, given the backdrop of earlier exhortative restraints and the acumen of policymakers. Yet, even the most skilled macroeconomic juggler will be able to keep growth and stability in balance only for so long. Eventually, the limitation of having only one tool to address two objectives will force policymakers to prioritize growth or stability – with the likely choice of growth entailing the acceptance

---

[51] Kennedy Council of Economic Advisers Chair Walter Heller (1966, 6) affirmed that "the political economist typically thinks in terms of trade-offs … rather than all-or-nothing thinking."
[52] Mankiw and Romer (1991); Taylor (1993); Yellen (1996).
[53] On desocialization, see Wendt (1999, 294).

of wage-price or asset-price inflation. Moreover, such losses of earlier gains are often only the beginning: even as intellectual conversion fuels this repression of *past* means of reconciling trade-offs through exhortative leadership and regulation, its most destabilizing effects are forward-looking, as it gives rise to a misplaced confidence that obscures speculative dynamics and accumulations of market power in ways that amplify *future* instability and crisis.

## Stage 3: Misplaced Certainty: Overconfidence and Iterative Crises

Intellectual conversion can eventually cause new inefficiencies, as it contributes to the onset of a misplaced certainty that sees policymakers overrate their ability to contain speculative excesses and abuses of market power.

First, intellectual overconfidence may see sustained reliance on models like the Phillips curve or Taylor rule obscure not only the dynamic nature of market expectations, but also lead to a convergence of market expectations in ways that result in intensified risk taking. In such settings, as Charles Goodhart has noted, policy beliefs not only *reflect* market beliefs but also *reshape* them, as the promulgation of rules drawn from past correlations reshapes expectations in ways that invalidate these same past correlations.[54] Similarly, Jacqueline Best has suggested that the formalization of policy rules can reduce the plurality of interpretations necessary to competitive efficiencies, reducing the diversity of expectations. For example, from this perspective, when Ben Bernanke lauded the convergence of monetary beliefs in the early subprime bubble – arguing that "more open communication" from the Federal Reserve had increased "the likelihood that financial market participants' rate expectations will be similar to those of the policymakers themselves" – he overlooked the potential for a mutual policy *and* market repression of mounting instability.[55] In this light, where policymakers overrate their acumen in fine-tuning – as the Neoclassical Keynesians of the 1960s lauded a "New Economics" and as New Keynesians of the 2000s heralded a "Great Moderation" – this

---

[54] Goodhart (1975).
[55] Bernanke (2004b).

can reduce markets' own sense of caution, accelerating the onset of crisis.

Second, overconfidence in intellectual frameworks may obscure mounting concentrations of labor or financial market power which, over time, grow more resistant to macroeconomic fine-tuning and enable market agents in key sectors to thwart the imposition of restraint. Given the potential reemergence of concentrations of market power, macroeconomic policymakers will be forced to either impose greater austerity across the entire economy in order to secure sector-specific restraint, or to "ease up" and accommodate the sectoral imbalance of market power in order to sustain growth. Moreover, where subsequent easing leads the economy to become more dependent on such key sectors, pressures for sustained accommodation can become increasingly difficult to resist, as such sectors take on the role of engines of demand – as was the case with labor into the 1970s and finance through the 2000s. Over time, as policy becomes locked into accommodating such market power on the "upside," this can raise the eventual "downside" costs of future crises.

However – and finally – such crises will seldom spur immediate or punctuated change. Given intellectual inefficiencies, early bouts of instability may in fact initially have limited effects on policy beliefs – reflecting not only the constructivist insight that crises do not "speak for themselves," but also Kahneman's insights regarding the tensions between types of interpretive biases.[56] In the early crises of a declining order, "hard times" may be interpreted as requiring not principled change but intellectual consistency, as the utilitarian imperative of recovery impedes value-laden reform. For this reason, crisis-driven change often has, on closer inspection, less a punctuated than an *iterative* character, as marked by moments of advance and partial retreat that accumulate across crises. Such dynamics may often play out across several crises. For example, the Mexican, Asian, "Dot-com" and Global Financial Crises were viewed as increasingly severe and so as justifying mounting reforms – as Sarbanes-Oxley in 2002 yielded to Dodd-Frank in 2010. Moreover, such utilitarian concerns to limit the extent of reform may have merit in crises, justifying resistance to fast thinking principled excess. Speaking to this balancing act, Keynes argued that "even wise and necessary Reform may ...

[56] Blyth (2002); Hay (1996); and Widmaier, Blyth, and Seabrooke (2007).

impede and complicate Recovery. For it will upset the confidence of the business world ... before you have had time to put other motives in their place."[57] This view was later advanced by the Obama administration in the early Global Financial Crisis as officials stressed the need to "do no harm." In this way, reformist adjustments are often advanced across moments of instability, as agents "repurpose" policies once meant to accommodate market power in ways that limit its abuse, and as interpretive leaders reinforce such efforts in appeals for speculative restraint. While the final crisis that sees the construction of new market expectations and institutions may appear, from a distance, to be an example of punctuated change, such developments are better seen as the final steps in an iterative process, as slow-thinking ratchets are successively overcome by fast-thinking advances.

## 1.4 Plan of the Book

Having developed this framework, I apply it to explain the development of the Progressive, Keynesian, and Neoliberal orders, tracing their principled construction, intellectual conversion, and the onset of misplaced certainty which led to the Great Depression, Great Stagflation, and Global Financial Crisis. To provide extra context on these shifts, I highlight at the beginning of each section the foundations of each order not only in principled ideas but also the broader American Hamiltonian and Jeffersonian philosophical traditions that can themselves often acquire new meaning across successive orders. In terms of the methodological "plan of attack," this requires an interpretive approach, offering a "structured, focused" analysis of the interplay of interpretive leadership, intellectual conversion, and misplaced certainty and crises.[58] In terms of choice of issue area and cases, these represent "least likely" contexts and case studies for a social psychological approach.[59] First, the economic issue area comprises a less likely one for any social perspective, as market agents possess relatively clear preferences and access to near-perfect information, which should limit the scope for social influences or inefficiencies. Second,

---

[57] Keynes (1933).
[58] On structured, focused analysis, see George and Bennett (2005, 67).
[59] On least likely cases, see Eckstein (1975).

regarding the case selection, to the extent that Progressive, Keynesian, and Neoliberal orders vary in terms of coalitional and ideological influences, this analysis highlights the similar social psychological tensions that can disrupt different types of coalitional and cognitive commitments, as each order was destabilized by similar inefficiencies and misplaced certainties.

Previewing these substantive arguments, I focus first in Chapter 2 on the construction, conversion, and collapse of the Progressive order, spanning Theodore Roosevelt's efforts at balancing the interests of labor, capital, and agriculture, the emergence of Wilson's more administrative state and antitrust focus, to economic collapse in the monetary hubris of the 1920s. In tracing these shifts, I begin with Theodore Roosevelt's *principled construction* of a regulatory order in a "Square Deal" balancing the interests of labor and capital, spanning the settlement of the 1902 coal strike, the passage of the Hepburn Act of 1906 regulating rail rates, and 1907 financial crisis. Second, I address Wilson's *intellectual conversion* of this order as his "New Freedom" saw the Revenue Act of 1913 set the bases of modern fiscal policy and the Federal Reserve Act of 1913 made possible the conduct of a deliberate monetary policy. However, I also note the implications of the war for a more Rooseveltian, regulatory "detour" on Wilson's part, and the role of a postwar antitrust revival that limited the scope for industrial collusion and saw Wilson move against labor. Finally, I highlight the onset of *misplaced certainty* in monetary policy, which accommodated the 1920s bull market and led to its collapse in the Great Crash.

In the second part, I trace over three chapters the construction, conversion, and collapse of the Keynesian order. In Chapter 3, I first address order construction, highlighting Roosevelt's interpretive leadership in the *principled construction* of the Keynesian order, as the Banking Acts of 1933 and 1935 contained finance, the Wagner Act strengthened labor, the 1937 recession justified fiscal activism, and wartime controls demonstrated the scope for containing wage and price pressures. Upon completion of the conflict, this set the template for Truman's and Eisenhower's efforts at using rhetoric to prevent a postwar inflationary surge in the 1940s and restrain a "New Inflation" marked by simultaneously rising prices and unemployment in the 1950s. In Chapter 4, I address the *intellectual conversion* of the Keynesian order in a

Neoclassical Synthesis, arguing that an intellectual aversion to populist appeals would find expression in the Kennedy-Johnson Council of Economic Advisers' opposition to wage controls and support for the fiscal fine-tuning of a Phillips curve trade-off between inflation and unemployment. In Chapter 5, I trace the Keynesian order's collapse, as *misplaced certainty* in gradualist fine-tuning obscured the role of labor's market power in self-reinforcing wage-price spirals, leading the Nixon, Ford, and Carter administrations to each accommodate unsustainable stagflationary surges with diminishing effectiveness.

In the final three chapters, I trace the construction, conversion, and crisis of the Neoliberal order. In Chapter 6, I address Reagan's libertarian construction of government as "the problem" in causing stagflation and of striking air traffic controllers as "violating the law" in seeking wage gains. Such efforts combined with the Volcker Federal Reserve's use of monetary restraint to break labor's market power and the Fed's support for financial power as it sought to enable large US banks to withstand the Latin American debt crisis.[60] In Chapter 7, I address the shift in the 1990s toward *intellectual conversion*, as the Clinton administration abandoned a stress on public investment to favor instead the accommodation of private investment, in the context of an implicit fiscal-monetary accord with the Greenspan Federal Reserve, efforts to advance a New Keynesian monetary activism via appointments to the Federal Reserve Board, and increasing support for financial deregulation. In Chapter 8, I highlight the onset of *misplaced certainty* in a "Great Moderation," which shaped reactions to the technology crash of the early 2000s and the Global Financial Crisis, as each spurred monetary, fiscal, and regulatory accommodation. Turning to the iterative construction of the Global Financial Crisis, I suggest that initial fast, principled responses were limited by the Obama administration's utilitarian concern that reform should "do no harm." Yet, while opposition to reform prevented efforts to end "too big to fail"-styled arrangements, initial efforts at macroprudential regulation and the promotion of increased competition in derivatives markets can be seen as providing bases for future iterations of progress. (See Table 1.2 on this framework, as applied over stages of construction, conversion, and misplaced certainty and crisis.)

---

[60] Reagan (1981a; 1981b).

Table 1.2. *Constructing Crises in Political Time – Chapter Overview*

| Order | Construction | Conversion | Certainty and crisis |
|---|---|---|---|
| Progressive (Ch. 2) | Theodore Roosevelt's rhetoric legitimates efforts to balance labor and capital | Federal Reserve and Revenue Acts of 1913 enable macroeconomic fine-tuning | Misplaced monetary confidence leads to Great Crash/Depression |
| Keynesian (Ch. 3, 4, 5) | Franklin Roosevelt's rhetoric enables efforts to contain finance and support labor | Council of Economic Advisers/Neoclassical Phillips curve guides fiscal fine-tuning during 1960–1970s | Misplaced fiscal overconfidence leads to Great Stagflation |
| Neoliberal (Ch. 6, 7, 8) | Reagan's rhetoric enables efforts to contain labor and support finance | Federal Reserve/New Keynesian Taylor rule guides monetary fine-tuning into the 2000s | Misplaced regulatory, fiscal, and monetary confidence leads to Global Financial Crisis |

In the conclusion, I address theoretical, historical, and policy implications. In theoretical terms, this analysis highlights the merit of a social psychological institutionalism in enabling a general theory of stability and instability – one capable of encompassing views of ideas as initially reducing uncertainty but – over time – causing misplaced certainty and crises. In historical terms, this analysis also has implications for International Political Economy debates, as hubris regarding wage-price or asset-price stability has been paralleled with respect to currency stability across the Progressive, Keynesian, and Neoliberal orders. In policy terms, this analysis finally offers new insights into the need to balance democratic accountability and intellectual expertise, providing insight into a "pragmatic paradox" – as ostensibly pragmatic efforts to enhance the quality of intellectual deliberation and limit populist excesses can see intellectual ideas acquire a rigidity of their own. In such settings, pragmatic refinement can devolve into technocratic hubris. Taken as a whole, this paradox reinforces the larger insight of this volume – that stability can impede efficiency, causing instability and crisis.

# 2 | *The Construction, Conversion, and Collapse of the Progressive Order*

> Combination and concentration should be, not prohibited, but supervised and within reasonable limits controlled.
>
> Theodore Roosevelt, First State of the Union Message, 1901[1]

> The history of liberty is a history of the limitation of governmental power, not the increase of it.
>
> Woodrow Wilson, Address to the New York Press Club, September 9, 1912[2]

> The very existence of the Federal Reserve System is a safeguard against anything like a calamity growing out of money rates. Not only have we the power to deal with such an emergency instantly by flooding the street with money, but I think the country is well aware of this.
>
> New York Federal Reserve President Benjamin Strong, 1928[3]

## 2.1 Introduction and Overview

Over the nineteenth century, US economic policy orders can be seen as driven by shifts between "Hamiltonian" and "Jeffersonian" visions. While Hamilton favored a mercantilist view, urging the establishment of high tariffs and a central bank to benefit manufacturing, Jefferson held more classically liberal views, favoring lower tariffs and easier money to benefit agriculture. These views would shift in relative influence over time, as wartime booms alternated with postwar busts. By the end of the century, while the inflationary Civil War had benefited

---

[1] Roosevelt (1901).
[2] Cooper (2009, 164).
[3] Greider (1987, 298–299).

agriculture, the post-1873 return to the gold standard would usher in a prolonged agrarian depression. Following the brief rise of the agrarian Populist movement, the early twentieth century would witness the onset of Progressive debate over the shift to a more industrial economy. In this context, one can trace Theodore Roosevelt's construction of the Progressive order, Woodrow Wilson's intellectual conversion, and New York Federal Reserve President Benjamin Strong's misplaced confidence which led to its collapse. These stages would in turn be marked by parallel shifts in forms of rhetoric, as Roosevelt's exhortative appeals would be narrowed in Wilson's more educative approach, before the Federal Reserve would come to rely on targeted, sector-specific pronouncements.

Over the course of this chapter, I trace these dynamics, first addressing Roosevelt's construction of key foundations of the Progressive order in appeals for an array of restraints on the power of labor, capital, and agriculture: specifically, Roosevelt sought a balanced settlement of the 1902 coal strike (favoring labor), passage of the Hepburn Act which regulated railroads (favoring agriculture), and acquiesced to J. P. Morgan's handling of the 1907 stock market crash (favoring capital). These positions would culminate in Roosevelt's 1912 campaign calls for "New Nationalism" and an enhanced role for the state in regulating economic activity. In the second section, I show how Wilson advanced the *intellectual conversion* of the Progressive order as he engaged in a more administrative advocacy on behalf of an antitrust-styled "New Freedom" and laid the foundations of modern macroeconomic policy – in the Revenue Act of 1913 and the Federal Reserve Act of 1913. While wartime exigencies led Wilson to pivot toward a more regulatory approach, he would close out his presidency by resisting efforts to extend wartime regulation and oversaw antitrust attacks on the market power of unions. In the third section, I argue that the 1920s would be marked by an increasingly misplaced certainty in deregulation and monetary fine-tuning, as Benjamin Strong would err in the direction of accommodating the 1920s bull market. Despite a late regulatory attempt to impose "direct pressure," overconfidence in monetary fine-tuning would eventually yield to crisis in the onset of the Great Crash and Great Depression. In this way, one can trace the construction, conversion, and misplaced certainty that fueled the collapse of the Progressive order.

## 2.2 Constructing a Progressive Order: From Roosevelt's Square Deal to a New Nationalism

The Progressive movement emerged from two decades of agrarian Depression, reinforced by a financial "Panic of 1893" which drove unemployment to double digits, where it remained for a half decade.[4] However, no clear policy departure would be immediately forthcoming. Instead, the Panic of 1893 led to a split within the Democratic Party. On the one hand, the pro-business "Bourbon Democrat" President Grover Cleveland hewed to orthodoxy by supporting repeal of the Sherman Silver Purchase Act in 1893 and supporting the gold standard. On the other hand, the Populist movement would assume an increasing influence, culminating in the 1896 Democratic nomination of presidential candidate William Jennings Bryan. While Bryan memorably campaigned against orthodoxy in his "cross of gold" speech, his agricultural coalition would be defeated three times by Republicans enjoying the backing of northeastern labor. However, Bryan's losses would not mean the defeat of reform, as the Democratic split would be mirrored on the Republican side, where the party's "Old Guard" would be rivaled by a more Progressive faction – and McKinley's conservatism at the top of the ticket would be balanced by the selection of New York Governor Theodore Roosevelt as 1900 vice presidential nominee. Yet, with McKinley's assassination in September 1901, the balance of power in the party would shift, and Roosevelt would channel Populist sentiment into a reformist Progressivism. Submerging Bryan's class-based rhetoric to a broader appeal to the common good, Roosevelt adopted a meditative approach to struggles between labor and capital, seeking a "Square Deal" that recognized the existence of market power but sought not to break so much as manage it. This effort to reshape the economic balance of power would be foreshadowed in Roosevelt's first State of the Union address. This advanced the case for a public interest in regulation, as Roosevelt held that "trusts are in certain of their features and tendencies hurtful to the general welfare," justifying a "conviction that combination and concentration should be, not prohibited, but supervised and within reasonable limits controlled."[5]

---

[4] Romer (1986, 31).
[5] Roosevelt (1901).

In policy terms, Roosevelt would apply this ethos across a series of disputes between capital, labor, and agriculture, with an eye to maintaining social balance across these realms. First, in the context of a 1902 anthracite coal strike, Roosevelt established a template for a more mediative federal intervention in labor disputes. In May 1902, approximately 150,000 miners of the anthracite brand of coal – used to heat homes throughout America – struck for higher wages, shorter hours, and recognition of their United Mine Workers (UMW) union. Even though Attorney General Philander Knox told Roosevelt that he had "no power or duty in the matter," Roosevelt would assemble industry and labor representatives at the White House in October, warning of "the catastrophe impending over a large portion of our people in the shape of a winter fuel famine," and pressing for an agreement.[6] Following much wrangling, the industry eventually agreed to the establishment of a commission that gave the union a 10 percent raise. In the end, the strike foreshadowed two sets of institutional and economic changes. Institutionally, while the draft of Roosevelt's statement to the coal operators and union leaders had stated that "no precedent of interference in strikes will be created," Roosevelt recognized this was an untenable promise, and removed this sentence – setting the stage for presidential efforts at stabilizing the economic balance of power to shape recurring disputes going forward.[7] Economically, the price of coal subsequently increased by 10 percent, foreshadowing the ways in which cost-push dynamics would complicate labor-capital mediation.[8] Put differently, the 1902 coal strike set the precedent for a number of mid-century interventions in both arriving at a coalitional compromise – and paying for it with inflation.

Second, providing a more enduring basis for regulatory authority – in a way that would see him take a step toward the emergence of a more rhetorical presidency – Roosevelt sought to limit abuses of market power in the rail industry. In a key early move, he had acted to prevent the 1901 establishment of the Northern Securities Company railroad by J. P. Morgan and E. H. Harriman, which would have combined the Northern Pacific and Great Northern lines. Morgan subsequently met with Roosevelt and Knox, suggesting that "If we have

---

[6] Rhodes (1922, 239–240).
[7] Grossman (1975).
[8] Donald (2008, 150).

done anything wrong send your man to my man and they can fix it up," to which Knox replied "We don't want to fix it up ... we want to stop it."[9] However, Roosevelt would subsequently focus less on fragmenting than managing market power in the rail industry. This could be seen most importantly in the Hepburn Act of 1906, which empowered the Interstate Commerce Commission to control rail rates and audit railroad accounts.[10] Roosevelt had foreshadowed this move in his first State of the Union, casting the railway as "a public servant" whose "rates should be just to and open to all."[11] In 1905, when the Senate held the bill up in committee, urging public hearings, Roosevelt took the opportunity to go on a rhetorical swing through the south and midwest. In the process, he advanced the case for the broader stress on fairness underlying what he termed a "Square Deal." Setting forth an egalitarian vision, Roosevelt argued in Dallas that the act embodied "no more intention of discrimination against the rich man than the poor man ... with the intention of safeguarding each ... and giving him nearly as may be a fair chance."[12]

Third, revealing the extent to which Roosevelt's progressivism was premised on the need to work with, rather than dismantle, market power, the Panic of 1907 would see Roosevelt acquiesce to J. P. Morgan's own role as de facto lender of last resort – a particular necessity given that the United States had lacked a central bank since the 1830s.[13] Morgan had, on his own, stepped into this role in response to the collapse of the Knickerbocker Trust Company, halting a wider run by standing behind the Trust Company of America – and in early November locking bankers in his library to enable a "bail in" that would provide a firewall against further panic. In addressing the crisis, Morgan called Treasury Secretary George B. Cortelyou to New York – a request which speaks to the distribution of power between Wall Street and Washington – while Roosevelt ceded power to private finance, staying incommunicado while hunting in Louisiana. When the worst of the panic had passed, Roosevelt wrote his treasury secretary a public letter in which he congratulated "those conservative and substantial businessmen who in this crisis have acted with

[9] Rhodes (1922, 222–223).
[10] Tulis (1987, 101).
[11] Roosevelt (1901).
[12] Tulis (1987, 108–109).
[13] Bruner and Carr (2007, 2).

such wisdom and public spirit."[14] Beyond the gratification to his spirit, Morgan would also profit from his intervention, having arranged during the crisis for U.S. Steel to purchase the Tennessee Coal, Iron and Railroad Company, a major steel producer, and so fueling increased market concentration. Nevertheless, Roosevelt would sign off on the purchase, which he believed necessary to stave off a market collapse – revealing the extent to which he aspired to be less a "trust buster" than a "trust regulator."[15]

Moving forward, while Roosevelt would yield the presidency to his Republican colleague William Howard Taft in 1908, differences between the two over Taft's more legal approach to dismantling corporate power would see Roosevelt reenter the arena in the 1912 campaign, running at the head of his "Bull Moose" party. To the extent that Taft was essentially marginalized in the public eye, the 1912 campaign pitted two versions of Progressivism against one another – in Roosevelt's regulatory New Nationalism and Wilson's antitrust oriented New Freedom. On one hand, speaking to differences of policy substance and rhetorical style, Roosevelt would critique Wilson for advancing "a bit of outworn academic doctrine ... after it had been abandoned by all who had experience of actual life." Condemning the "laissez-faire doctrine of the English political economists three-quarters of a century ago," Roosevelt argued that it was suited only to "a primitive community under primitive conditions" at odds with the "highly organized industries" of the United States.[16] On the other hand, from a more competitively oriented view – in tune with his party's Jeffersonian heritage – Wilson placed a more legal stress on antitrust efforts. In his Labor Day campaign address, Wilson warned that Roosevelt's regulatory approach risked backfiring, on grounds that "once the government regulates the monopoly, then monopoly will see to it that it regulates the government." Later that month, Wilson would similarly affirm that "the history of liberty is a history of the limitation of governmental power, not the increase of it."[17] Wilson also alluded to their differences of rhetorical style, countering objections that he was an overly academic "schoolteacher" by

---

[14] Harbaugh (1961, 311–312).
[15] Bruner and Carr (2007, 132).
[16] Roosevelt (1912).
[17] Cooper (2009, 163–164).

suggesting that "there is one thing a schoolteacher learns that he never forgets, namely, that it is his business to learn all he can and then communicate it to others."[18] With the two Republicans splitting the vote, Wilson's more legally focused New Freedom would prevail – setting the stage for a larger intellectual conversion of the Progressive order.

## 2.3 Converting the Progressive Order: Wilson's New Freedom

In broad terms, Wilson sought to promote a more competitive order, based not only on antitrust principles but also on a more enlightened, intellectualized style of governance. Over his first year, these goals would be embodied in his efforts to lower tariffs, establish the bases of modern fiscal policy, and construct the foundations of the Federal Reserve. Moreover, in using presidential rhetoric, Wilson saw his leadership as embodying not Roosevelt-styled exhortation, but rather cognitive appeals for a more refined deliberation. In early April 1913, Wilson would accordingly break with tradition and deliver his first postinaugural address – on tariff reform – to a joint congressional session. In the address, he further drew a contrast with Roosevelt's view of the presidency as a "bully pulpit," arguing that "I do not know how to wield a big stick ... but I do know how to put my mind at the service of others for the accomplishment of a common purpose."[19]

First, in terms of policy initiatives, Wilson advanced the long-standing Democratic goal of tariff reduction in a way that also expanded the fiscal capacities of the state. In his April address to Congress, he framed the tariff issue in antimonopolist terms, arguing that the United States had "built up a set of privileges and exemptions from competition behind which it was easy by any, even the crudest, forms of combination to organize monopoly." Looking forward, he argued that "[o]nly new principles of action will save us from a final hard crystallization of monopoly."[20] In terms of legislative output, the ultimate Revenue Act – or Underwood Tariff – worked in the immediate sense by lowering the average tariff rate to 25 percent. Perhaps more importantly, Wilson accomplished this in a way that expanded the scope for the

---

[18] Cooper (2009, 164).
[19] Cooper (2009, 214–216).
[20] Wilson (1913a).

exercise of fiscal policy, as lost tariff revenues were supplanted by a progressive income tax – raising $71 million in its first year, making up for the losses of tariff revenues.[21] Over the long run, this act provided the foundation for modern-day fiscal fine-tuning as a tool of managing aggregate demand.

Second, building on a debate that had raged since the 1907 financial crisis, Wilson synthesized a desire for improved monetary governance with a preference for disaggregated power in the initial Federal Reserve System. To be sure, debates over a potential central bank had a long pedigree, encompassing concerns for both credit creation and crisis management. From one side, the Populists had long demanded provisions to increase the seasonal stock of currency in circulation, stressing the need to reduce agrarian dependence on Wall Street, and so favored a publically held, decentralized bank. From another vantage point, representatives of capital – particularly following the 1907 Panic – favored private, concentrated control of the money supply that could provide lender of last resort assistance. Wilson sought to reconcile the views by establishing privately owned regional banks which would be overseen by a presidentially appointed Federal Reserve Board. Making the case for this vision, he would revisit Congress in June 1913, again striking a moderate tone while evoking antimonopolist principles. Wilson urged legislation that would prevent "the concentration anywhere in a few hands of the monetary resources of the country." Elaborating, he argued that any control "must be public, not private … so that the banks may be the instruments, not the masters, of business and of individual enterprise and initiative."[22] Building on this need to limit the regulatory reach of the bank, as well as the intellectualization of debate, Senator Carter Glass argued in congressional debate that the Federal Reserve should aspire to be a "nonpartisan organization whose functions are to be wholly divorced from politics."[23]

Yet, despite these accomplishments, the Wilson administration's focus would soon undergo a shift toward an increasingly New Nationalism–styled stress on regulation. While this shift reflected, in part, domestic political concerns for reelection, the key impetus was

---

[21] Berg (2013, 297).
[22] Wilson (1913b).
[23] Greider (1987, 281).

the outbreak of war in Europe and mobilization pressures. As Arthur Schlesinger, Jr. would put it, Wilson became "the best New Nationalist of them all," as the imperatives of war made necessary "central direction of the economy."[24] To be sure, Wilson was well aware of this possibility, suggesting to Secretary of the Navy Josephus Daniels in late 1916 that "if we enter this war, the great interests which control steel, oil, shipping, munitions factories, mines, will of necessity become dominant factors, and when the war is over our government will be in their hands ... and neither you nor I will live long enough to see our country wrested from the control of monopoly."[25]

This regulatory transformation could be seen most clearly in the realm of price control, as Wilson would establish a War Industries Board, Price Fixing Committee, and Food and Fuel Administrations – the latter established via the Lever Act, which would ironically be redeployed after the war to limit not manufacturing abuses but *labor's* market power.[26] Taking its first steps toward price control in August 1916, the administration established a Council of National Defense and associated Advisory Commission. Wilson supporter and prominent financier Bernard Baruch saw the Advisory Commission as a "Business Men's Commission" that would oversee mobilization, to enable the "leading men" in each industry to advance "quick and economic action."[27] In light of later criticisms for having too close a relationship with business, Baruch would later protest that he made frequent use of hardball tactics, such as threats of curtailment or de-licensing. For example, in a dispute over steel consumption with leaders of the auto companies, Baruch recalled placing a call to the head of the Railroad Administration, instructing him to "take down the names of the following factories, and ... stop every wheel going in and going out," forcing the automakers' capitulation.[28]

However, more lasting lessons could also be drawn from patterns of regulatory success, particularly as imperfectly competitive industries seemed most susceptible to market control. Speaking to these structural bases of restraint, the Price-Fixing Committee's chief economist Frank Taussig cited the stabilization of nickel, where the

[24] Schlesinger (1957, 37).
[25] Cuff (1969, 386–387).
[26] Rockoff (1984, 43).
[27] Cuff (1969, 387–388).
[28] Rockoff (1984, 46).

American Nickel Company stood as "a single producer, in possession of a complete monopoly." Taussig noted that "notwithstanding heavy increase in public demand and an eventual absorption for military use of virtually the entire supply, the price remained the same as that before the war, and was so maintained throughout."[29] Moving from this structural extreme, Taussig described a policy mix combining the application of a "bulk line" pricing principle with the use of an excess-profits tax. To identify these levels, economists constructed cost curves ranging from low-cost to high-cost producers, in which "a price was fixed which would 'protect' four-fifths or nine-tenths of the entire output." To prevent low-cost producers from reaping windfall profits, Taussig finally argued that they would be subject to a "heavy excess profits tax."[30]

Such successes aside, the war's end would see the Wilson administration move – if erratically – to curtail regulatory controls in favor of revived antitrust efforts. Such dynamics can be seen in the rise and fall of the Commerce Department's Industrial Board, which was set up to enable industry coordination in easing reconversion. The impetus for the Board came from business, as the Chamber of Commerce organized a December 1918 "Reconstruction Congress," at which participants called for reforms to enable "reasonable trade agreements." These proposals were supported by Treasury Secretary Carter Glass and Commerce Secretary William Redford, who cabled Wilson in Paris that the Industrial Board would seek "to secure by voluntary action the establishment of a reduced level of prices." While accepting the merit of the Industrial Board, Wilson also qualified his approval by noting that "it may be in contravention of [the] Sherman Anti-trust law." However, a postwar recession spanning August 1918–March 1919 initially kept such objections in check.[31] In its initial measures, the Board sought to reach a price-fixing agreement with steel firms, holding a conference, in March, at which steel producers were prematurely told that any agreement would enjoy antitrust immunity and would be

---

[29] Taussig (1919, 217).
[30] Taussig (1919, 218–220).
[31] Anticipating objections that the Board would violate antitrust law, Chairman Peek wrote to Attorney General A. Mitchell Palmer in March, and argued that "[e]very combination in restraint of trade" was not necessarily out of line, and that the Sherman Act was not meant to limit governmental coordination. Himmelberg (1968, 7–9, 13).

respected by government purchasers – most importantly the Railroad Administration.[32] Yet, these guarantees would incite backlash from *within* the government, as the Railroad Administration argued it was not bound by Industrial Board agreements and the Justice Department and Treasury revived antitrust concerns. While the Industrial Board initially felt that such objections could be overcome through higher appeals, Treasury Secretary Glass and Attorney General Palmer cast the Board's efforts as "in violation of the anti-trust laws."[33] On May 7, Wilson moved to dissolve the Board.[34] The brief attempt at a postwar regulatory order had been defeated, with revived New Freedom–styled antitrust appeals playing a key role.

Ironically – in a way that highlights the importance of ideas – the Wilson administration's antitrust commitment would be seen even more clearly in its relations with labor, which deteriorated amid a postwar Red Scare exacerbated by domestic violence – perhaps most importantly for administration figures in an attempted bombing of Attorney General Palmer's home. More broadly, late 1919 saw two strikes represent key setbacks for labor, which would limit its aggressiveness going forward. First, September 1919 would see Boston police officers strike to obtain union recognition and improved working conditions. Successfully constructing the strike as an assault on public safety, Massachusetts Governor Calvin Coolidge would dismiss and refuse to rehire the strikers, famously asserting that there was "no right to strike against the public safety by anybody, anywhere, anytime."[35] Second, in a reversal of Theodore Roosevelt's balanced stance from the 1902 anthracite coal strike, the Wilson administration moved against the United Mineworkers (UMW) union in a November 1919 coal strike. Invoking the wartime Lever Act – which had been created to limit corporate price-fixing – Attorney General Palmer issued an injunction against the strike and threatened criminal charges against union leader John L. Lewis, prompting the UMW to retreat. These trends were reinforced in the context of Federal Reserve monetary restraint and a recession over 1920–1921 – one Milton Friedman and Anna J. Schwartz later termed "the sharpest price decline ... perhaps

---

[32] Himmelberg (1968, 13–15).
[33] Himmelberg (1968, 17–19).
[34] Himmelberg (1968, 20–21).
[35] Schlaes (2014, 171).

also in the whole history of the United States."[36] Given this backdrop, labor assertiveness – and so wage-based demand – would be curtailed for much of the next decade.

Indeed, coming at the end of two decades of Progressive advance, the early postwar years would witness a diminution of reformist ardor – as Republican presidential candidate Warren Harding urged a "return to normalcy." Speaking to a mounting disillusionment among Progressives, Arthur Schlesinger Jr. would later argue that just "as Clemenceau slew the liberal dream in Paris, so Palmer slew it in America; and, in each case, Woodrow Wilson was the accomplice."[37] In the absence of reformist energies, economic policy would be reduced to monetary fine-tuning – with the residue of Progressive faith in apolitical policymaking fueling misplaced confidence in the ability of the Federal Reserve to reconcile growth, wage-price stability, asset-price stability, and currency stability.

## 2.4 The Collapse of the Progressive Order: Monetary Overconfidence and the Great Crash

Having followed its monetary restraint of 1920–1921 by facilitating milder slowdowns in the 1923 and 1926 efforts to limit inflation, the Federal Reserve oversaw what Milton Friedman and Anna J. Schwartz would describe as the "high tide" of monetary policy, "a period of high prosperity and stable economic growth" in which "recessions were clearly registered only on the delicate seismographs economists and statisticians were developing."[38] Indeed, monetary policy was largely "on its own" over this decade, reflecting widespread confidence in its potential ability to keep the economy on an even keel. In contrast, fiscal and regulatory policy were "locked in" to expansionary tacks. Over the decade, Treasury Secretary Andrew W. Mellon pushed to cut marginal tax rates four times, overseeing a reduction from 77 percent to 25 percent. Likewise, Federal Trade Commission Chairs such as William Humphrey came to see its purpose as meant to *encourage* industry collusion, as antitrust efforts fell by the wayside.[39]

---

[36] Friedman and Schwartz (1963, 232).
[37] Schlesinger (1957, 44).
[38] Friedman and Schwartz (1963, 296).
[39] Schlesinger (1957, 65).

In this light, the 1920s would be marked by increasing confidence in the Federal Reserve's ability to reconcile concerns for exchange-rate stability and asset-price stability with economic growth. Yet, regarding exchange-rate stability, no hegemonic or institutional mechanism existed to reconcile the deflationary gold standard with growth. Moreover, the British decision in 1925 to return the pound to prewar parity at its prewar level resulted in intensified pressures within Britain to cut wages and generate balance of payments surpluses. In this context, Keynes himself emerged as a leading critic, lamenting, in a piece on "The Economic Consequences of Mr. Churchill," that the chancellor of the exchequer was, in restoring the prewar parity

> committing himself to force down money wages and all money values, without any idea how it was to be done. Why did he do such a silly thing? Partly, perhaps, because he has no instinctive judgment to prevent him from making mistakes; partly because, lacking this instinctive judgment, he was deafened by the clamorous voices of conventional finance; and most of all, because he was gravely misled by his experts.[40]

Exchange-rate stability would in turn clash with a second priority, of asset-price stability. In mid-1927, New York Federal Reserve Governor Benjamin Strong cut interest rates from 4 percent to 3.5 percent, in large part at the urging of British, French, and German monetary policymakers who had met with Strong in New York and argued that a reduction would help in sending funds back toward London. Federal Reserve Board member Adolph Miller later cast these moves as "father and mother to the subsequent 1929 collapse."[41] Nevertheless, Strong would dismiss concerns for an asset-price bubble, arguing that monetary policy could limit any collapse, expressing misplaced confidence that

> the very existence of the Federal Reserve System is a safeguard against anything like a calamity growing out of money rates. Not only have we the power to deal with such an emergency instantly by flooding the street with money, but I think the country is well aware of this and probably places reliance upon the common sense and power of the System.[42]

Strong's successor at the New York Federal Reserve, George Harrison, would in early 1929 encounter further tensions between

---

[40] Keynes (1931, 248–249).
[41] Greider (1987, 297).
[42] Greider (1987, 298–299).

policy objectives as he pushed for a discretionary tightening to rein in speculation – only to encounter opposition from the Federal Reserve Board in Washington, concerned about the costs of asset-price restraint for real economic growth.[43] In February 1929, reflecting a Strong-styled confidence in the flexibility of monetary policy, Harrison argued that a "sharp, incisive action" to raise interest rates could break speculative demand and enable the Federal Reserve to "get back to a lower rate position ... as speedily as possible in order to provide business, commerce and industry with lower rates." The Board countered that "a rate increase was a most serious step ... and that [the Fed] should not do so except as a last resort."[44] Complicating matters, exchange-rate concerns remained relevant. As Barry Eichengreen later noted, New York Federal Reserve Governor Harrison and Bank of England head Montagu Norman each had concluded by February 1929 "that the Fed would have to raise interest rates temporarily to prick the stock market bubble, after which they would be reduced to stem the capital inflow," steps that would cause a "short-run inconvenience" but offer "long-term benefits."[45]

To the extent that these tensions might be eased, the long-neglected possibility of regulation offered a brief promise, but the feint in that direction came too late. In early 1929, the Federal Reserve Board moved to use moral suasion to limit the speculative use of Federal Reserve loans by brokers as an alternative to restraint. On February 2, 1929, the Board issued a warning against "the use of the resources of the Federal Reserve Banks for the creation or extension of speculative credit," and member-bank borrowing "for the purpose of making speculative loans."[46] Yet, in the midst of these efforts at "direct pressure,"

---

[43] Friedman and Schwartz (1963, 412–413) later held that "if Strong had still been alive and head of the New York Bank in the fall of 1930, he would very likely have recognized the oncoming liquidity crisis for what it was, would have been prepared by experience and conviction to take strenuous and appropriate measures to head it off, and would have had the standing to carry the System with him." This may be overrating the ability of any single agent to fine-tune economic growth and asset-price stability. Ben Bernanke would later voice admiration for Strong – and was likely more sophisticated in his later view of markets – but even Bernanke, eighty years later, could not devise the appropriate monetary policy to keep growth going while restraining a speculative mania.
[44] Eichengreen (1992, 219–220).
[45] Eichengreen (1992, 218–220).
[46] Galbraith (1954, 33).

the Board resisted regional banks' calls for monetary restraint, and would do so another ten times over the year.[47] In the immediate context, the February 2 statement was followed by decline in stock prices. By late March, momentum toward a more prolonged decline appeared to have accumulated, as the rate for call money hit 20 percent – the highest since the 1921 slump.[48] Yet, the Board would also be countered in late March by New York banks on grounds of averting a potential panic. On March 27, National City Bank President Charles E. Mitchell declared National City willing to lend $25 million dollars on call, arguing that this move was "paramount to any Federal Reserve warning, or anything else, to avert any dangerous crisis in the money market."[49] While the National City move was denounced by leading figures such as Senator Carter Glass, the thwarted Federal Reserve would not move again to tighten.[50]

The effects of such direct pressure have been the subject of long-standing debate. Following the Board's warning, the market stabilized, and rose by only 3 percent in the first half of the year.[51] Arguing for the effectiveness of the Federal Reserve's moral restraints, John Kenneth Galbraith later noted that given that the market ascent had only been temporarily halted, this was widely seen as demonstrating the limits of moral suasion. However, he countered that "the opposite conclusion could and probably should have been drawn" on the grounds that it would be difficult to imagine "a milder, more tentative, more palpably panic-stricken communiqué than that issued by the Board."[52] In contrast, Friedman and Schwartz condemned direct pressure for failing to address fundamental monetary sources of inflation, casting "hopes placed in direct pressure [as] ... doomed to disappointment."[53] Striking a middle ground, Barry Eichengreen later noted that the "most dramatic increase in stock prices took place in July and August, immediately after moral suasion was relaxed." From this vantage point, Eichengreen concluded that although "it is not certain that the policy of direct pressure was responsible for the stability of

---

[47] Eichengreen (1992, 218).
[48] Allen (1931, 255); Galbraith (1975, 179).
[49] Galbraith (1975, 179).
[50] Galbraith (1954, 41); Friedman and Schwartz (1963, 264–265).
[51] Eichengreen (1992, 218).
[52] Galbraith (1954, 34–35).
[53] Friedman and Schwartz (1963, 266).

share prices between January and June, neither is it obvious that the policy was ineffectual."[54] Ultimately, even Friedman and Schwartz conceded that the Federal Reserve faced a trade-off between growth and asset-price stability, as the goal of "promoting business activity" conflicted with "the desire to restrain stock market speculation." Unable to reconcile this trade-off, the Federal Reserve's policy was "not restrictive enough to halt the bull market yet too restrictive to foster vigorous business expansion."[55]

Yet, confidence in monetary policy would die hard. On October 19, the Harvard Economic Society held out the hope that "if recession should threaten serious consequences for business (as is not indicated at present) there is little doubt that Reserve System would take steps to ease the money market to check the movement."[56] Barely a week later, the onset of the Great Crash marked the first step in discrediting an array of conventional wisdoms. The first casualty pertained to the *private* monetary policy embodied in J. P. Morgan-styled efforts at providing "organized support." In contrast to the "bailing in" of bankers in the 1907 crisis, private efforts would now prove ineffective. On the first day of the crash, Thursday, October 24, the New York financial elite attempted both monetary intervention and moral suasion, with Morgan partner Thomas Lamont suggesting that there had been "a little distress selling," but arguing that "the heads of several financial institutions" had met and found that "margins are being maintained satisfactorily."[57] Such efforts sparked a rally, but only a brief one. Having lost 11 percent of its value on Thursday the 24th, the market lost another 12 percent on "Black Tuesday," October 29. As Friedman and Schwartz put it, "[b]y the second week after the crash the phase of organized support of the market was over."[58]

Over a longer term, Classical doctrines that counseled acquiescence to deflation would also lose ground. These stressed the need to accept wage, price, and share value losses as the cost of recovery, on the grounds that lower wages would spur more hiring, lower prices would spur more purchases, and such moves could together revive growth. From this perspective, in accord with Irving Fisher's quantity theory of

---

[54] Eichengreen (1992, 218).
[55] Friedman and Schwartz (1963, 213).
[56] Allen (1931, 270).
[57] Allen (1931, 274); Galbraith (1954, 101–102).
[58] Friedman and Schwartz (1963, 305n).

money, fiscal or monetary stimulus would only fuel inflation. Speaking up for this view, Treasury Secretary Andrew Mellon would stress the need to "[l]iquidate labor, liquidate stocks, liquidate the farmers, [and] liquidate real estate." Moreover, Mellon's view was attached to a set of asserted principles, as he argued such deflation would "purge the rottenness out of the system. High costs of living and high living will come down. People will work harder, live a more moral life."[59] Hoover would reject such views, albeit at first pursuing a range of ad hoc measures to deal more with the human costs of the crash than to implement any formal macroeconomic attempt at raising demand. In the early post-Crash setting, Hoover sought to aid labor and successfully exhorted business to avoid wage reductions as a means to limit suffering.[60] Looking back, he would argue that "seventeen months from the stock-market crash in October, 1929, to April, 1931 ... was a period of a comparatively mild domestic readjustment," in which "unemployment of the family breadwinners rose to about 2,000,000, or probably not more than 1,000,000 over the normal." In this light, Hoover argued that his program was working and that – by January, 1931 – the United States "had paid the price for our own economic misdeeds and were convalescing."[61]

However, with the onset of the European crises of mid-1931, Hoover would initiate a more direct effort at working with private agents to make up for the unwillingness of the Federal Reserve to act as lender of last resort, enabling financial collusion and providing direct aid to lenders. Hoover's efforts to promote action by capital would fuel the October 1931 establishment of a National Credit Corporation, which sought to push better-capitalized banks to lend to their weaker rivals. Unfortunately, as Hoover later put it, "[a]fter a few weeks of enterprising courage the bankers' National Credit Association became ultra-conservative, then fearful, and finally died" as "[i]ts members – and the business world – threw up their hands and asked for governmental action."[62] Hoover would accordingly go a step further and establish in early 1932 the more autonomous Reconstruction Finance Corporation (RFC) to lend more than $3 billion directly to troubled

---

[59] Hoover (1952, 30–32).
[60] Hoover (1952, 41–43).
[61] Hoover (1952, 38).
[62] Hoover (1952, 97).

financial institutions. To be sure, the RFC would encounter difficulties of its own, as charges of cronyism and favoritism spurred calls to make public the identity of borrowing institutions. Such difficulties aside, however, the RFC was accompanied by a temporary easing of the cascade of bank failures.[63]

Moving into the 1932 campaign, there were also limits that neither Hoover nor his Democratic rival Franklin D. Roosevelt would initially breach – as each voiced a principled aversion to fiscal or monetary stimulus. Hoover argued that a balanced budget was an "absolute necessity" and "the foundation of all public and private financial stability."[64] Roosevelt likewise promised to cut spending, on grounds that "Any government, like any family, can for a year spend a little more than it earns" but that "a continuation of that habit means the poorhouse."[65] Moreover, there were also larger limits on the scope for budget stimulus, as the federal government was as yet too small to have fiscal policy exert a meaningful influence, comprising little more than approximately 3 percent of GDP.[66] Yet, even as Roosevelt would be as constrained as Hoover by the initial limits to fiscal possibilities, he would soon break with *monetary* orthodoxies. These inclinations could be seen in the transition period between Roosevelt's victory and inauguration: on February 18, 1933, Hoover wrote Roosevelt to urge that he provide "prompt assurance that there will be no tampering with or inflation of the currency; that the budget will be unquestionably balanced ... [and] that the government credit will be maintained" – later privately noting to a colleague that "if these declarations be made by the president-elect, he will have ratified the whole major program of the Republican Administration." Roosevelt would wait a week before replying, suggesting that he had "mislaid" the letter, before dismissing Hoover's analysis and request.[67] While Hoover's policy evolved in iterative fashion across the postcrash period, he was no closet Keynesian, leaving Roosevelt wide scope for ensuing monetary, regulatory, and fiscal innovations.

---

[63] Friedman and Schwartz (1963, 320).
[64] Schlesinger (1957, 232).
[65] Roosevelt, Radio Address on the National Democratic Platform from Albany, New York; July 30, 1932.
[66] Stein (1996, 14).
[67] Feis (1966, 82–83).

## 2.5 Conclusions

Over its construction, conversion, and collapse, the Progressive era would see Theodore Roosevelt's principled fast thinking appeals for regulatory restraints undergo an intellectual conversion in favor of Woodrow Wilson's more restrained, slow thinking antitrust efforts, only to see monetary overconfidence in turn presage the order's collapse in the Great Crash. Initially, Theodore Roosevelt constructed the foundations of the Progressive order on appeals for regulatory efforts to advance a coalitional balance – culminating in his 1912 campaign "New Nationalist" agenda. In the process, Roosevelt would employ rhetoric in affective appeals that foreshadowed Franklin Roosevelt's construction of the New Deal and Ronald Reagan's advocacy of a more Neoliberal order. Subsequently, as the Progressive order matured, Woodrow Wilson countered Roosevelt in urging a "New Freedom" agenda that advocated not only a more legalistic approach to promoting perfect competition, but also laid the foundations – in the Federal Reserve Act of 1913 and the Revenue Act of 1913 – for the increasing reliance on fiscal or monetary fine-tuning. In seeking to justify this approach, Wilson would foreshadow the efforts of successors such as John F. Kennedy and Bill Clinton as they sought to remove debate from the realm of exhortative appeals in favor of more technical, "third way" styled approaches. Finally, over the 1920s, regulatory and legal efforts would yield to the increasing use of monetary fine-tuning to reconcile tensions between currency stability, financial stability, and growth. While early 1929 would see the New York Federal Reserve belatedly impose "direct pressure" on speculative lending, this would prove to be too late, and the October crash would accelerate the onset of the Great Depression. Hoover's iterative response to the crisis would be marked by a ratcheting up of governmental involvement in the economy, but it was also limited as – across the shifts from October 1929 to the aftermath of the European crises – he kept moving in the direction of supporting finance, resisting innovations that might have strengthened labor or raised demand in any sustained way. In sum, taken as a whole, even as the Progressive order provided a foundation for prolonged stability, its evolution would fuel increasing misplaced certainty in fine-tuning, eventually engendering renewed instability and crisis.

Taken as a whole, the Progressive order's rise and fall tracked stages of order construction, conversion, and misplaced certainty which led to collapse in crisis. Moreover, it is worth stressing that this rise and fall of the Progressive order would not simply prefigure the evolution of its Keynesian and Neoliberal successors. It witnessed the construction of *three* new institutional features of the American political order that would make possible their further refinements of economic institutions. These encompassed not only the use of fiscal policy in the income tax and monetary policy as employed by the Federal Reserve, but also the emergence of the modern rhetorical presidency itself – marked by ongoing expectation of presidential involvement in policy deliberation, particularly during crises.[68] This increasing importance of presidential rhetoric would pose a problem where subsequent orders would be initially dependent on the principled leadership of rhetorical presidents, who would cede authority over time to institutional and intellectual elites favoring reliance on macroeconomic fine-tuning. In such settings, where instability might recur, and rhetorical presidents sought to reengage late-order debates, they would often find that the moral capital that had enabled earlier regulatory and exhortative appeals had lapsed. This suggests that policy effectiveness is not simply a function of ahistorical institutional design, but rather of political time.

---

[68] On the institutional evolution of the rhetorical presidency, see Tulis (1987).

PART II

# The Construction, Conversion, and Collapse of the Keynesian Order

# 3 Constructing the Keynesian Order: Breaking Finance and Boosting Labor

The achievement of victory in war and security in peace requires the participation of all the people in the common effort for our common cause.

Franklin D. Roosevelt, 1942[1]

Wage policy raises far-reaching psychological and political issues. It can only be handled by a simple, trustful and imaginative policy which covers a wider field than technical finance.

John Maynard Keynes, 1940[2]

## 3.1 Introduction

If the Progressive era began with Theodore Roosevelt seeking a truce between Hamilton and Jefferson – by striking a balance between capital, labor, and agriculture – the Keynesian era began with Franklin Roosevelt advancing a new egalitarian synthesis by reinterpreting Hamilton and Jefferson in light of Keynes. Where Hamiltonian "big government" initially favored capital against Jeffersonian agriculture and labor, Roosevelt offered a reconstructed view of Hamiltonian big government as *supporting* agriculture and labor through Keynesian policies promoting demand and growth. Employing principled fast thinking appeals, Roosevelt evoked and sustained positive attitudes toward the state. Moreover, Roosevelt would employ this rhetoric in a way that would have a reflexive, self-reinforcing effect on market structures and sentiments. This could be seen across his early successes in assuaging popular anxieties in the March 1933 banking crises, as he employed rhetoric to limit self-reinforcing bank runs, through to his April 1942 efforts to contain any self-reinforcing wage-price spiral. Such appeals would be refined by Truman and Eisenhower, who would

---

[1] Roosevelt (1942a).
[2] Keynes (1940b).

mix principled exhortation with efforts at inculcating self-reinforcing wage-price expectations – in order to minimize the inflationary concerns that could preclude a potential macroeconomic stimulus. The result would be to provide principled foundations for prolonged stable growth.

Over this chapter, I accordingly trace these early foundations of the Keynesian order, as its principled construction across the Roosevelt, Truman, and Eisenhower administrations enabled their use of exhortation, guidelines, and controls to stabilize tensions between inflation and unemployment. In the first section, I highlight the evolving accord between Keynesian values and Roosevelt's principled claims – as Keynes's principled stress on "macro" or collective interests accorded with Roosevelt's egalitarian approaches to addressing the 1930s depression and containing the 1940s inflation. In the second section, I address the postwar efforts of the Truman administration in constructing crises as stemming from steel, railroad, and mining strikes to legitimate continued wage-price restraint while enabling ongoing growth. In the third section, I address the Eisenhower-era construction of a "New Inflation" – combining rising inflation and unemployment – as driven by corporate and labor power, justifying appeals to shared interests in limiting inflation and stabilizing the Bretton Woods fixed exchange rates. Finally, I pull back to address the broader institutional and societal context, as societal trust provided a key backdrop supporting wage-price restraint. Taken as a whole, this analysis highlights the importance of principled leadership to stabilizing expectations and preempting trade-offs between growth and wage, price or currency stability.

## 3.2 Roosevelt: Constructing the Keynesian Order in a Regulatory-Macroeconomic Mix

While the construction of the Keynesian order rested heavily on the cognitive innovations in Keynes's *General Theory*, its popular accessibility depended on accord with Roosevelt's principled egalitarian rhetoric. In cognitive terms, the essential insight of Keynesian macroeconomics pertains to the existence of a "fallacy of composition," as private "micro" incentives can produce perverse public "macro" outcomes – justifying efforts to promote a uniquely common good. To be sure, Keynes himself acted as a public intellectual, and recognized the need to situate cognitive appeals in principled settings. For example, Keynes would stress the self-defeating nature of wage-price competition – offering principled arguments that "what is to the advantage of each of us regarded as a solitary individual is to the disadvantage of each of us regarded as members of a community."[3] In this light, Keynes's principles accorded with Franklin Roosevelt's arguments regarding the need for cooperation to alleviate the two broad goals spanning his administration – first, to recover from the Great Depression by promoting inflation and full employment, and second, – once war had bought a return to full employment – to contain revived wartime inflation. For example, in early 1933 – in his first "fireside chat" on the banking crisis – Roosevelt condemned private "hoarding" as contrary to the public interest.[4] Nearly a decade later, Roosevelt would advance a parallel appeal in containing the 1940s wage-price spirals, urging "common effort for our common cause."[5] In this way, the sentiments stayed the same, even as the policy ends varied.

## Keynesian Sentiment in the 1930s: Reversing the Downward Spiral

In his inaugural address, Roosevelt articulated a common interest in addressing the spreading bank panic. To reverse the tide, Roosevelt's construction of the crisis appealed to a public interest in private restraint. Little more than a week into his presidency, Roosevelt broadcast a nationwide appeal. Condemning private "hoarding" as "exceedingly unfashionable," Roosevelt argued that "when the people find that they can get their money – that they can get it when they want it for all legitimate purposes – the phantom of fear will soon be laid." In contrast, in the absence of a sufficient public spirit, Roosevelt warned that markets would be "stampeded by rumors or guesses."[6] Having issued his principled appeal, Roosevelt then described a process by which all banks would be closed, with those the government deemed solvent to be reopened soon after, and – after a slightly longer interregnum – less stable banks would be shored up

---

[3] Keynes (1940a, 5).
[4] Roosevelt (1933b).
[5] Roosevelt (1942a).
[6] Roosevelt (1933b).

with government aid. In the end, however, those banks held to be fundamentally insolvent would be permitted to fail. Through such rhetorical appeals, Roosevelt succeeded in stabilizing expectations and limiting the crisis.

Having stemmed the banking crisis, the administration then shifted to reforms meant to contain abuses of financial power. The first such initiative came in the Banking Act of 1933, which established the Federal Deposit Insurance Corporation (FDIC) to limit the potential for self-reinforcing bank runs and sought to break financial power by separating investment from commercial banks. Two years later, the Banking Act of 1935 strengthened the ability of the state to act as a source of countervailing power, reorganizing the Federal Reserve and increasing the power of the Board of Governors and Federal Open Market Committee relative to the district banks. Where money and banking interacted, Roosevelt moved to break with gold and its deflationary pull, taking the United States off the gold standard after less than two months in office and urging Congress to give him power to devalue the dollar and issue $3 billion in new currency.[7] Stressing the need to promote inflation, Roosevelt argued that the key problem was to "raise commodity prices" and otherwise let the dollar "take care of itself." Congress quickly passed legislation abrogating contracts stipulating payment in gold, with even J. P. Morgan terming the move "the best possible course under existing circumstances."[8] Moving to oppose the gold standard at an international level, Roosevelt would capsize the June 1933 London Economic Conference which had been meant to restabilize the international monetary system. Speaking at a June 30 news conference, Roosevelt declared that the "the United States was not going to be pushed around" and – once the conference had started – warned in a cable to London that currency agreements were secondary to concerns for the "sound internal economic system" of any state. To be sure, some limited cooperation would ensue, as the Gold Reserve Act of 1934 created an Exchange Stabilization Fund to bolster the dollar during periods of instability and a 1936 Tripartite Agreement with the English and French governments worked to enable

---

[7] Ahamed (2009, 461); Feis (1966, 144).
[8] Signaling the fading of Federal Reserve influence, the New York Federal Reserve's George Harrison later told the Bank of England's Montagu Norman that he had been surprised by the devaluation, having been left "completely in the dark." Ahamed (2009, 465); Smith (2007, 328–329).

monetary cooperation.⁹ Yet – having broken the gold standard – a formal alternative would emerge only in the context of a wartime commitment to the more inflationary Bretton Woods order.¹⁰

Indeed, inflationary sentiments would provide a key foundation for what was initially the signature act of the New Deal, as the establishment of the National Recovery Administration (NRA) broke with antitrust norms and was established to craft a series of codes to enable wage and price-fixing. The NRA permitted trade associations to write codes prescribing maximum hours and minimum wages, balancing against them an increased scope for collective bargaining. To the extent that demand required a degree of macroeconomic accommodation, the act provided $3.3 billion in government spending by a Public Works Administration (PWA).¹¹ However, despite a flurry of initial enthusiasm in NRA parades and the distribution of "Blue Eagle" decals, PWA Head Harold Ickes proved reluctant to spend. This led Roosevelt to shift funds from Ickes's Public Works budget and appoint Harry Hopkins as head of a Civil Works Administration, which found employment for 4 million by 1934.¹² Nevertheless, its complexities would undermine support for the NRA, which would be ruled unconstitutional by the Supreme Court in 1935. Roosevelt privately conceded that the NRA had itself become too cumbersome, remarking to Labor Secretary Frances Perkins that it had been "an awful headache" and stressing that he had not wished to "set aside the anti-trust laws on any permanent basis."¹³ In this light, the significance of the Supreme Court's dismantling of the NRA can be overrated, particularly as the administration moved to promote labor's bargaining power even more directly by throwing its support behind the Wagner Act, which sought to redress the "inequality of bargaining power" between employees and employers. Rather than seek a cooperative accord between labor and capital in raising wages and prices – as Theodore Roosevelt had attempted in 1902 or as had been embodied in the NRA – the expanded scope for collective bargaining would increase the importance of wage-driven demand vis-à-vis investment-driven growth.

⁹ Helleiner (1994, 24).
¹⁰ On the benefits of a break with gold, see Romer (1992).
¹¹ Smith (2007, 331).
¹² Smith (2007, 345).
¹³ Smith (2007, 344–345).

Yet, even as the administration had successfully staunched the bleeding from the depths of 1933 – when unemployment had peaked at a historic high of 25 percent – fiscal activism remained limited both by value-laden wariness of deficits and the underdeveloped theoretical edifice of the Keynesian model. While fiscal policy had moved in an expansionary direction – with the deficit reaching 5.5 percent of GDP in 1936 and unemployment falling to 14.3 percent by 1937 – inflation fears would spur a move back toward balance as the deficit was brought to 0.1 percent of GDP in 1938.[14] This produced a reversal of economic fortunes, as unemployment shot back up to 19 percent. In this light, Keynes's *General Theory* would play a key role in providing a basis for macroeconomic activism, leading economists to stress the merit of fiscal policy as it could put funds directly in consumers' pockets. Keynes would memorably argue that if the Treasury "were to fill old bottles with banknotes, bury them at suitable depths in disused coalmines which are then filled up to the surface with town rubbish, and leave it to private enterprise on well-tried principles of laissez-faire to dig the notes up again ... there need be no more unemployment." While granting that it would be "more sensible to build houses and the like ... the above would be better than nothing."[15] Such were the principled restraints on fiscal policy that, even after the 1937 slump, only war would make the necessary spending politically respectable – as deficits rose from 17.8 percent of GDP in 1942 to 37.1 percent of GDP in 1942. In turn, unemployment would plummet – from 9.9 percent in 1941 to 4.7 percent in 1942 and 1.9 percent in 1943.[16] Yet, success in promoting demand would give rise to a second phase of policy, as the return to full employment would raise concerns for inflationary wage-price spirals.

## Keynesian Sentiment in the 1940s: Containing an Upward Spiral

Having moved from efforts to avert deflation, the Roosevelt administration now faced a new challenge – of reconciling full employment with price stability. Shaping debate by modifying insights from *The*

[14] Council of Economic Advisers (2000, 398; 2014, 378).
[15] Keynes (1936a, 129).
[16] Council of Economic Advisers (2000, 398; 2014, 378).

*General Theory* in a pamphlet on *How to Pay for the War*, Keynes himself would emphasize the anti-inflation merit of fiscal contraction, urging a "deferred earnings" plan to limit demand. However, highlighting the need for controls, Keynes would also note that "some measure of rationing and price control should play a part" in any anti-inflation efforts. This would prevent "wages and prices chasing one another upwards," as during World War I.[17] Nevertheless, the US shift to a recognition of the need for controls would occur gradually, as economists would move from an early support for piecemeal or sectoral controls to support the use of "universal" guidelines. For example, Director of the Price Division of the Office of Price Administration (OPA) John Kenneth Galbraith initially resisted calls by Wilsonian-era price controller Bernard Baruch for a "cap on all prices, once and for all," employing a sector-by-sector approach.[18] Yet, this ultimately proved inadequate, given differentials in the rate of control across sectors. Galbraith later wrote that the OPA "faced a hitherto unforeseen problem, one that should have been foreseen" as "each price-fixing action took time ... [and] some divisions ... were more deliberate than others ... Since one firm's prices could be another's costs, the uncontrolled or later-controlled prices were beginning to unhinge those under earlier control."[19]

By March 1942, Galbraith had come to accept that the piecemeal approach "had been very wrong. We needed, somehow, to move on all prices at once – place a general ceiling over all."[20] Moreover, the need for popular consent meant that Roosevelt himself would need to advance a principled appeal, employing the sort of communicative rhetoric that had prevented the deflationary run on the banks in 1933 – now to prevent inflationary wage-price spirals. Roosevelt would accordingly issue in April 1942 the General Maximum Price Regulation or "General Max" ruling, freezing all US prices at their March levels. In an address to Congress, Roosevelt further stressed the need for a sense of public responsibility, arguing that preventing inflation would require "common effort for our common cause."[21] In effect, Roosevelt recast his criticisms of hoarding from 1933, applying them to the new

[17] Keynes (1940a, 51, 73).
[18] Galbraith (1981, 142).
[19] Galbraith (1981, 164).
[20] Galbraith (1981, 164).
[21] Roosevelt (1942a).

context of the wage-price spiral, as he warned in a national-broadcast fireside chat that "a few seem very willing to approve self-denial – on the part of their neighbors," and called instead for a "comprehensive, all-embracing program covering prices, and profits, and wages, and taxes and debts."[22] Such rhetoric both accorded with and facilitated private restraint on behalf of a wider public good.

Nevertheless, the General Max ruling would prove only a partial remedy. Criticism of the OPA would mount over 1942, given the persistence of inflation, even though the OPA lacked the ability to regulate commodity prices and the War Labor Board (WLB) similarly lacked the ability to set wages. In October 1942, having warned Congress that he would act even in the absence of legislative support, Roosevelt secured passage of a new Stabilization Act, which would centralize control of wages, prices, and rents under a broader Office of Economic Stabilization, which would work through the OPA and WLB.[23] Yet, also recognizing a latent libertarian wariness in business opposition, the administration would accept a new mandate that OPA officials possess five years of business experience, forcing out a number of academics, including OPA Director Leon Henderson and Galbraith.[24] Following the 1942 electoral Republican gains, Henderson would be replaced by former Michigan senator Prentiss Brown, who would appoint as information director former advertising executive Lou Maxon, a vocal critic of OPA "slide rule boys, professors, theorists, and lawyers."[25] Ironically, Maxon himself would resign in July 1943, after having lost a struggle to ensure that all regulations went through his office. On leaving, he would issue a last parting shot, denouncing OPA efforts to prohibit price premiums for branding. Maxon argued that this represented an opening attack on advertisers' freedom of speech, terming it "the greatest threat to American industry and our way of life that ever existed, because it is without question the spearhead in the drive to eliminate brands, trademarks, and eventually free enterprise."[26]

---

[22] Roosevelt (1942b).
[23] Mansfield (1947, 52).
[24] Following the 1942 midterm Republican gains, OPA Director Leon Henderson would resign, and Galbraith would last only a few more months, departing in May 1943. Rockoff (1984, 96).
[25] Rockoff (1984, 94).
[26] Rockoff (1984, 95).

Taking these difficulties together, as OPA administrators faced persistent appeals to permit price increases, the administration moved again to bolster the agency's power. On April 8, 1943, Roosevelt issued a "Hold the Line" order, which denied the OPA price administrator the ability to grant any price relief unless explicitly required by law, and only then to the absolute minimum permitted. In announcing the order, Roosevelt again stressed the need for a recognition of uniquely public interests to halt the wage-price spiral, arguing that "the only way to hold the line is to stop trying to find justifications for not holding it here or not holding it there."[27] The order more specifically tightened up standards at the Department of Agriculture and the War Labor Board. Later in the year, the promotion of former advertising executive Chester Bowles to replace Brown would enable the OPA's recovery from the struggles of 1942–1943. OPA efforts would subsequently remain quite effective. Inflation, which had hovered at around 10 percent for most of 1940 and until early 1942, remained below 3 percent for the remainder of the war. More significantly, in terms of later debates over Phillips curve-styled inflation-unemployment trade-offs, this price stability was accompanied by unemployment of less than 2 percent.[28]

However, these successes cannot be explained in abstraction from ongoing communicative appeals, which were rooted not only in Roosevelt's interpretive leadership, but also in popular mobilization efforts, particularly under OPA Consumer Protection Division Director Harriet Elliott. Providing a communicative support for Price Division efforts, the Consumer Division concentrated "on price restraint at the local level, where community pressure and grassroots groups, if properly mobilized, could work most effectively."[29] As early as August 1940, the Consumer Division had convened representatives of nearly one hundred such groups at a Washington summit, seeking to establish a national network for monitoring and enforcing price control. It would go on to broadcast a national radio program, "The Consumer Wants to Know," and engage in the publication of pamphlets with titles such as "132 Million Consumers" and "Shock Troops," designed to – as Elliott put it – equip "American consumers ... to perform their

---

[27] Rockoff (1984, 85).
[28] Council of Economic Advisers (1998); Rockoff (1984).
[29] Jacobs (2005, 186).

function as economic citizens."[30] In fall 1943, the OPA would launch a nationwide Home Front Pledge campaign, obtaining promises from twenty million consumers – often reaffirmed in placards in their front windows – to "pay no more than top legal prices [and] ... accept no rationed goods without giving up ration stamps."[31] In a more formal sense, the Consumer Division oversaw the establishment of more than five thousand local War Price and Rationing Boards or "little OPAs" charged with monitoring compliance and investigating complaints. In July 1945 – the final full month of the war – OPA efforts were supported by 127,075 volunteer board members, whose activities were further supplemented by 300,000 "peak load" volunteers.[32] Such mobilization efforts played a key role in OPA success in reconciling growth and price stability.[33]

These principled shifts in turn prefigured changes in economists' causal frameworks. In later debates over the lessons of wartime efforts, OPA successes would be cast as affirming the importance of efforts at both containing market power and stabilizing self-reinforcing wage-price expectations. First, with respect to market structures, Galbraith echoed Taussig's views from World War I, later arguing that OPA efforts had been *least* effective in "the part of the economy which, with important exceptions, most closely approaches pure competition."[34] In contrast, in oligopolistic or monopolistic sectors, price trends were "subject to an informal control by the seller." Given such a structure, consumers were more able to "police the price regulations imposed on the sellers" and firms were more able "to minimize the frequency of price changes."[35] Galbraith summed up the importance of market structure by noting that "it is relatively easy to fix

[30] Jacobs (2005, 187).
[31] Jacobs (2005, 187).
[32] Jacobs (2005, 203–204).
[33] Support also existed in the business community, as price controls minimized uncertainty regarding labor and input costs, and as business itself remained receptive to appeals to the common interest. For example, in October 1940, *Fortune* magazine published a survey of executive opinion, posing varied means to containing wage-price pressures. The greatest support – 35 percent – went to direct controls, with 25 percent favoring trade association efforts, 27 percent favoring reliance on the market, and 14 percent offering no view. Rockoff (1984, 89, 95–96).
[34] Galbraith (1952, 26).
[35] Galbraith (1952, 10–15).

prices that are already fixed."[36] Highlighting the importance of popular expectations, Galbraith also stressed the importance of wartime collective identification in arguing that "a community that has come to regard war as a tragedy stigmatizes illegal profiteering."[37] In this light, in contrast to a prewar wariness, economists came to anticipate a substantial postwar role for incomes policies.[38]

Moving outside the domestic setting, it is worth noting that incomes policies also had implications for monetary cooperation, providing oft-overlooked foundations for the Bretton Woods fixed exchange rates. Highlighting these links, Keynes stressed in proposals for postwar arrangements the need to *simultaneously* address prices and exchange rates, arguing that monetary stability would depend upon "(i) measures to control capital movements and (ii) the existence of a tendency for broad wage movements to be similar in the different countries."[39] Moreover, Keynes built this recognition into his plans for postwar domestic and international stabilization. Stable exchange rates would limit the adverse effects of depreciation on inflation, while the transnational use of incomes policies to limit purchasing power *disparities* would enable states to sustain competitiveness without accepting austerity. Such mechanisms would, moreover, reduce the need for the "hegemonic" support of the United States in using its monetary resources. To be sure, reconciling these goals would require continued exhortation – which would follow over the early postwar order.

## 3.3 Truman's Confrontations and Rhetorical Restraints

Building on Roosevelt's interpretive template and the institutional backdrop of experience in restraining wages and prices, the Truman administration's efforts at containing inflation while promoting growth

---

[36] Galbraith (1952, 17).
[37] Galbraith (1946, 481).
[38] Support for price controls was coupled with a dismissive view of monetary policy, even at the Federal Reserve. The Federal Reserve Board of Governors (1943, 10) stated in its 1943 *Annual Report*: "It is believed by many that inflation and deflation can be prevented by monetary action ... This is a greatly magnified view of the influence of monetary action ... In the past quarter century, it has been demonstrated that policies regulating the quantity and cost of money cannot by themselves produce economic stability or even exert a powerful influence in that direction."
[39] Keynes (1936b, 501).

evolved over three phases. First, initial efforts to reconcile growth and stability occurred in a context marked by the renewed desire of labor and capital to "catch up" with wartime opportunities for wage and profit advances. Given these pressures, Truman frequently employed presidential rhetoric to induce noninflationary settlements. Second, once the postwar inflationary surge had been contained, debate over controls often concerned the relative culpability of labor or capital in undermining wage-price stability, culminating in the Korean War revival of controls by the Office of Price Stabilization (OPS). Finally, the scope for official restraint was also curtailed in Korea-era debates, most importantly as the Supreme Court rejected Truman's seizure of the steel mills – placing a legal limit on controlling authority.

### *Postwar Conversion: From the OPA to Presidential Rhetoric*

Efforts to manage the transition from wartime controls were complicated by the unexpected early end of the war in August 1945 and by uncertainty as to whether recessionary headwinds or inflationary tailwinds would prove stronger. On August 16, 1945, as a first step toward decontrol, Truman announced the relaxation of wage controls, appealed for a continuation of wartime no-strike and no-lockout pledges, and announced plans to convene a national Labor-Management conference on reconversion. Nevertheless, even while this conference was being held in the fall of 1946, the United Steelworkers union (USW) announced that it would push for a substantial wage increase.[40] U.S. Steel President Benjamin Fairless in turn informed the OPA that the industry could not meet the steelworkers' wage demands without administration assent to price relief. On January 18, the USW accepted a fact-finding board's proposal for an 18.5 cent per hour increase, which U.S. Steel then rejected as impossible in the absence of higher prices. In the face of this deadlock, on January 21, 750,000 steelworkers struck, marking the largest work stoppage in US history to that point.[41] Truman himself eventually interceded to grant price relief, bypassing OPA Director Chester Bowles and acceding to industry desires for a $5 per ton price increase, ending the strike on February 15.[42]

---

[40] Goodwin and Herren (1975, 19).
[41] Brecher (1997; 2005).
[42] Donovan (1977, 167–168).

However, this rapid assent to USW demands would have unappreciated consequences. Only three months later, the railworkers' union, emboldened by a view of the administration as unwilling to "hold the line" on prices, adopted a hard line in its own negotiations. On May 23, after prolonged administration efforts at mediation, the union rejected its final settlement proposal and commenced a nationwide strike, one which threatened to paralyze transportation throughout the country. In contrast to his accommodative stance during the steel dispute, Truman adopted a more confrontational position, reflecting not only his personal frustrations with the railworkers' negotiators, but also the importance of rail transportation to the national economy. Over the next two days, Truman twice addressed the public – in a May 24 national radio broadcast and May 25 address to Congress.[43] In his radio address, Truman cast the union leaders as traitors to the public trust, comparing them to wartime enemies. Unlike the "crisis of Pearl Harbor," which had been "the result of action by a foreign enemy," Truman argued, the rail crisis had been "caused by a group of men within our own country who place their private interests above the welfare of the nation." Insisting that he was a "friend of labor," Truman nevertheless stressed a larger national interest in ensuring that any settlement remained "within the wage stabilization formula."[44] In his May 25 address to Congress, Truman reprised his construction of the crisis as one "brought about by the obstinate arrogance" of the union leaders, and requested that Congress authorize the drafting of striking workers into the armed forces in order to maintain "price control and stabilization laws."[45] These rhetorical and legal assaults would prove sufficient to compel a settlement, as union negotiators conceded to the administration during Truman's broadcast. This would in fact prompt a dramatic mid-speech interruption, as Truman announced that the strike had been settled on his terms.[46] In contrast to the accommodative approach employed with steel, Truman had demonstrated the effectiveness of communicative-styled rhetoric as a means to wage-price restraint.

[43] Providing a window into his own views, Truman drafted a rough version of his radio address, in which he urged the public to "put transportation and production back to work, hang a few traitors and make our own country safe for democracy." Donovan (1977, 212, 213).
[44] Truman (1946a).
[45] Truman (1946b).
[46] Clifford with Holbrooke (1991, 91–92); Donovan (1977, 213–215).

Even following the Republican recapture of Congress in 1946, Truman employed continued exhortation on behalf of wage-price restraint.[47] Just weeks after the midterm setback, Truman would exploit a confrontation with United Mine Workers (UMW) President John Lewis. In October 1946, Lewis had accused the administration of "unilateral misrepresentations" of a strike settlement reached the previous spring. Secretary of the Interior Julius Albert Krug warned Truman that the negotiation of a new contract would be seen as "another surrender to Lewis" and would exacerbate inflationary tendencies. Truman's political aide Clark Clifford argued that in order to establish his post-Roosevelt standing, it would be necessary to affirm the primacy of the national interest over private wants. Facing a November 20 UMW deadline, Truman accepted this advice, confronting Lewis by seeking a court injunction to prevent the strike.[48] This strategy worked both substantively, as the Supreme Court eventually upheld the administration's position, and politically, by helping Truman to move out of Roosevelt's shadow and establish his own identity.

## Stagflation in Early Form and Social Struggles over Shared Responsibility

With the immediate transition completed, the establishment of a more explicit postwar framework remained necessary. While the OPA had been abolished, inflationary trends – running at more than 18 percent in 1946 and more than 8 percent in 1947 – combined with concerns for wage-price pressures (particularly regarding steel), an aversion to monetary restraint, and an egalitarian emphasis on the common good to sustain support for incomes policies.[49] In this context, Truman repeatedly pushed the Republican Congress for greater authority over wages and prices and urged business to exercise greater social responsibility in raising prices. Such pressures were maintained to the extent that even in the context of the 1949 recession, uncertainty over inflation would remain, anticipating discussions of the 1950s New Inflation and 1970s Stagflation. For example, when asked at a press conference

[47] Donovan (1977, 239).
[48] Clifford with Holbrooke (1991, 93); Donovan (1997, 241).
[49] Council of Economic Advisers (1998, 354).

whether "the [wage-price] spiral is going down [or] ... going up," Truman answered "it's going both ways."[50]

In the context of ongoing concerns for such a self-reinforcing wage-price spiral – one that might persist even in the context of an economic slump – Truman called Congress into special sessions in both October 1947 and July 1948, in each case urging more direct action. Moving closer to the 1948 elections, Truman ratcheted up such rhetoric, affirming in one campaign speech that there existed "no great mystery about how to stop the cost of living from going higher and higher ... Everybody knows that when we had price control the average family was not gouged by inflated prices."[51] Shifting to a more cognitive argument, Council of Economic Advisers (CEA) member Gerhard Colm urged the definition of "[wage-price] principles [as] ... guideposts for specific negotiations and agreements for particular industries."[52] This support for incomes policies also reflected the Council's concerns for the likely effects of macroeconomic restraint on growth. Indeed, Treasury Secretary Snyder warned that tighter money would penalize "legitimate business operators" and "affect production adversely."[53] The Council similarly warned of the consequences of any Federal Reserve interest rate increase, noting that the "stability of the Government bond market has been a significant element in the smooth postwar reconversion" and that it would risk "a serious error to introduce new elements of uncertainty ... which would follow a change of policy with respect to the support of bond prices" by raising interest rates.[54] Incomes policies in this light represented a key contribution to the policy mix, enabling lower interest rates and increased growth.

In coalitional terms, the emphasis on public responsibility should not be seen as having obviated labor-business conflict so much as having reshaped its terms, to revolve around the distribution of responsibility for wage or price restraint. In this context, business groups blamed not macroeconomic excess but rather labor militancy for inflation. Urging the imposition of limits on union power, the

[50] Goodwin and Herren (1975, 64–65).
[51] Goodwin and Herren (1975, 60).
[52] Goodwin and Herren (1975, 53).
[53] Goodwin and Herren (1975, 50).
[54] Council of Economic Advisers (1949 [January], 43).

National Association of Manufacturers (NAM) issued advertisements decrying "labor monopoly" for "rais[ing] the prices of the things you need," warning consumers that "[t]he price of monopoly comes out of your pocket."[55] General Electric President Charles Wilson argued more broadly that "labor has no right, any more than any group has a right, to starve, endanger, or destroy the society of which it is a part."[56] In this way, the construction of inflation as caused by market power did not negate capital-labor tensions so much as it reoriented them to focus on the relative burden of sacrifice. This enabled Truman – who had condemned labor so harshly in the early postwar months – to shift by April 1947 to assert that "private enterprise must display the leadership to make our free economy work by arresting this [inflationary] trend."[57]

Such concerns for abuses of market power would be most pressing in the steel industry. Not only Democrats and Keynesians but also Republicans and Classical economists argued that market imperfections necessitated greater private wage-price restraint. In early 1948, Republican Senator Ralph Flanders urged the steel companies to mind the public interest, warning that any steel price increase "has to be defended on public grounds as well as for business reasons."[58] These appeals for public restraint even found their way into the statements of Classical economists. In mid-1950 congressional hearings on monopolistic pricing, Classical economist George Stigler highlighted the need "for further social controls," on the grounds that "the forces of competition in the steel industry are not now sufficiently strong to justify us to leave the industry alone."[59] These pronouncements accorded with public sentiment, which saw the government as a source of price stability and private agents as driving the wage-price spiral. For example, in an April 1947 poll, 49 percent of the public blamed societal agents – labor or business – for inflation, and only 25 percent blamed government.[60]

---

[55] Jacobs (2005, 232).
[56] Jacobs (2005, 233).
[57] Goodwin and Herren (1975, 41).
[58] Tiffany (1988, 55).
[59] Tiffany (1988, 89).
[60] Nine percent had no opinion, with the remainder blaming each other. Gallup Poll 395 qn1 (April 23, 1947).

## Wartime Challenges – and Judicial Limits

With the onset of the Korean War, inflation returned to the top of the agenda, as the administration revived earlier wartime designs in an Office of Price Stabilization (OPS) and Wage Stabilization Board (WSB). Of particular concern was the prevention of any steel strike that might interrupt wartime production and spur a renewed wage-price spiral. However, despite obtaining a postponement of a scheduled December 1951 strike, the administration failed to secure a wage settlement that the steel industry would accept in the absence of government price relief.[61] With the arrival of an April 8, 1952 strike deadline, Truman declared in a nationwide address that the nation faced "times of crisis" and announced his intention to seize control of the steel industry. While he conceded that in "normal times," unions and firms were entitled to whatever "they can get," he argued that war justified limitations, lest a "wage-price spiral ... send prices through the roof."[62] However, the subsequent legal battle saw the industry prevail, as the Supreme Court ruled Truman's actions unconstitutional. This would be followed by a 53-day strike, in which the administration eventually conceded on price relief. Foreshadowing the rise of the conservative media of later decades, Edward L. Ryerson, chair of the American Iron and Steel Institute's (AISI) Public Relations Committee, cited its campaign to reshape public opinion as crucial to the Supreme Court ruling.[63]

Nevertheless, the defeat of the seizure only affected the outer limits of administrative possibilities.[64] It did not undermine the scope for communicative leadership. This would be deployed over the next administration as Eisenhower officials advanced Keynesian constructions of a New Inflation driven by market power and self-fulfilling expectations, justifying principled appeals for a "shared responsibility" in wage-price restraint.

---

[61] Tiffany (1988, 97).
[62] Truman (1952).
[63] Tiffany (1988, 226).
[64] Price stability was arguably overdetermined during the Korean War, as advocates of controls, monetary restraint, and fiscal restraint could all claim success for their favored policies. See Rockoff (1984, 179).

## 3.4 Eisenhower's Crises: The New Inflation

Despite the Eisenhower administration's initial aversion to incomes policies, it would grow increasingly concerned over the decade with a "New Inflation" paradoxically combining rising prices with declining employment.[65] CEA Chairman Arthur Burns would warn of "a new kind of inflation," resistant to macroeconomic restraint, necessitating the greater use of incomes policies.[66] In this light, the history of Eisenhower policy is one of increasing recourse to incomes policies, moving through three stages, over recognition of the New Inflation, to the use of informal presidential exhortation in the 1959 steel strike; to poststrike support for the formalization of guidelines. Not coincidentally, these shifts paralleled administration concerns for the dollar foundation of the Bretton Woods order, and a transnational convergence on the use of incomes policies to enable exchange-rate stability.

*Constructing the New Inflation*

The Eisenhower administration initially permitted the Truman controls, along with its own standby authority over wages and prices, to expire as scheduled on April 30, 1953. Nevertheless, CEA Chairman Burns would also concede in congressional testimony that the administration "would not exclude direct controls under all circumstances," and that "[i]n a time of grave national emergency, direct controls might be desirable."[67] While the need to reflect more substantially on anti-inflation policy would be delayed by a 1954 recession, the administration would be troubled by the rigidity of prices during this initial downturn, particularly by a steel wage increase that demonstrated the potential resistance of steel- and labor-market power to reduced demand. Burns's Council stated in its 1955 *Economic Report* that "the

---

[65] Even as this interpretation reflected the influence of Keynesian frameworks, nothing precluded explaining the New Inflation in terms of monetary or fiscal abuses. Consider that the Eisenhower administration ran recurring budget deficits, which peaked at 2.6 percent of GDP in 1959 – a level not surpassed until 1968. Council of Economic Advisers (2000, 398).

[66] Burns (1957, 1); Kennedy economist Kermit Gordon later remarked that the "1955–1958 episode ... shook many preconceptions about the nature of the inflation process [and] ... the compatibility of full employment and price stability." US Congress. Joint Economic Committee (1966, 62).

[67] Gordon (1975, 112).

apparent stability of prices in the face of falling manufacturing activity was one of the striking features of the recent contraction."[68] Burns would respond to this instability in the face of slackening growth by making greater use of administrative measures. For example, in the spring of 1955, he sought to limit the availability of credit by establishing a "new informal organization, where representatives of various credit agencies of the government frequently met ... to supplement what the Federal Reserve did."[69]

The administration's concerns for inflationary settlements in a softening economy increased in 1955, as a rivalry between United Auto Workers (UAW) leader Walter Reuther and USW President David McDonald, coupled with the recent replacement of U.S. Steel Chairman Benjamin Fairless by Roger Blough, led to the adoption of more aggressive negotiating postures: While McDonald aimed to surpass a recent UAW settlement, Blough sought to demonstrate his firmness in his inaugural negotiations. In this context, the 1955 steel settlement was signed only at the last minute, temporarily idling four hundred thousand workers. The settlement provided the USW with a wage increase double that obtained by the auto workers, and led the steel companies to announce – the next day – their own price increase. Eisenhower was, by 1955, increasingly dismayed with such practices, remarking that he "was pretty disgusted with business men [who] ... can't wait more than a few hours to raise the price of steel 7 dollars a pound."[70] The administration's patience would be again tested the next year, as the steel industry was idled by a 26-day stoppage, leading Eisenhower to engage in a covert intervention. Prior to the strike, Secretary of Labor James Mitchell had invited USW President McDonald to meet with Eisenhower and Treasury Secretary George M. Humphrey to stress "the necessity of his exercising statesmanship and responsibility in the steel negotiations because of the possible inflationary tendency of an unrealistic wage settlement."[71] Eisenhower counseled the labor leader to offer only a muted response to industry attacks.[72] Over the next twenty-six days, Mitchell and Humphrey mediated a settlement, with the unions receiving scheduled 8–9 percent wage increases over

[68] Council of Economic Advisers (1955, 95).
[69] Hargrove and Morley (1984, 116).
[70] Tiffany (1988, 147–149).
[71] Gordon (1975, 128).
[72] Tiffany (1988, 149–150).

the next three years. The steel companies then announced 7.4 percent average price increases, in turn raising concerns for the balance of payments and the dollar, as steel imports had already increased by 38 percent from their 1955 levels against the backdrop of the strike.[73]

In a communicative effort to bring the power of presidential rhetoric to bear on capital and labor, Eisenhower declared in his 1957 State of the Union Address that "increases in wages and other labor benefits, negotiated by labor and management, must be reasonably related to increases in productivity." He urged that wage negotiations should "take cognizance of the right of the public generally to share in the benefits of improvements in technology." Eisenhower more broadly stressed the need to identify with the common vantage rather than the individual view, arguing that the national interest

> must take precedence over temporary advantages, which may be secured by particular groups at the expense of all the people. In this regard I call on leaders in business and in labor to think well on their responsibility to the American people.[74]

Integrating this communicative rhetoric with a more refined, cognitive analysis, the 1957 *Economic Report of the President* stressed the importance of private wage-price restraint to the reconciliation of price stability with economic expansion. The *Report* argued that "fiscal and monetary policies must be supported by appropriate private policies to assure both a high level of economic activity and a stable dollar." In the absence of societal cooperation, policymakers would be forced to "depend exclusively on monetary and fiscal restraints as a means of containing the upward movement of prices," an approach that "would raise serious obstacles to the maintenance of economic growth and stability." Further, because of the market power of large firms, the Council argued that macroeconomic "restraints would bear with undue severity on sectors of the economy having little if any responsibility for the movement toward a higher cost-price level."[75]

These attitudes were also reflected in congressional discourses that condemned "administrative pricing" and placed a particular stress on steel prices.[76] In August 1957, Senator Estes Kefauver, chairman of the

[73] Tiffany (1988, 151–153).
[74] Eisenhower (1957).
[75] Council of Economic Advisers (1957, 44).
[76] Tiffany (1988, 147).

Senate Antitrust and Monopoly subcommittee, began an investigation of the steel companies after a July 1957 wage increase was accompanied by 11.4 percent average price increase.[77] In May 1958, confronting rumors that the steel companies were preparing yet another July price increase, Kefauver wrote to Eisenhower suggesting that he develop a more explicit plan to restrain prices, particularly in the steel industry. Kefauver did not advocate controls, but urged that Eisenhower marshal public opinion, convene an industry-labor conference, and offer voluntary wage and price guidelines. Eisenhower's reply failed to engage most of Kefauver's suggestions, save to specifically *oppose* a labor-management summit. With press reports regarding a potential steel price increase mounting, Kefauver telegraphed the president again on June 20 to urge that Eisenhower employ "the full powers of your office in order to prevent this disastrous occurrence."[78] On June 24, the president replied, again demurring. In late July, the steel companies again announced a price increase, and Kefauver privately urged Eisenhower to "persuade the steel industry to rescind this latest and most unfortunate price action" and more broadly "to formulate a wage-price program to arrest what appears to be a permanent inflationary trend, which continues unabated *regardless of whether the economy is in a state of prosperity or recession.*" Eisenhower's last reply in this exchange noted that the Council was studying the issue and invited future suggestions from Kefauver.[79] Yet, although Kefauver's background pressures were not unimportant, a 1959 steel strike would ultimately force a more public administration response.

## The 1959 Steel Strike: Public Intervention on Behalf of Guidelines

The administration's resistance to public intervention in labor-management disputes would finally collapse in the context of the July 1959 steel strike, which would total 116 days and close plants accounting for approximately 85 percent of the industry's output. Some of these steps toward a more visible role also reflected the approach of the 1960 election, and concerns that the public saw the Democrats as

---

[77] Tiffany (1988, 157).
[78] Gordon (1975, 120).
[79] Gordon (1975, 120–121; emphasis added).

better suited to dealing with inflation. In January 1959, the administration had sought to supplement its behind-the-scenes exhortatory efforts by establishing a Cabinet Committee on Governmental Activities Affecting Costs and Prices (under Eisenhower's second Council Chairman Saulnier) and a Cabinet Committee on Price Stability for Economic Growth (under Vice President Richard Nixon). Saulnier's committee would have the lesser impact, having been established to monitor the effects of official procurement and spending decisions on wage and price stability.[80] In contrast, Nixon's committee would prove more visible, charged with not only an investigative role but also enhancing "public understanding of the problem of inflation."[81]

These new mechanisms would be tested with the July 1959 beginning of the steel strike, providing the most serious crisis yet of the New Inflation. In early September, following the absence of progress over two-and-a-half months of negotiations, Eisenhower issued an open letter in which he declared it "disheartening … that so little apparent progress toward settlement has been made thus far."[82] Prior to meeting with union and industry representatives on September 28, Eisenhower declared himself "sick and tired" of the strike and asserted that it was "up to both sides, labor and management, to recognize the responsibility they owe to our Nation and settle their differences reasonably and promptly."[83] With no action by November, Eisenhower ordered the steelworkers back to work for the Taft-Hartley eighty-day "cooling-off" period. The administration also held a November 1959 conference on price stability, at which Eisenhower cast fiscal restraint as necessary but insufficient and urged that private agents "exercise self-discipline" in order to maintain price stability.[84]

In December 1959, the administration would redouble its efforts to settle the strike. When the companies issued a "final" offer that looked likely to guarantee a resumed strike in January, Secretary of Labor Mitchell secured further union concessions, which he and Nixon relayed to industry officials at a January 1960 private meeting. Eisenhower later recalled in his memoirs, that Nixon "'laid the issue on the line,' reminding them that if the strike resumed, 'the

[80] Gordon (1975, 122–123); Hargrove and Morley (1984, 139–140).
[81] Gordon (1975, 123).
[82] Eisenhower (1959a).
[83] Eisenhower (1959b).
[84] Eisenhower (1959c).

country will have no place to go for a remedy but to the [Democratic] Congress,'" and that management would not benefit from the likely "labor-management legislation such a Congress will produce." Following their meetings with the vice president and labor secretary, the steel firms capitulated.[85] On January 4, 1960, the strike ended, with the union receiving an approximately 3.5 percent wage increase, while the steel companies held prices steady.[86]

In ensuing constructions, the 1959 strike was widely interpreted as affirming the contributions of incomes policies as permanent features of the economic landscape. The 1960 Eisenhower Council's *Economic Report* itself affirmed the "need to supplement [fiscal and monetary] policies with appropriate private actions."[87] The 1961 *Economic Report* went further still by linking wage and price stability to the balance of payments and affirming the importance of "appropriate action by management and labor to insure the competitiveness of United States goods." The Council even subtly threatened that further instances of labor-management stalemate might compel recourse to firmer controls, urging labor and management to "settle their differences in a responsible manner and thus avoid inviting new Government controls and new limitations on their initiative."[88]

## 3.5 The Social Context: Societal, Institutional, and Public Influences

By the end of the 1950s, this policy mix would be accepted across an array of political, institutional, societal, and public contexts – including some ideologically unlikely settings. First, among the Republican party – ostensibly the party of capital – potential ideological objections to the use of incomes policies would be muted by an appreciation for their contributions to the economic policy mix. For example, looking back on his tenure as Eisenhower's vice president, Richard Nixon pointed with pride to his efforts at mediation in the steel dispute, offering a guidepost-styled justification that the "new contract provided for an average [wage increase] of less than 3 per cent – almost exactly in

---

[85] Eisenhower (1965, 458).
[86] Gordon (1975, 132).
[87] Council of Economic Advisers (1960, 70).
[88] Council of Economic Advisers (1961, 39, 59).

line with the annual 'productivity' factor."[89] Lamenting his loss as the 1960 Republican presidential nominee, Nixon would express frustration that the administration had failed to seize this space to prevent the fall 1960 economic downturn. Nixon recalled a March 1960 warning from Arthur Burns that "unless some decisive governmental action were taken, and taken soon, we were heading for another economic dip which would hit its low point in November, just before the elections." Yet, Eisenhower rejected Nixon's call for fiscal action, questioning Burns' judgment and arguing that a stimulus should be used only to prevent a "major recession." When October 1960 would see the jobless rolls increase by 452,000, Nixon characterized this development as one which "[a]ll the speeches, television broadcasts, and precinct work in the world could not counteract."[90]

Similarly, in business settings, support for incomes policies reflected their utility as mechanisms to obtain wage restraint and enhance the scope for macroeconomic stimulus and growth. Into the 1950s, the Committee for Economic Development (CED), a pro-Keynesian business group, would stress the need for "the voluntary exercise of restraint in price and wage policies by business and labor."[91] Conversely – and perhaps ironically, given the notion that the New Deal coalition was premised on labor support – labor often opposed incomes policies for impeding the full scope of potential wage gains.

Likewise, in institutional contexts, Federal Reserve Chairman William McChesney Martin would view the New Inflation as revealing the limits to monetary restraint. Indeed, the Federal Reserve's Open Market Committee (FOMC) found the 1959 strike particularly disconcerting, as the slowdown in economic growth combined with a potential rise in steel prices to leave the appropriate monetary policy unclear. While a substantial minority on FOMC favored cutting rates to spur recovery, Martin favored restraint, but with little conviction, as wage-push dynamics were beyond the Federal Reserve's influence. At the December 15 meeting, Martin accordingly conceded that "[w]hat the System does will not really make too much difference" given the inability of monetary restraint to affect wage-push pressures.[92]

[89] Nixon (1962, 304–311).
[90] Nixon (1962, 304–310).
[91] Committee for Economic Development (1958, 15).
[92] Bremmer (2004, 140).

Finally, the popular willingness to accept an egalitarian stress on the public interest also reflected a widespread trust in government – as 73 percent of Americans stated that they could trust the government either "just about always" or "most of the time" in a 1958 poll. These views would be paralleled by a public skepticism in the efficiency of market competition – as 56 percent of the public blamed labor or business for inflation, while only 14 percent blamed government in a 1959 poll.[93] In this context of communicative rhetoric and public trust, the Keynesian order seemed to have enabled prolonged economic stability.

## 3.6 Conclusions: Popular Legitimacy and Postwar Cooperation

In the early Great Depression, Franklin Roosevelt advanced principled appeals to enable the iterative construction of a Keynesian order that would contain financial market power, restrain speculative excesses, and enable stable wage-driven growth. In a foundational sense, Roosevelt's inaugural address combined a commitment to the public good with a sector-specific condemnation of pre-crash financial excesses. In his early term, Roosevelt sought to halt a deflationary downward spiral by breaking with the gold standard and stabilizing the banking sector. Having averted collapse, Roosevelt then pursued more active efforts to promote inflation-driven demand, limiting the power of finance through the Bank Acts, empowering labor in the Wagner Act and – following the 1937 downturn – making increased use of expansionary fiscal policy. With the onset of wartime full employment, the problem of recovery would yield to that of wage-price stability, as the OPA successfully contained wartime inflation, in ways reinforced by Roosevelt's rhetorical appeals.

Taken together, the Great Depression and wartime inflation set the template for the Keynesian order. Over the ensuing decades, the Truman and Eisenhower administrations employed presidential rhetoric to sustain wage-price stability – with Eisenhower-era constructions of a "New Inflation" justifying restraint to limit not only inflation but also stabilize the dollar foundations of the Bretton Woods order. In this way, across recurring moments of crisis, Keynesian sentiments reshaped cognitive

---

[93] Gallup Poll #614 qn 29 (May 29 to June 3, 1959).

ideas, institutional and coalitional interests, and public dispositions, advancing a policy mix that saw incomes policies enable wage, price, and currency stability and limit the need for macroeconomic restraint. Nevertheless, these principled foundations would subsequently undergo intellectual conversion in the advance of a Neoclassical Synthesis, spurring the repression of rhetorical appeals and regulatory possibilities. In their stead, there would emerge increasing reliance on a fiscal fine-tuning that would exhibit diminishing effectiveness in containing the market power of labor and self-reinforcing wage-price dynamics. In this way, postwar stability would enable practices that contributed to mounting instability.

# 4 Converting the Keynesian Order: Toward the Neoclassical Synthesis

What is at stake in our economic decisions today is not some grand warfare of rival ideologies ... What we need is not labels and clichés but more basic discussion of the sophisticated and technical questions involved in keeping a great economic machinery moving ahead.

John F. Kennedy, June 1962 Address at Yale University.[1]

## 4.1 Introduction

In the aftermath of the Great Crash, Roosevelt's egalitarian rhetoric combined with Keynesian principles to enable the construction of public interests in private restraint – from early responses to the 1933 bank panic through to the wartime adherence to wage-price guidelines. Such was the broad nature of these early successes that Roosevelt's approach would evolve into a macroeconomic template under Truman and Eisenhower: employing communicative appeals to the national interest, Truman and Eisenhower each worked to fix wage-price expectations by exhorting firms and unions possessing market power to exercise private restraint, in a way that might help to sustain low inflation. Moreover, having used social appeals to obtain wage-price restraint, the scope would be increased for employing fiscal or monetary policy in a way that might help to reduce unemployment and raise growth. However, even in the context of this presidential leadership, the refinement of economic models in the context of an emergent Neoclassical Synthesis would see economists seek to abstract away from the rhetorical appeals in favor of a greater focus on ostensibly underlying-macroeconomic fundamentals. Put more formally, postwar success in achieving stable growth would over time see Keynesian values undergo an intellectual conversion into a Neoclassical Synthesis – and wage-price guidelines would in parallel fashion undergo an

[1] Kennedy (1962a).

intellectual displacement in favor of fiscal fine-tuning. Stability would accordingly begin to yield to increasing instability.

Over this chapter, I trace the evolution of these intellectual and institutional shifts, as early Kennedy-era debates over the need for wage-price guidelines and a tax cut yielded to later Johnson-era struggles over Vietnam War spending, incomes policies, and the need for a tax increase. In the first section, I address a split within the Kennedy administration between varieties of Keynesianism, highlighting the broader social dynamics that saw more institutionally oriented Keynesians such as John Kenneth Galbraith remain supportive of incomes policies while Neoclassical figures such as Council Chairman Walter Heller opposed their use. In a second section, I examine the implications for Kennedy administration policy, tracing early debates as Council economists initially accepted wage-price guideposts to deflect objections that their preferred tax cut risked inflation, but then used the steel confrontation of April 1962 to argue for the adverse effects of the guideposts on confidence. In the third section, I address Johnson-era debates over the Vietnam War inflation, as Neoclassical efforts at displacing guidelines would persist even as inflationary pressures mounted, with Council officials engaging in the construction of domestic and international crises to justify fiscal restraint in the 1968 tax increase. In a final section, I pull back to address the institutional and societal context, as an erosion of trust provided a key backdrop limiting the scope for regulation, foreshadowing an overburdening of fiscal and monetary policy in a way that would lead to the accommodation of the wage-price spirals over the next decade.

## 4.2 Converting Keynesianism: The Neoclassical Synthesis and Fiscal Fine-Tuning

Over the early 1960s, Keynesian ideas themselves underwent an intellectual conversion, as the Institutionalist emphasis placed by economists such as John Kenneth Galbraith on the need for incomes policies yielded to a more Neoclassical stress on the part of economists such as Paul Samuelson and Walter Heller on fiscal measures. Moreover, such changes were themselves part of a broader reevaluation of the scope for communicative or coordinative appeals, as McCarthy-era Red Scare tensions prompted in turn the emergence of an "intellectual anti-populism," as intellectuals sought to limit principled debates involving the public in favor of more technocratic forms of deliberation. This reflected a latent aversion to the populist appeals of the 1930s on the part of intellectuals such as Arthur Schlesinger and Daniel Bell, who highlighted the dangers of ideological politics and sought to treat the political as more technical. Where Schlesinger, later a Kennedy adviser, argued for the need to govern technocratically from a "vital center," Bell similarly heralded an approaching "end of ideology."[2] Perhaps the most enduring expressions of these intellectual anxieties were to be found in the writings of Richard Hofstadter, who offered historical analyses of "anti-intellectualism in American life" and "the paranoid style in American politics."[3]

Such wariness of public engagement was not altogether unreasonable in the aftermath of the McCarthy era – as intellectuals viewed their careers as threatened by populist demagogues and sought refuge in technocratic formalisms. For example, MIT economist Paul Samuelson – a key postwar advocate of discretionary fiscal policy – would later justify the Neoclassical redefinition of Keynesianism as a partial response to postwar Red Scare pressures, confessing that he had been influenced by the experience of Keynes's onetime colleague, Lorie Tarshis, whose textbook had been "killed … in its tracks" by "vicious political and personal attacks on him as a 'Keynesian-Marxist.'"[4] In the 1948 first edition of his textbook, Samuelson accordingly sought to abstract away from any social context, asserting that his analysis was "neutral" and denouncing the "narrow band of zealots associated with some of the policy programs that Keynes himself espoused during the great depression."[5] By the mid-1950s, carving out a niche for an economic "vital center," Samuelson would christen the Neoclassical Synthesis by arguing that "90 percent of American economists … have worked toward a *synthesis* of whatever is valuable in older economics and in modern theories of income determination. The result might be called *neoclassical* economics and is accepted by all but about 5 percent of extreme left-wing and right-wing writers."[6] Similarly characterizing the evolution of economists' issue-specific ideas, Herbert Stein – later chair of Nixon's Council of Economic

[2] Bell (1960); Schlesinger (1949).
[3] Hofstadter (1962; 1965).
[4] Samuelson (1997, 157–158).
[5] Samuelson (1948, 253–254).
[6] Samuelson (1955, 212; emphases added).

Advisers (CEA) – would argue that a "domestication of Keynes" had been "necessary before Keynesianism could become national policy," resulting in less a "straight-line movement towards more and more acceptance of Keynesian ideas" than "a convergence between the ideas of 'Keynesian' economists on the one hand, and national fiscal policy on the other hand, in which both sides moved."[7]

To the extent that such efforts at abstracting away from principled concerns reshaped policy debates, the most important postwar divides among economists were intra-Keynesian affairs, pitting Institutionally oriented Keynesians such as Galbraith, who saw uncertainty as a more pervasive constraint and favored regulatory efforts and more communicative engagement, against more Neoclassical Keynesians who favored fine-tuning and a reduction in the scope for debate to educational, coordinative appeals. From the former vantage point, Galbraith had become one of the most prominent economists of the postwar era, as he advanced – in efforts like *The Affluent Society* and *The New Industrial State* – principled arguments for incomes policies.[8] In *The Affluent Society*, published in the context of *Sputnik*-era concerns for excesses of consumerism, Galbraith echoed Keynes's stress on the conventional bases of expectations by highlighting the role of a "conventional wisdom" in limiting policy possibilities. Characterizing conventional ideas as those which have power because they are familiar or respectable, Galbraith highlighted the importance of a conventional wisdom on wage and price controls, stressing the degree to which the "specter of such controls invokes the ancient resistance to the intrusions of government." Galbraith argued that the scope for such measures had been limited where "Social Darwinists and the utilitarian philosophers have successfully identified vitality and liberty with the free market," leaving controls to be seen "as an even more far-reaching menace."[9]

Moving from the principled plane to the cognitive context of debates over the policy mix, Galbraith argued against the increasing Neoclassical formalization of a trade-off between inflation and unemployment, lest it obscure the ways in which labor or capital could abuse wage or price power – even in the midst of an overall slowdown in

---

[7] Stein (1996, 132).
[8] Galbraith (1958; 1967).
[9] Galbraith (1958, 195).

the economy. Highlighting the importance of expectations, he argued that monetary and fiscal policies could often fail to contain inflation because they made "no direct contact with the wage-price interaction" by which wage and price expectations could take on self-reinforcing lives of their own, and only worked "by reducing the aggregate demand for goods." Moving from a stress on market expectations to market structures, Galbraith warned that macroeconomic restraint would be resisted in oligopolistic sectors and fall more heavily on competitively structured ones. Viewing the entire policy mix, Galbraith urged a combination of "fiscal policy [to maintain full employment] with control over prices and wages [to contain inflation]," so that policymakers could "reconcile capacity output with price stability."[10] In *The New Industrial State*, Galbraith expanded on these arguments, suggesting that large corporations would be more concerned with minimizing uncertainty than maximizing profits, and would work with government and labor to contain wage-price pressures.[11] Such cooperation could reduce the intensity of any Phillips curve trade-off by providing a social basis for wage-price restraint.

In contrast to Galbraith's stress on market psychology and structure, Neoclassical Keynesians –as advocates of what Kennedy CEA Chair Walter Heller termed a "New Economics" – urged a greater reliance on fiscal fine-tuning to reconcile full employment and price stability.[12] This reflected a view of market efficiencies as limiting the need for regulation over the long run, while leaving open the scope for policy activism in the short run. In contrast to Keynes and Galbraith, Samuelson and Solow cast wage and price trends as shaped by competitive pressures that would increase with the approach to full employment. This underlying view was essential to the popularization of a Phillips curve trade-off between inflation and unemployment. To be sure, Samuelson and Solow would offer in the last lines of their piece arguing for the Phillips curve trade-off a "final disclaimer," conceding that they had left unaddressed "the important question of what feasible institutional forms might be introduced to lessen the degree of disharmony between

---

[10] Galbraith (1958, 194).
[11] Galbraith (1967a, 397–398).
[12] Heller's (1971, 28) definition of the New Economics excluded incomes policies, stressing the "conscious use of budget expenditures and tax policy for economic stabilization, for full employment and related policies."

full employment and price stability."[13] In limiting discussion of "institutional forms," Samuelson and Solow would foreshadow a broader shift as economists would increasingly treat wage and price trends as beyond the reach of institutional mechanisms. Samuelson himself would later argue that incomes policies could be at best supplements to, but "not substitutes for proper macroeconomic fiscal and monetary policies."[14] Similarly, Solow argued that incomes policies would be potentially useful in "a zone of economic conditions, neither too tight nor too slack, in which there is some tendency toward inflation, but a weak enough tendency so that an informed and mobilized public opinion can have effect."[15] In the long run, however, Samuelson held that the only dependable cure for inflation was "tighter money and/or more restrictive fiscal policy."[16] Solow echoed this skepticism, arguing that no other instrument was as "weak, uncertain, and uneven in its effects as exhortation" and rejecting the idea that "when demand is excessive ... the price level can be talked out of rising."[17] Samuelson would more bluntly dismiss Galbraith's arguments for incomes policies as "absurd" and warn that "the more you are trying to push the Phillips curve down, while also operating in the inflationary part of it, the less the situation can be maintained, particularly in the longer run."[18] In short, even as the final lines of their article suggested that one might seek to shift the Phillips Curve "downward and to the left," this possibility would be minimized in Neoclassical debates going forward.

The reduction of economic debate to technical questions would be accelerated as coming decades would see economic policymakers take the Samuelson-Solow analysis as the starting point in debate over trade-offs between unemployment and inflation – one that would often leave discussion of incomes policies to the margins. First, Milton Friedman argued that as policymakers sought to exploit the trade-off, short-run successes would yield to long-run accelerating inflation, as agents formed lagged "adaptive expectations" and the Phillips curve would take on a vertical shape. In this light, Friedman argued that "there is always a temporary trade-off between inflation

[13] Samuelson and Solow (1960, 193–194).
[14] Burns and Samuelson (1967, 53–54).
[15] Solow (1966, 42–45).
[16] Burns and Samuelson (1967, 53).
[17] Solow (1966, 42–45).
[18] Burns and Samuelson (1967, 64–65).

and unemployment; there is no permanent trade-off."[19] Second, in a more fundamental critique, Robert Lucas and Thomas Sargent would argue that where agents formed fully efficient "rational expectations," fiscal and monetary stimulus would immediately spillover into higher inflation. Taken together, while these critiques may have advanced the technical rigor of debate, they also narrowed its scope, facilitating the repression of regulatory or legal concerns.

These differences also paralleled divergent views of the role of economists in public debate, as Samuelson and Solow stressed the importance of the construction of causal models and cast Galbraith's efforts at public engagement as lacking rigor, if not likely to muddle public thinking. For example, in a debate with Galbraith over *The New Industrial State*, Solow distinguished the concerns of a public intellectual and "big thinkers" such as Galbraith from those of more professionally focused "little-thinkers" such as Samuelson and himself. While Galbraith was preoccupied with large issues related to "[w]hither we are trending," Solow argued that "little-thinkers" were testing hypotheses regarding less glamorous questions such as "what will happen to the production of houses and automobiles in 1968 if Congress votes a 10 percent surcharge on personal and corporate tax bills." In this division of labor, Solow suggested that the public might enjoy Galbraith's effort, but serious economists would find *The New Industrial State* to be "a book for the dinner table and not the desk."[20] Not coincidentally, these debates also accorded with a shift in the nature of political rhetoric over the Kennedy administration, as Kennedy's inaugural appeal stressed the primacy of the public good – to "ask not what your country can do for you, ask what you can do for your country." In contrast, following the steel price dispute and May 1962 market collapse, Kennedy would argue in his June 1962 Yale

---

[19] Friedman had acknowledged the short-run merit of income policies as supplements to fiscal and monetary restraint at a 1966 University of Chicago conference on the Kennedy-Johnson guideposts. Friedman paralleled Samuelson and Solow in conceding a scope for the short-term use of income policies, arguing that they could have a temporary utility in breaking inflationary expectations. Similarly, Friedman cited an Argentine effort to "end an inflation" in which, "by altering people's expectations," income policies "did succeed in rather substantially reducing the rate of inflation with relatively little cost in the way of unemployment." Quoted in Rockoff (1984, 5). Quote in text from Friedman (1968, 11).
[20] Solow (1967, 100–101, 103, 108).

address that economic debate should involve "not some grand warfare of rival ideologies" but rather address "sophisticated and technical questions."[21] This shift in rhetorical forms is not epiphenomenal, however, as the reduction of economic debate to "technical questions" limits the scope for public involvement – and so technical skepticism in incomes policies can assume the force of a self-fulfilling prophecy in the absence of official exhortation to their use.

## 4.3 The Kennedy Administration: The Gradual Displacement of Incomes Policy

Through the Kennedy administration, debate over incomes policies evolved across three broad stages, as the intellectualization of debate limited the scope for their use. First, from January to September 1961, institutional and Neoclassical Keynesians moved toward a brief convergence on support for incomes policies, as the Neoclassical Council accepted their merit as short-term economic palliatives and political prerequisites to a tax cut. Second, from September 1961 to May 1962, this convergence was most clearly manifested in relations with the steel industry, culminating in a confrontation in which Kennedy employed communicative rhetoric to compel the companies to rescind an announced price increase. Finally, following the May 1962 stock market decline, Neoclassical economists backed away from support for incomes policies and Kennedy himself tamped down on his own rhetoric, pushing instead for a tax cut to regain business confidence and promote growth.

### *Toward the Wage-Price Guideposts*

Over its initial months, Kennedy administration support for incomes policies was linked most importantly to foreign economic policy concerns for the dollar's value. Just before the election, in response to a late-October 1960 increase in the price of gold, Kennedy – advised by Galbraith – not only declared that "If elected President, I shall not devalue the dollar," but also argued that the "present downward trend in our balance of payments" reflected a domestic inflation that had priced US exports "out of many foreign markets."[22]

---

[21] Kennedy (1962a).
[22] Given concerns for growth, Kennedy also declared that he would "reject monetary policy as an instrument of controlling inflation," emphasizing

During the transition and early months of administration, Kennedy officials further stressed this link between wage-price pressures and the dollar. For example, a Kennedy-commissioned study by former Federal Reserve Bank of New York president Allen Sproul on the balance of payments argued that "part of our difficulty in maintaining a stable price level has arisen because [of] our wage-making arrangements."[23] In a February message on the domestic economy, Kennedy himself announced the establishment of an Advisory Committee on Labor Management Policy, to be chaired by Secretary of Labor Arthur Goldberg and designed to highlight "actions that may be taken by labor, management, and the public" to promote "sound wage policies [and] sound price policies," and so enhance "America's competitive position in world markets."[24]

Yet, this emphasis on inflation and the dollar was viewed warily by Kennedy's Council, which was more concerned to promote growth. Chairman Walter Heller argued that inflation was a comparatively remote concern, with "a lot of sluggishness in the private economic outlook." He suggested that this provided "a lot of leeway to introduce fairly long lasting government recovery programs ... without the stultifying fear that they will aggravate an inflationary boom." Heller also downplayed concerns for a gold outflow, countering that "many informed foreign observers are now beginning to worry about a continued U.S. recession."[25] Still, Kennedy resisted Heller's tax cut, stressing his own concerns for inflation and the possibility that a tax cut would undercut his inaugural call for public sacrifice. Kennedy had also pledged in his January 1961 State of the Union address to seek a balanced budget – albeit leaving escape hatches pertaining to "the development of urgent national defense needs or a worsening of the economy."[26] Instead of acceding to Council pressures for a fiscal

---

    instead a desire to "work closely with labor and management to develop wage and price policies consistent with reasonable price stability." Roosa (1967, 268–270).

[23] Sproul, Blough, and McCracken (1961).
[24] Kennedy (1961b).
[25] Council of Economic Advisers (1961b).
[26] The Council was later dismayed to learn that Kennedy had promised congressional leaders that he would not only refrain from seeking a major tax cut, but would strive to submit a balanced budget. Kennedy conceded the Council a second review of the economy in April, but – to the Council's dismay – the recovery from the 1959–1960 recession was continuing. Heller (1966, 31–32); quote in text from Kennedy (1961a).

stimulus, Kennedy actually sought to educate his own advisers regarding alternative mechanisms to limit inflation, instructing Heller to examine recent British experiments with incomes policies.[27]

Given this Council opposition, the administration's initial development of incomes policies would occur in the absence of Council support. Its early efforts were instead driven by John Kenneth Galbraith – particularly over the period prior to his departure to serve as Indian ambassador – Deputy Special Assistant for National Security Affairs Walt W. Rostow, and Secretary of Labor Arthur Goldberg. In early transition debates, Rostow had taken the lead in arguing for "breaking the institutional basis for creeping inflation, notably in the key steel and automobile industries; and on driving hard to earn more foreign exchange." Such efforts were needed, Rostow continued, because European bankers were "waiting to see if we are capable of dealing with the hard core of our balance of payments problem." The persistence of inflationary wage-price settlements, he warned, "might set in motion a gold drain which could upset our present tenuous equilibrium."[28] In a June 1961 letter to Kennedy, Galbraith placed a similar stress on the need to restrain cost-push pressures, anticipating that over "the next year, the active force shoving up prices will be wage contracts that force up prices with the latter leading, in turn, to further pressure on wages. Higher interest rates make no contact with this cause of inflation. The only hope is by direct negotiation through Secretary Goldberg's new machinery [the Labor-Management Committee]."[29]

In June 1961, Rostow took the lead in negotiations with United Auto Workers (UAW) President Walter Reuther as a first step in seeking auto industry wage-price restraint. Reuther began their meeting by arguing "that it was inappropriate, as the first initiative of the new administration, for 'White House professors' to throw their weight against a labor movement whose efforts had elected the first Democratic President in eight years." Rostow responded by stressing the national interest in wage-price stability and by assuring Reuther that the administration would not permit the UAW or labor to bear the entire burden of restraint. Reuther then turned to the issue of intra-labor rivalries or wage-wage pressures, asking Rostow if "Kennedy [could] assure

---

[27] Barber (1975, 170).
[28] Barber (1975, 147).
[29] Goodman (1998, 43–44).

him that [USW leader] McDonald wouldn't do better?" When Rostow provided this assurance, Reuther pressed further to have "Kennedy assure [him] that [labor] restraint wouldn't be exploited by a rise in steel prices?" Rostow responded that there "was no intention to shift the distribution of income in favor of profits." Reuther then suggested he might be able to help the administration with automobile prices, affirming that he could "look after them."[30] This meeting represented a crucial first move toward securing labor restraint, as September 1961 saw the UAW settle for a 2.5 percent wage increase. However, Rostow's efforts remained somewhat improvised, as the administration now faced the more politically problematic task of encouraging wage-price restraint in the steel industry.

## The 1962 Steel Crisis

Over these early months, Council economists came to recognize the potential contributions of incomes policies to a policy mix including their thus-far frustrated tax cut.[31] While the Council had achieved some successes, most notably in convincing Kennedy to refrain from seeking a tax increase during a summer 1961 Berlin crisis, Council economists still saw these steps as insufficient. This increased the appeal of incomes policies as economic and political support for a tax cut. First, incomes policies might make a discrete macroeconomic contribution given that the economy existed in a "band" between inadequate or excessive growth. Council member Kermit Gordon later suggested that the economy had been "*within* the band [where] the guideposts could have a constructive influence in restraining inflationary wage and price behavior."[32] Second, incomes policies might offset political concerns for the effects of any fiscal stimulus on domestic prices and the balance of payments. Council member James Tobin later conceded that the Council wanted to ensure that any potential wage and price spiral would not provide "any excuse for deflationary

---

[30] Rostow (1972, 140–141).
[31] Heller (1971, 23–24, 35–36) also sought to forestall Galbraithian calls for a stimulus via a spending, recalling that, "I had to say to Ken Galbraith one time, 'The way to get to your objective of more expenditures most rapidly is through the tax cut route. This is one case where the long way around is the short way home.'"
[32] US Congress. Joint Economic Committee (1966, 64).

measures by the monetary authorities or others," affirming that "this was the essential reason for the wage and price guideposts." Tobin further acknowledged that "price stability was unusually important because of U.S. balance of payments difficulties."[33] Given the failure thus far to secure a tax cut and the desire to alleviate inflation fears, the Council by late 1961 began to move toward the articulation of its formal wage-price guideposts.

The challenge of maintaining wage-price restraint itself intensified at this point, as the automobile industry's restraint was seen as unlikely to be obtained in upcoming steel negotiations scheduled for spring 1962. Given the October 1, 1961 approach of a scheduled steel industry wage increase, the administration was wary that the steel firms might argue for an inflationary price hike, and so issued a preemptive presidential letter to the heads of the steel companies. Heller recalled that the essence of Kennedy's message to the firms was that "If you play ball on this I'll help get labor into a more receptive mood on a reasonable settlement in 1962."[34] In the letter, Kennedy noted that if the industry exercised price restraint, it would then be the "turn of the labor representatives to limit wage demands."[35] Despite some misgivings, the companies exercised restraint, and administration attention moved to the March 1962 wage negotiations. It was here that the Council made its formal entry into the wage-price arena, introducing in its 1962 *Economic Report* the notion of wage and price "guideposts." Heller later recalled that "between that September when the letter went out to the steel companies and that April when there was the first steel crisis in the Kennedy Administration, there had been a lot of quiet work done within the Council ... to develop general principles of non-inflationary wage and price behavior."[36] Justifying their use, the Council spoke explicitly to the policy mix, casting guideposts as preferable to austerity, on the grounds that "to accept heavy

---

[33] US Congress. Joint Economic Committee (1966, 17–18).
[34] Heller (1971, 50).
[35] Council of Economic Advisers (1962, 182–183).
[36] While the CEA would claim that the guideposts were neutral with respect to industry, they were crafted with steel's market power very much in mind. Heller wrote to Goldberg in December 1961 that "we are really aiming at a dual economic target: (i) avoiding a price rise in steel itself; and (2) avoiding wage-induced price rises in other industries whose wage settlements (and materials costs) will be affected by the basic steel settlement." Quoted in Barber (1975, 166). Quote in text from Heller (1971, 50–51).

unemployment and persistent slack as the necessary cost of price stability is to undermine the vitality and flexibility of the economy."[37] The *Report* also stressed the interplay of domestic wage-price restraint and international monetary stability, arguing that "the success of the U.S. in solving the international payments problem ... will depend to a major extent on our ability to avoid inflation."[38] Writ large, in justifying the guideposts, the Council asserted that there existed a public interest in private wage and price decisions where "[private] decisions affect the progress of the whole economy."[39]

However, almost as soon as they had been formally introduced, the guideposts became the focus of controversy. When steel negotiations concluded on March 31, 1962, the administration breathed a brief sigh of relief that the United Steelworkers union (USW) had acquiesced to the absence of any wage hike, accepting only a 2.5 percent increase in fringe benefits. Kennedy later praised the USW for recognizing that the nation "could not afford another inflationary spiral [that] ... would affect our competitive position abroad."[40] Indeed, Kennedy telephoned identical congratulations to each side, lauding the agreement as one that "should provide a solid base for continued price stability."[41] Yet, this success would last only a little more than a week. On April 10, U.S. Steel President Roger Blough arrived for a last-minute Oval Office appointment, handing Kennedy a press release announcing that U.S. Steel would that next day "raise the price of the company steel products by an average of about 3.5 percent." After reading the announcement, Kennedy accused Blough of having deceived him, while Blough protested that he had never promised not to raise prices. To USW President McDonald, Kennedy later remarked, "you've been screwed and I've been screwed" – or words to that effect.[42]

---

[37] The CEA argued against mandatory controls as "neither desirable in the American tradition nor practical in a diffuse and decentralized continental economy." Council of Economic Advisers (1962, 183; 185–186).
[38] Council of Economic Advisers (1962, 167).
[39] The 1962 *Report* did not offer a quantitative guidepost figure, as the 3.2 percent standard would emerge in the 1964 *Report*, justified as the "annual average percentage change in output per man-hour during the last 5 years." Council of Economic Advisers (1964, 114); quotes in text from Council of Economic Advisers (1962, 185–186).
[40] Sorensen (1965, 446).
[41] Sorensen (1965, 447).
[42] Reeves (1993, 295).

The administration subsequently responded on a number of fronts, deploying antitrust threats, diverting contracts, floating legislative proposals, and appealing to smaller companies.[43] However, the most prominent use of executive influence came in a White House press conference, as Kennedy employed broadly affective rhetoric to accuse the industry of flouting the public interest, condemning "a tiny handful of steel executives whose pursuit of private power and profit exceeds their sense of public responsibility." Kennedy warned that the price increase "would seriously handicap our efforts to prevent an inflationary spiral ... make it more difficult for American goods to compete in foreign markets ... and thus more difficult to improve our balance of payments position." Finally, Kennedy affirmed a market failure construction of the crisis, noting that "the suddenness by which every company ... came in with ... almost identical price increases ... isn't really the way we expect the competitive private enterprise system to always work."[44] Taken as a whole, Kennedy stressed concerns for market structure and the public interest, and linked them in turn to concerns for the dollar.

On April 12, Blough held his own news conference, at which he was subjected to aggressive questioning. For example, well-known news anchor Walter Cronkite pressed him on whether he had abused the administration's trust, noting that "at your joint news conference with Mr. McDonald, he mentioned the non-inflationary nature of the agreement ... I wonder if you can tell us why there was no denial at that time ... on your part that an [anti-inflationary] agreement ... was intended?" Other reporters questioned whether he was motivated by partisan opposition to the Democratic Party, and his very commitment to the national interest.[45] Given such mounting pressures, the steel companies rescinded the increase within days.

### Reconstructing the Steel Crisis: Avoiding a "Kennedy Recession"

In the immediate setting, the steel crisis was seen as demonstrating the power of presidential exhortation on behalf of guidelines,

---

[43] Barber (1975, 171–176).
[44] Sorensen (1965, 450–451).
[45] Reeves (1993, 299).

as public condemnation had proved successful in obtaining the rollback.[46] However, subsequent narratives would call the administration's conduct into question, condemning these same affective excesses and warning of threats to economic freedom. Chamber of Commerce President Richard Wagner noted pointedly that "dictators in other lands usually come to power under accepted constitutional procedures."[47] Perhaps more significantly, labor was also coming to view the guideposts with wariness. In February 1962, AFL-CIO President George Meany responded to Arthur Goldberg's assertion of the need for government to "define the national interest" by protesting that "[s]uch a course would represent an infringement on free collective bargaining in a free society [and] ... a step in the direction of saying that the federal government should tell either or both sides what to do."[48] Perhaps most prominently, Milton Friedman denounced the guideposts as based in a "fundamentally subversive doctrine," noting that the crisis had demonstrated "how much of the power needed for a police state was already available." Rather than highlight the notion of a uniquely public interest, Friedman suggested that the guideposts posed threats to private freedoms, warning that the steel crisis had shown that "[i]f the price of steel is a public decision, as the doctrine of social responsibility declares, then it cannot be permitted to be made privately."[49]

Closer to home, the Kennedy Council would distance itself from the steel confrontation. In explaining the steel price retreat, Council officials minimized the role of presidential exhortation, stressing instead their own coordinative-styled market interventions. Heller would later argue that "what really broke the price increase was economics," as the Council had concluded "that if you held out as

---

[46] See Perry (1967) for the most developed argument regarding the success of the Kennedy guideposts in holding wages and prices to a level below what might otherwise have been the case.
[47] Matusow (1984, 40–41).
[48] Robinson (1981, 224).
[49] Such constructions would draw upon reports of middle-of-the-night phone calls by FBI agents to steel executives, 3:00 a.m. visits to journalists, and by the leak of a Kennedy comment that "my father told me all businessmen were sons-of-bitches, but I didn't really believe that he was right until now." Kennedy would argue he had said only "steelmen." Reeves (1993, 298–316) argues that Robert Kennedy believed Hoover had timed the raids to embarrass the administration. Quoted in text from Friedman (1962, 134).

much as 15 percent of steel capacity, then the price increase would collapse." Heller elaborated that "[w]e did our work – I knew some people at Armco, others knew people at Inland Steel and Kaiser, and when those three ... promised to hold out, there was just no way that U.S. Steel could hold its price increase."[50] With respect to subsequent debate over fiscal or incomes policies, the Council also used the *aftermath* of the crisis – particularly after the stock market suffered its largest single day drop since 1929 on May 28, 1962 – to justify a revived push for its tax cut.[51] Barely more than a week after the May 28 crash, meeting with Kennedy and other advisers, a Neoclassical tag-team of Heller, Samuelson, and Solow advanced an "administration failure" construction of a coming recession. Kennedy aide Ted Sorensen recalled that Heller "used language that hit the President where it hurt" as he suggested that "for the first time the prudent odds for a so-called 'Kennedy Recession' have ceased to be negligible." Heller warned that the "first Kennedy expansion may last no longer than the 25 months of Eisenhower's last recovery," and urged that "[o]nly an early tax cut appears to be capable of giving the economy the stimulus it needs in time."[52] Tobin would later highlight the links between the Kennedy market and the fiscal stimulus, terming "the hesitation in the expansion in summer 1962 ... the major reason for the President's personal conversion" to support for a tax cut.[53] The Council also stressed the political need to improve poststeel relations with business. Heller later affirmed that the administration "had to sell modern fiscal policy to an unbelieving and highly suspicious public," and that "a fringe benefit of going the tax route was to get business on board to help sell modern economics through a tax cut, which was dear to their hearts."[54]

These arguments against incomes policies and for fiscal mechanisms would soon be manifested in a shift in presidential rhetoric. This would be most clear in Kennedy's June 1962 Yale commencement address, in which he argued that "the problems of fiscal and monetary policies in the sixties as opposed to the kinds of problems we faced in the thirties demand subtle challenges for which technical answers, not political answers, must be provided."[55] Kennedy's eventual shift to favor a

[50] Hargrove and Morley (1984, 212).
[51] Reeves (1993, 316).
[52] Sorensen (1965, 421–424).
[53] Tobin (1966, 25).
[54] Heller (1971, 35).
[55] Kennedy (1962a).

tax cut – and muted support for incomes policies – would be advanced by the year's end. In his December 1962 speech at the Economic Club of New York, Kennedy explicitly urged a tax cut, stressing the need to "strengthen ... demand among consumers and business" through an "across-the-board, top-to-bottom cut in personal and corporate income taxes." Omitting any mention of the guideposts, Kennedy echoed Heller's earlier administration arguments regarding the extent of economic slack, holding that the scope for a fiscal stimulus remained open to the extent that "resources and manpower are not being fully utilized," and "increased competition, both at home and abroad ... will help keep both prices and wages within appropriate limits."[56]

In later narratives of this evolution toward a tax cut, the contributions of incomes policies – and Kennedy's own plans to follow the Heller tax cut with Galbraithian spending increases – would be increasingly obscured, not least by Council economists themselves. For example, Samuelson later argued that the Council had merely tolerated the establishment of the Goldberg Labor-Management Committee, seeing the sprawling committee as likely to affirm the limits of incomes policies.[57] Given the amount of slack in the economy over 1962–1964, Samuelson cast the maintenance of price restraint as "a very easy victory, and ... *not a victory that necessarily belongs to guideposts*," arguing instead that increased imports may have deserved more credit.[58] Such a construction, in which guideposts would be disregarded in favor of fiscal policy, would emerge with even greater force in debates over Vietnam-era inflation as attitudes toward the state shifted toward more minimalist views of policy possibilities.

## 4.4 The Johnson Administration: The Gradual Emergence of Fiscal Fine-Tuning

Over the next five years, the evolution of Johnson administration economic policy saw the CEA increasingly advocate for the displacement of incomes policies by fiscal policy. This shift was advanced over three stages. First, into mid-1966, Johnson would successfully employ exhortation of behalf of wage-price restraint, building on the steel crisis success. Second, from late 1966 through the fall 1967 sterling

---

[56] Kennedy (1962b).
[57] Council of Economic Advisers (1964b, 52–53).
[58] Burns and Samuelson (1967, 60; emphasis added).

devaluation, fears of a "recessionette" led the Council to urge a fiscal stimulus, while permitting the guideposts to atrophy in the absence of inflation concerns. Third, as concerns for the slowdown faded, the Council nevertheless resisted calls to strengthen incomes policies, emphasizing instead the primacy of fiscal policy into early-1968 struggles with Congress over a tax increase. This analysis suggests the need to reexamine the conventional wisdom regarding Johnson's ostensible fiscal failures, highlighting instead his Neoclassical advisers' repression of concerns for market psychology and power in their displacement of incomes policies.

### Vietnam and the Guideposts: Early Successes

On November 23, 1963, following the Kennedy assassination, the Council presented Johnson with an overview of wage-price issues, attributing recent price stability in part to "the opposition of the Administration to inflationary wage and price decisions, as spelled out in the 1962 and 1963 Annual *Economic Reports*, statements by President Kennedy, and the big Steel Episode." While the Council warned that, "[a]s the economy approaches fuller utilization of capacity, it will be more difficult to restrain prices and excessive wage increases," it also suggested that inflation would not become a major concern for another two years.[59] Instead, from late 1963 into early 1965, the Council was more worried about growth – and so stressed the need for a fiscal stimulus. Heller's replacement as Council chairman, Gardner Ackley, later recalled that the Council "thought that the economy had responded very well to the tax cut of '64," but that their "forecast suggested that the steam was likely to run out if we didn't get some more stimulus in." The Council accordingly convinced Johnson in June 1965 "to advocate the repeal of all the Korean War excise taxes, another tax cut."[60]

Given this support for a stimulus, when Johnson requested added Vietnam funding in late July 1965 the guideposts temporarily stood as the primary means to wage-price stabilization. In the Johnson administration's summer 1965 handling of the first post-1962 steel contract negotiations, Johnson aide Joseph Califano later recalled

---

[59] Cochrane (1975, 196).
[60] Ackley (1973, 26).

that the administration accordingly sought to avoid a strike, obtain "a settlement within the administration's wage-price guideposts," and guarantee that there would be "no increase in steel prices."[61] Indeed, the administration enjoyed the support of the steel companies themselves, who countered USW President I. W. Abel's goal of a 5 percent wage increase by pointing to the 3.2 percent wage guideposts. On August 17, Johnson met with Abel to lodge a personal appeal for labor restraint, followed by an invitation to the unions and companies to conduct negotiations at the White House. On September 3, 1965, in a nationally televised address, Johnson unveiled a successful 3.2 percent settlement, lauding the willingness of each side to compromise and to "put the interest of their Nation first."[62] Through the negotiations, each side had been aware of the force of public opinion in support of restraint. Addressing the negotiations, presidential aide George Reedy spoke to the popularization of the guidepost framework, noting that the steel companies "are afraid that they will get clobbered if they increase the price of anything and they are looking for some release from this fear."[63]

However, the steel companies would also adapt to this public prominence, as they would often schedule price increases to minimize administration and public awareness. For example, on December 31, Bethlehem Steel announced a $5-per-ton increase in structural steel prices, one that frustrated Johnson, given the administration's September efforts in restraining the USW, the holiday timing, and the wartime context. On January 1, 1966, Bethlehem Chairman Edmund Martin met with Ackley and Califano and "gave little justification for the increase and no indication that he would rescind it." Johnson responded with both private and public pressures, sending a telegram which urged the heads of the other steel firms to "put the interest of your country first" and by directing Ackley and Califano to anonymously charge that Bethlehem officials were "open to warranted charges of profiteering." U.S. Steel President Roger Blough stepped in at this point to announce that U.S. Steel was considering a more limited $2.75-per-ton increase, with offsetting reductions elsewhere. Johnson accepted this compromise, and Bethlehem scaled back

---

[61] Califano (1991, 88, 91).
[62] Johnson (1965).
[63] Dallek (1998, 304–305).

its increase. Nevertheless, this partial victory foreshadowed difficulties to come.[64]

Into mid-1966, Johnson officials would struggle to uphold the 3.2 percent standard. Califano later recalled the period as one of improvisation, during which Johnson seemed like "a Dutch uncle with a thousand thumbs plugging holes in economic dikes to hold off the floodwaters of inflation."[65] Perhaps the most public disappointment came in summer negotiations between the International Association of Machinists (IAM) and the nation's air carriers. While the companies proposed a "guidepost settlement" of 2.8 percent, the IAM stressed the need for a 5 percent increase. In the face of mounting pressure on the dollar, this was seen as a particularly important settlement, as Ackley noted in a memo on the airline dispute, warning that "with our balance of payments situation – we cannot afford inflation, even if it could be tolerated domestically."[66] In late July 1966, in an attempt to reprise the prior summer's steel triumph, Johnson moved negotiations into the Old Executive Office Building, obtaining a tentative 4.4 percent agreement, which he in fact lauded in a nationally televised address – Johnson justified the higher figure on the grounds of increased labor productivity, a violation of the broader guidepost principle that called for price decreases where productivity increased. However, the union rank-and-file would later repudiate the agreement by a 3-1 margin, eventually obtaining a 4.9 wage percent increase. IAM President Roy Siemiller, who Secretary of Labor Willard Wirtz termed "one of the two or three most bitter public critics of the guideposts," would declare that the increase "destroys all existing wage and price guidelines now in existence."[67] When Wirtz returned from an AFL-CIO meeting, he likewise informed Johnson that "Everybody is assuming 5 percent is the new guideline."[68] In this context, as Califano would later recall, Johnson was forced "to face the limits on his own power to manipulate the economy and to consider wage and price controls and fiscal action on the tax front." Between these options, Johnson would increasingly break away from incomes policies and pursue the fiscal course, in accord with Council preferences.[69]

[64] Califano (1991, 102–104).
[65] Califano (1991, 137).
[66] Cochrane (1975, 262).
[67] Cochrane (1975, 259, 262).
[68] Cochrane (1975, 259–263); Rowen (1994, 16–17).
[69] Califano (1991, 146).

## Neoclassical Displacement of the Guideposts

Over the remainder of the Johnson years, opposition to incomes policies would steadily increase, with the opposition of the Council playing a key role at several points. First, in late 1965, Johnson accepted the Council's recommendation that he refrain from raising the 3.2 percent guidepost figure to a more politically viable 3.6 percent, which would acknowledge the weight of price increases.[70] This decision ran counter to political pressures from labor, as Ackley conceded that labor would "call it a betrayal if we don't go to 3.6." Secretary of Labor Wirtz likewise warned that the administration's failure to permit higher wage increases would lead to "a great deal of trouble with labor unless this is part of a general 'austerity' program," encompassing "both a very tight domestic budget plus a tax increase, and tighter guideposts for prices."[71] Ackley himself later came to view the Council's resistance as having been a mistake, on the grounds that wages were not the sole source of inflation. He later conceded that "after the inflation really began to take hold, 3.2 per cent became no longer appropriate" and that the Council "may have waited too long in recognizing that," admitting that it had been "stupid to say that you should continue to take no account of a rising cost of living in setting wages."[72] To be sure, some administration figures urged a revision of the guidepost framework to acknowledge both political realities and

---

[70] Interestingly, the Council rejected its own technocratic formula, as the increase to 3.6 would have been in accord with the definition of the guidepost as a five-year moving average of productivity trends. Solow later rationalized the decision to keep it at 3.2 percent as "right ... in substance," because the original formula had been something of a political device. Solow suggested that the very notion of a "five year moving average as the 'official' method" for calculating the guidepost figure had been "not a technician's method," but rather a "compromise expedient – a method anyone could understand which happened to give the same answer as the technicians' methods." Solow went on to assert that "the technicians' methods should prevail," lest opening the guidepost figure up to bargaining "destroy any claim that the guidepost figure might have to be an objectively determined number." The Council itself noted that, moving into 1966, the "last recession year (1960) drops out of the average; yet the unsustainable productivity gains of a year of recovery (1961) and four years of improving utilization of productive capacity are retained." In this light, "3.6 percent would not be an accurate measure of the true trend of productivity." Council of Economic Advisers (1966, 92); Solow (1966, 53).
[71] Ackley (1965).
[72] Ackley (1974, 26).

the non-wage-based sources of inflation. However, this ran counter to the technocratic views of the Council.

Second, the Council resisted congressional efforts to institutionalize incomes policies and bring them into the deliberative arena, opposing a bill introduced by Democratic Representative Henry Reuss to transform the Council from a purely advisory body into one with a statutory responsibility for maintaining wage-price guideposts. In September 1966, Reuss proposed mandating that the Council publicize an annual guidepost figure to cultivate "an informed public opinion in order to restrain ... price or wage behavior." This figure would then be submitted to the Joint Economic Committee for legislative review. Just as the Federal Reserve was responsible for monetary policy, and the Treasury was responsible for fiscal policy, the Council would be responsible for the guideposts.[73] However, in congressional testimony, Ackley rejected this grant of authority on the grounds that its "implied direction" was "toward giving legal status and a flavor of compulsion to what must – in order to be successful in the long run – remain a matter of understanding and freely volunteered cooperation."[74] Solow similarly warned against the politicization of the guideposts on the grounds that "the guidepost figure is not something one sets," but rather "something one finds out" through economic analysis. Solow warned further that while "Congress can investigate," it was "far from clear that its methods are ideal for investigating the subtler properties of economic time series," again reflecting a technocratic skepticism of popular influences.[75]

Third, in early 1967 – one year after having resisted raising the guidepost to 3.6 percent – the Council abandoned quantitative guideposts altogether. At this point, the Johnson administration faced a choice among three options. First, it could reiterate the 3.2 percent wage guidepost, knowing – as it put it in its *Administrative History* – "that it would be resented as unfair by labor and ignored in practice." In turn, it might temporarily deviate from the 3.2 percent figure to "some other figure which would give at least partial recognition to the rise in living costs" but which might create a precedent "difficult to deviate from after the price advantage slowed down." Lastly – the

[73] US House of Representatives (1966).
[74] Ackley, Okun, and Duesenberry (1966, 36–37).
[75] Solow (1966, 53).

course eventually taken – the Council might admit "that some adjustment for rising prices was inevitable, and urge restraint without setting any new numerical guidepost." Yet, just as Ackley had conceded that the failure to revise 3.2 upward had been a misstep, the Council came to view this third choice as a mistake, acknowledging that it had been "the omission of any number, rather than the reason for the omission, that received the widest attention and publicity." The omission was interpreted by "both business and labor as an abandonment of the guideposts [and so] ... the prevailing view was that the guideposts were dead."[76]

Fourth and finally, Neoclassical opposition also weighed against the imposition of mandatory controls. This possibility had been rejected by Johnson himself in August 1966, just after the airline defeat. Seeking an understanding of his statutory options, Johnson ordered Califano to oversee a "top-secret-eyes-only" study into whether the President could impose wage and price controls without congressional authorization. Califano found that "in a national emergency declared by the President, the 1917 Trading with the Enemy Act might be invoked to impose wage and price controls without going to the Congress." Providing added weight, the Truman administration's declaration of national emergency from the Korean War remained in effect.[77] Johnson also discussed the legality of such efforts with Attorney General Nicholas Katzenbach. While Katzenbach was sympathetic, he was also "concerned that a court might overturn presidential action to impose controls," unless Congress moved quickly to provide legislative backing.[78] Johnson then conferred with Supreme Court Justice Abe Fortas, who could provide no clear sense of the Court's likely views, suggesting instead that "the outcome might well depend on the severity of the situation at the time."[79]

Neoclassical objections heavily influenced these debates, as Califano recalled the "vehement opposition expressed by those who had helped administer economic controls during World War II and the Korean

---

[76] Council of Economic Advisers (1969b, ch. 3).
[77] Califano (1991, 146).
[78] Katzenbach later provided memo more formally making these arguments, but kept it from the Justice Department itself, because he wanted to keep a "free hand to support any such action" with respect to presidential wage-price authority. Califano (1991, 146–147).
[79] Califano (1991, 147).

War" noting that this was "persuasive to Johnson."[80] For example, in January 1966, Budget Director – and former Kennedy Council member – Kermit Gordon responded to a Johnson inquiry on controls with a memo explaining "why economists – particularly those who served with OPA or OPS – tend to flinch when mandatory price control is mentioned." Gordon argued first that "general price control inevitably generates serious economic distortions, and the distortions tend to become more damaging the longer price control survives." He further warned that "the administrative problems of general price control are staggering," on grounds that it requires "an army of federal employees to administer and enforce price control" many of whom "are inevitably recruited from the industry they will regulate, with the result that the integrity of the whole process comes under a cloud." Gordon finally stressed the impact on public morals, asserting that "[a]ny clever and unscrupulous seller can find loopholes in the price regulation; Thus general price control tends to reward scofflaws and penalize honesty."[81]

## Constructing a Fiscal Crisis

The Council's displacement of incomes policies was paralleled by its support for fiscal fine-tuning, which provided an apolitical avenue to fighting inflation. In the fiscal realm, administration debate began, according to Ackley, shortly after Johnson's July 1965 request for additional funding in Vietnam. By October, Ackley recalled, the president began to confront "two alternatives that really weren't alternatives because, in a sense, they were ruled out by his values." Initially, Johnson "might have substantially cut government expenditures – not defense expenditures – which meant his Great Society programs," or he might have accepted the need "to tighten monetary policy instead of fiscal policy." Ackley argued that Johnson's values precluded either of these options, as the burden would have fallen on more vulnerable elements of society – recalling that it made Johnson "ill to think about those bankers collecting 12 percent interest."[82]

---

[80] Califano (1991, 147).
[81] Cochrane (1975, 269–270).
[82] Hargrove and Morley (1984, 247–248).

Nevertheless, one should not overlook early proactive administration measures in the direction of a tightening. For example, at the Council's urging, in his January 1966 State of the Union Address – only six months into the Vietnam escalation – Johnson called for the postponement of a number of enacted tax cuts. Over late 1965 and early 1966, the Council also succeeded in convincing Johnson to mute his opposition to monetary restraint. When the Federal Reserve raised the discount rate from 4 to 4.5 percent in December 1965, the Council countered Johnson's initially hostile reaction and expressed guarded support for the move. Council Chair Ackley later recalled receiving memos from Johnson and key advisers through April 1966, asking whether the president should not "come out and condemn this tight money and these high interest rates?'" Ackley would reply by citing Council warnings from "about ten different places in which we had said in so many words, 'If you don't have a tax increase, one of the things you're really going to get is tight money and high interest rates.'"[83]

Nevertheless, the Council and the Federal Reserve each reversed themselves, urging a fiscal and monetary *easing* into 1967 in light of recessionary fears. In December 1966, discussing the upcoming State of the Union Address and budget message, Ackley urged a "new *stimulus*, both from fiscal and monetary policy, to minimize the risk of a dangerous stall" and recommended that Johnson seek "the maximum degree of flexibility to back away from a tax increase."[84] Breaking with calls for restraint, Ackley warned Johnson that "the tax increase should be put on the shelf."[85] In its December 1966 economic assessment, the Council more formally "foresaw a weak outlook for the first half of 1967," justifying "a need for a new stimulus, both from monetary and fiscal policy."[86] Looking back on the whole period, Ackley later recalled that "around the beginning of the year [1967] there was some reason to consider the possibility that there might be a genuine recession," and so the Council was not "pushing very hard" for a tax increase. It would take until mid-1967 for the Council to "see that the recovery was coming and that the problem was soon to be

---

[83] Hargrove and Morley (1984, 232–233, 248–249).
[84] Dallek (1998, 311; emphasis added).
[85] Bremner (2004, 225).
[86] Council of Economic Advisers (1969b, ch. 2–19).

back with us and then we really began to push" once again for a tax increase.[87] Monetary policy would also ease over this period, with the Federal Reserve reducing the discount rate from 6 to 5.5 percent, its first reduction since 1960.[88] In this context, in his 1967 State of the Union Address, Johnson requested a 6 percent income tax surcharge, but in light of concerns about growth, he requested that it not take effect until July 1, 1967.[89] Conventional wisdom notwithstanding, later denunciations of Johnson for resisting austerity are difficult to square with contemporaneous Federal Reserve and Council pressures for stimulus. Johnson could not have resisted pressures for austerity, as technocratic concerns had pivoted to press him for a stimulus.

In this light, while inflation and monetary instability were potential problems, they were not – from the perspective of early 1967 – obvious or pressing. Moreover, when support for restraint reemerged over the fall of 1967 and into the spring of 1968, it would stem to a greater degree from international developments, particularly the November 1967 devaluation of the pound. Yet, in contrast to the early-1960s Kennedy reliance on incomes policies as a first line of defense for the dollar, the Council would resist their use to support the dollar. The Council even refused to include in its 1968 *Economic Report* a full discussion of proposed alternative wage-price frameworks. Ackley himself conceded that "[t]he suggestions contained herein go only a little way toward meeting [Treasury] Secretary Fowler's need for a tough wage-price policy as part of the balance-of-payments program for 1968."[90] Instead, on January 1, 1968, when Johnson imposed direct controls on foreign investment, these measures went unaccompanied by similar wage-price efforts. Johnson himself declared, "I do not hold to the view that wage or price controls are imminent at all."[91]

This contrasted with the Council's revived lobbying for fiscal restraint. In a May 1968 memo, newly appointed chairman Arthur Okun warned Johnson that the failure to secure passage of the tax surcharge could precipitate a "world financial crisis." Okun warned that "the failure of the tax bill would demonstrate to the world that the United States is not serious about preserving the dollar." In this memo,

[87] Hargrove and Morley (1984, 263).
[88] Bremner (2004, 234).
[89] Dallek (1998, 311); Bremmer (2004, 228).
[90] Ackley (1967).
[91] Johnson (1968a).

which Johnson read aloud to key congressional figures, Okun went so far as to suggest that "the first casualty might be the Paris peace talks."[92] These crisis constructions succeeded in securing congressional support, and when Johnson signed the resulting tax increase on June 28, 1968, he offered a Neoclassical narrative of fiscal pragmatism, juxtaposing the Kennedy tax cuts which had spurred "88 months of sustained prosperity" with an inflation that now required pressing "the fiscal brakes" to enable continued reliance on "free markets, unfettered by damaging Government controls."[93]

While Council-styled constructions of Stagflation as brought on by fiscal policy failures would gain ground in later decades, they weaken on closer inspection, as they overlook early guidepost-driven successes in containing inflation, the 1966–1967 consensus push for stimulus, and the relatively quick Johnson shift to enable successful passage of the 1968 tax increase.[94] First, in comparison with earlier episodes, a case can be made that the guideposts initially helped contain World War II– or Korean War–styled price surges. Consider that in 1942 – the first full year of World War II – inflation reached 9 percent, and in 1951 – the first full year of the Korean conflict – inflation totaled 6 percent. In contrast, in 1965 inflation increased by 1.9 percent, and in 1966 by 3.5 percent.[95] Second, while there would be some delay in obtaining the Johnson administration's ultimate tax increase – in part reflecting the consensus on the need for a stimulus, given the brief 1967 "recessionette" – the ensuing deficits of 1967 (1.1 percent of GDP) and 1968 (2.9 percent of GDP) were hardly significant in

---

[92] Califano (1991, 286–288); Okun (1968).
[93] Johnson (1968b).
[94] David Halberstam (1972, 604) in particular overrates Johnson's duplicity, asserting that he "would not give accurate economic projections, would not ask for a necessary tax raise, and would in fact have *his own* military planners be less than candid with *his own* economic planners." Such analyses downplay the Johnson CEA's support for fiscal stimulus over 1966–1968 and their opposition to controls. Halberstam's account is also undermined by the admission of CEA Chair Gardner Ackley that the Council "knew what numbers were being talked about, and ... [that] they weren't nearly big enough in terms of what was going to happen to defense expenditures." While conceding that Johnson may have tried to conceal matters in "July and maybe August [1965]," Ackley argued that the Council possessed "all the evidence we needed ... by November or early December, that a tax increase was absolutely necessary" (Hargrove and Morley 1984, 247–248).
[95] Council of Economic Advisers (2007, 304).

historical terms.[96] Third and finally, over this entire period, Johnson had supported overlooked tax increases, suggesting that the costs for his Great Society and his ostensible ideological objections may have been overrated: Johnson accepted the need to adjust the tax code in 1966 along a range of fronts and obtained the 1968 surcharge and budget surplus. The failure of fiscal restraint to contain inflation is supportive less of claims for presidential duplicity than its limits in the face of market power and psychology.[97]

Indeed, having secured fiscal restraint, Okun conceded in a July 15 memo to Califano that there had been "lull in our efforts to get business and labor cooperation on wage-price restraint" and that "so far this year" the administration's "record of activity here is considerably below any other period of the Kennedy-Johnson era." Okun then went on to concede that "economic conditions indicate that this is the time for an energetic price-wage stance."[98] However, the administration at most engaged in occasional ad hoc efforts at holding the line against forthcoming wage and price increases. For example, the summer of 1968 saw Bethlehem Steel follow the conclusion of contract negotiations with an announcement of a 5 percent price increase. The administration condemned this move, and the Defense Department moved again to shift purchases toward lower-priced suppliers. While most companies initially followed Bethlehem, U.S. Steel backed down the next week, announcing that it would still implement a 2.5 percent price increase. Bethlehem and the other producers accordingly modified their increases, conforming to U.S. Steel's "responsible" move.[99] Such improvised pressure proved effective as far as the administration would go. Indeed, the 1969 *Economic Report* – like its predecessor – failed to provide any specific quantitative guidepost. Instead, the *Report* stressed micro-level options to reduce prices, such as deregulation, education, and improvements in infrastructure.[100] Moving across 1967, 1968, and 1969, inflation would steadily rise from 3.0 to 4.7 to 6.2 percent.[101] The limited effectiveness of the Johnson administration's

---

[96] The 1968 deficit came to barely more than the Eisenhower deficit of 1959, which had been only 2.6 percent of GDP. Council of Economic Advisers (2007, 324).
[97] Galbraith (1958, 194).
[98] Cochrane (1975, 285).
[99] Hall (1997, 80–81); see also Cochrane (1975, 286).
[100] Council of Economic Advisers (1969b, 98–102, 142).
[101] Council of Economic Advisers (2007, 304).

fiscal restraint combined with the displacement of incomes policies to enable continued inflation.

## 4.5 The Social Context: Societal, Institutional, and Public Influences

The collapse of incomes policies cannot be understood in abstraction from the mutually reinforcing erosion of government authority and institutional support for efforts at public mobilization. First, in societal terms, skepticism toward incomes policies stemmed from an increasing trend to state-societal alienation, most importantly among representatives of labor and consumer groups. Regarding labor, even in 1964, AFL-CIO President George Meany would declare to the administration, "they're your guidelines and not mine," and proceed to "question this whole idea of guidelines ... to protect the public interest."[102] In mid-1966, as noted above, the IAM union would deal the guideposts perhaps their most explicit public defeat. With respect to consumer groups, consumer advocate Ralph Nader questioned the democratic nature of the Johnson efforts, arguing in a 1968 letter to Okun, "General Motors has been reviewing prices in strict secrecy with the CEA since 1964 ... Such a government policy, contrary to its usual justification, does not, in my judgment, maximize the government's leverage nor does it serve the public by keeping it in the dark about the issues, the facts, and what the government does or does not do."[103] While consumer groups had been incorporated into the Office of Price Administration (OPA) system of the 1940s, in the more Neoclassical 1960s they found themselves on the outside looking in. Finally, as noted earlier, representatives of business would increasingly seek to evade limits on price increases through discrete adjustments – as seen in Bethlehem Steel's testing of guidelines in December 1965 and mid-1968.

Second, in terms of public opinion, the emergence of a "credibility gap" with respect to foreign policy facilitated economic policy cynicism as narratives stressing Johnson's mendacity accorded with public opinion trends.[104] These marked the beginning of a prolonged decline

---

[102] Cochrane (1975, 211).
[103] Cochrane (1975, 292).
[104] Journalists who covered economic policy during this period, including Leonard Silk (1984, 19) of the *New York Times* and Hobart Rowen (1994, 3)

in trust in government and an increasing tendency to blame state rather than societal agents for inflation. Even over the 1966–1968 period, those declaring that they could "just about always" trust the government would fall by more than half, from 17 percent to 7 percent. Pulling back to a view of shifts from 1958 to 1970, those declaring they could trust the government either "just about always" or "most of the time" would likewise decline, from 73 percent to 53 percent.[105] Paralleling this decline in trust was a wider support for policy failure constructions of inflation. In 1959, only 14 percent of respondents had declared that they found government to be more responsible than business or labor for inflation. In contrast, by 1968, 46 percent of the public would come to blame government for inflation.[106]

Third, in overlapping ideational and institutional terms, where Neoclassical Kennedy-Johnson economists were committed to a more cognitive model of argumentation, they saw their role as more educational rather than exhortative, and so communicative rhetoric was increasingly displaced by a coordinative alternative. Where this impeded societal mobilization on behalf of restraint, it had the effect of a self-fulfilling prophecy. Johnson CEA Chair Gardner Ackley would later concede this Council failure to mobilize public support, noting that "[e]ven the most fully compulsory system cannot work for long" unless it enjoys "broad support" from "the general public," and so whether a "wage ceiling survives ... surely will depend on the extent to which other unions – and the general public – support the restraint system." Likewise, with respect to business support, Ackley noted "there are many ways – legal, questionable, and illegal" – to evade "almost any price regulation." He concluded that the absence

---

of the *Washington Post*, commenced later narratives of economic decline with Johnson's deceit and failure to raise taxes. Silk stressed presidential "duplicity," which kept the costs of Vietnam "secret from the American people." Rowen similarly began by declaring that Johnson "made two decisions that would have a profound effect not only upon his presidency, but also upon the future of the American economy. In February [1965], he started the systematic bombing of North Vietnam. Then, in July, he made the commitment – kept secret from the nation – to bring troop strength in Vietnam up to 500,000."

[105] Trust the Federal Government, 1958–2004 *The American National Election Survey Guide to Public Opinion and Electoral Behavior* www.electionstudies.org/nesguide/text/tab5a_1.txt.

[106] Gallup (1978).

of popular consent had weakened the Kennedy-Johnson guideposts, which he lamented for having been "dreamed up by economists." In this light, the "greatest weaknesses of the guidepost system" had been "the absence of any real participation by the interest groups in the origination and modification of the guideposts – and, as a consequence, the absence of any sense of responsibility on their part for the success or failure of the effort."[107] In the absence of consent, incomes policies lost their effectiveness, which rendered consent more difficult to secure, which only increased the need for recourse to macroeconomic fine-tuning.

## 4.6 Conclusions: Intellectual Conversion, Institutional Displacement, and Fiscal Fine-Tuning

Over the early postwar decades, the Keynesian order saw principled appeals restrain the market power driving potential wage-price spirals and expand the scope for expansionary macroeconomic policies to promote growth. However, this success would over time provide the foundation for an intellectual hubris that obscured the social bases of wage-price restraint and spurred increasing confidence in the potential fine-tuning of Phillips Curve-styled trade-offs. In this way, the Keynesian order would undergo an intellectual conversion in the rise of a Neoclassical Synthesis. This would be paralleled in rhetorical forms of debate, as Kennedy sought to abstract away from the communicative "grand warfare of rival ideologies" and reduce economic debate to a more coordinative, slow thinking set of "sophisticated and technical questions."[108] Given these shifts, the early Kennedy administration would see the eclipse of Institutional Keynesians such as Galbraith and Rostow by more Neoclassical Keynesians on the CEA such as Heller and Ackley who favored the fiscal fine-tuning of a Phillips curve trade-off between inflation and unemployment. While an early truce within the Kennedy administration could be attributed to the merit of the wage guideposts in providing "political space" for a fiscal stimulus, this accord would prove short-lived. Following the 1962 steel confrontation, Kennedy grew concerned to regain his credibility with business, and the Council saw guideposts as having outlived their usefulness

---

[107] US Congress. Joint Economic Committee (1971, 245).
[108] Kennedy (1962a).

in providing insulation from charges that the eventual 1964 tax cut would spur inflation.

Intellectual conversion would in turn be followed during the Johnson years by the institutional displacement of incomes policy by fiscal policy, as the guideposts were permitted to wither on the vine. Nevertheless, the Council would judge Johnson's ostensible failure to engage in timely fiscal tightening a key source of rising prices – as Johnson's last Council Chair Arthur Okun described Stagflation as reflecting "the defeat of the New Economics by the old politics."[109] In the context of diminishing trust in government, the next decade would witness a furthering of this displacement of incomes policies – which would be used not in any systematic way, but at most as short-term policy alibis. In their place, a misplaced confidence in fiscal "gradualism" would justify the fiscal accommodation of recurring bouts of Stagflation – setting the stage for the next decade's final eclipse of the Keynesian order.

---

[109] Greider (1987, 333).

# 5 Constructing the Great Stagflation: From Accommodation to Transformation

> We were always, in terms of an anti-inflationary program, six months to a year behind the game.
>
> Carter CEA Chairman Charles Schultze.[1]

## 5.1 Introduction

Over the early Keynesian era, presidential appeals had enabled the use of incomes policies to contain wage-price pressures, while increasing the space for expansionary policies and economic growth. However, by the 1960s, an intellectual conversion of debate saw the Neoclassical Phillips curve used both to guide fiscal fine-tuning and justify wage-price deregulation. Into the 1970s, this Neoclassical framework would fuel a misplaced certainty in the ability of "gradualist" fiscal and monetary fine-tuning to contain inflation. Yet, while the Nixon, Ford, and Carter administrations each pledged that they would wring inflationary expectations out of the system, each proved unwilling to impose sustained restraint, as inflation instead continued to rise across iterations of stagflation. To be sure, each administration would at points "reach back" and make intermittent recourse to incomes policies in order to maintain a degree of anti-inflation credibility – but each also did so in ways marked by an absence of sustained engagement with the public. To the extent that incomes policies would suffer a diminishing credibility as a result of this erratic and uneven application, Paul Volcker would by the decade's end argue that their use might paradoxically *raise* expectations of inflation – as market actors might see official recourse to incomes policies as suggestive of a lack of policy credibility. Taken together, the combination of intellectual conversion, institutional displacement, and misplaced certainty in gradualist fine-tuning brought the Keynesian order to the brink of collapse.

[1] Hargrove and Morley (1984, 479–480).

In this chapter, I trace this increasing misplaced certainty across the Nixon, Ford, and Carter administrations, as each combined gradualist restraint with ad hoc recourse to incomes policies, spanning Nixon's "New Economic Policy" (NEP), Ford's "Whip Inflation Now" (WIN) program, and Carter's Tax-Based Incomes Policies (TIPs). In the first section, I address the early-1970s Stagflation, as the Nixon administration moved from an initial gradualism to the August 1971 New Economic Policy which saw "phases" of freezes alternate with voluntary guidelines through to the administration's collapse in the Watergate scandal. Although these efforts worked to sustain growth and contain inflation prior to the 1972 elections, they were not sustained, and early 1973 would see the collapse of fixed exchange rates and reemergence of inflation. In the second section, I address the brief efforts of the Ford administration to address the revived inflation by imposing fiscal and monetary restraint – only to back off in the face of a late-1974 slowdown, substituting a short-lived WIN program and limited fiscal contraction. Even as these restraints proved too weak to defeat inflation, they proved just strong enough to slow growth going into the 1976 elections, contributing to Ford's loss. In the third section, I describe how the Carter administration initially promised an expansionary approach, only to see a revival of inflationary pressures. In this setting, it belatedly proposed – and quickly abandoned – a set of technocratic TIPs that envisioned the taxing away of inflationary wage increases. In a fourth section, I address the institutional, coalitional, and public tensions which led former Federal Reserve Chair Arthur Burns to lament "the anguish of central banking" in a 1979 speech – setting the stage for the Neoliberal order. Taken as a whole, this analysis highlights the combination of misplaced certainty and diminishing policy returns that fueled Stagflation and the final crises of the Keynesian order.

## 5.2 Nixon's Stagflation: From Gradualism to the New Economic Policy

Over the Nixon administration, macroeconomic policymaking evolved across two stages, as an initial stress on fiscal and monetary gradualism yielded to the adoption of a New Economic Policy and a second period of shifts in the use of controls from "freezing" to "easing." First, the administration renounced wage and price guideposts in favor of gradualist monetary and fiscal fine-tuning. However, this would have the effect of liberating agents possessing wage and price power, while weighing more heavily on more perfectly competitive sectors of the economy. The result would be to slow growth while permitting an increase in prices – a New Inflation–styled result that would be rechristened as "Stagflation" – and which initially prompted business groups and the Federal Reserve to push for a strengthening of incomes policies. Second, in the context of this pressure, the Nixon administration would in August 1971 adopt a New Economic Policy, one which initially brought price stability and growth, but would yield to a shifting array of controls, mandatory guidelines, and voluntary restraints that exhibited diminishing returns. Perhaps most importantly, the January 1973 abandonment of "Phase II" mandatory guidelines led to a second dollar devaluation and collapse of the Bretton Woods fixed exchange rates. Taken as a whole, the Nixon administration would move from its early gradualism to accommodate inflation in a way that anticipated the practices of its successors.

## Nixon's Gradualism: From Fine-Tuning to the New Economic Policy

Despite the change of party control, the Nixon administration initially exhibited broad continuity with the later Johnson administration in its support for fiscal and monetary fine-tuning and wariness toward guidelines. At his first press conference, Nixon himself endorsed "fine tuning of fiscal and monetary affairs" but rejected "the suggestion that inflation can be effectively controlled by exhorting labor and management and industry to follow certain guidelines." Instead, he argued, "the primary responsibility for controlling inflation rests with the ... handling of fiscal and monetary affairs."[2] This aversion to controls was also shared by key advisers, including Secretary of Labor George Shultz and self-proclaimed "Friedmanesque" Council Chairman Paul McCracken. Shultz explicitly argued that incomes policies "had not been very effective while in force" and argued that they may have strengthened inflation "by diverting attention away from the fundamental weapons of monetary and fiscal policy."[3]

[2] Nixon (1969).
[3] De Marchi (1975, 300); Shultz and Dam (1977, 1).

In place of reliance on guidelines, the administration initially adopted a policy of gradualism, to impose fiscal or monetary restraint while avoiding the pain associated with what McCracken saw as a "cold turkey" approach.[4] Gradualism would slowly – and hopefully less painfully – wring inflationary expectations from the system by reducing the rate of monetary growth and increasing fiscal austerity. In February 1969, Federal Reserve Chairman Martin expressed support for this "constructive effort to disinflate without deflating."[5] However, over the first two years of the administration, Nixon himself would grow skeptical. Reflecting not least memories of his defeat in 1960 – when Eisenhower had refused a stimulus – Nixon was less willing to accept a gradual disinflation. In April 1969 when Council member Herbert Stein expressed support for the Federal Reserve's recent monetary tightening as "consistent with [administration] objectives," Nixon countered that, in 1958, "[w]e cooled off the economy and cooled off 15 Senators and 60 Congressmen at the same time."[6] McCracken and Shultz then moved to criticize the Federal Reserve, suggesting that Federal Reserve Chairman Martin's tightening had been too severe – and out of line with a truly *gradual* policy.[7] By mid-1970, Nixon had become increasingly convinced that gradualism had accomplished the worst of both worlds. Foreshadowing Stagflation, it had reduced growth but failed to contain inflationary pressures. Even as tax revenues had risen from 17.6 percent of GDP in 1968 to 19.1 percent in 1970, and the prime rate had climbed from 6.3 percent to 7.9 percent, inflation had nevertheless increased from 4.7 percent in 1968 to 5.6 in 1970.[8]

In response, business and institutional agents would call for more direct efforts at securing wage and price restraint. In October 1970, at a meeting of the Business Council, subsequent Director of Nixon's Cost of Living Council Arnold Weber saw administration figures "subjected to harsh criticisms for failing to check excessive wage increases and price inflation." Weber noted that the "fact that the Business

---

[4] McCracken stressed the need "to avoid the stop-start strategy of seeming to see a recession and stepping on the accelerator – then seeing inflation and stepping on the brakes." Matusow (1998, 14–15).
[5] Matusow (1998, 20).
[6] Matusow (1998, 22).
[7] Matusow (1998, 60).
[8] Council of Economic Advisers (1998).

Council was comprised of the top executives of the largest corporations in the nation indicated that the administration could not dispel demands for economic activism by appeals to conservative ideology." The Business Council persisted instead with "a demand for some form of comprehensive incomes policy."[9] Similarly, in November 1970, the probusiness Committee for Economic Development issued a statement urging that the administration define "the wage and price behavior that is ... consistent with overall price stability."[10]

Notwithstanding its expected bureaucratic interests in monetary restraint, the Federal Reserve provided another source of pressure for wage and price regulation. In May 1970, newly appointed Chairman Arthur Burns publicly pressured the administration, suggesting that "an incomes policy, provided it stopped well short of direct price and wage controls ... might speed us through this transitional period of cost-push inflation."[11] In a December speech, Burns called for "the establishment of a high-level price and wage review board ... to investigate, advise, and recommend on price and wage changes."[12] By June 1971, Burns would stress the link between "cost-push inflation" and the deterioration in "our international competitive position," arguing for the need to "bring inflation under control [in order to] ... compete more effectively with foreign producers in our domestic markets."[13] Although these arguments reflected Burns's desire that the Federal Reserve not bear the entire burden of anti-inflation policy, they also led to a cooling of relations with the administration.[14] This deterioration would continue as Burns would raise the discount rate on July 15, 1971, in part due to his "concern over the continuation of substantial cost-push inflation." In response, the White House leaked the charge that Burns had sought a $20,000 raise, though Nixon later retreated and lauded Burns as "the most responsible and statesmanlike of any Chairman of the Federal Reserve."[15]

In light of these pressures, Nixon had begun in mid-1970 a shift away from gradualism and toward a revival of incomes policies. In

---

[9] Weber (1973, 5–6).
[10] Committee for Economic Development (1970).
[11] Burns (1978, 99).
[12] Burns (1978, 114).
[13] Burns (1978, 99).
[14] Hetzel (1998, 22).
[15] Matusow (1998, 111–112).

June, Nixon announced a series of measures in a nationally televised address, appointing a National Commission on Productivity, directing the Council to issue periodic "Inflation Alerts," and establishing a Regulations and Purchasing Review Board to align procurement and anti-inflation policies. More broadly, Nixon called for the greater exercise of "social responsibility ... on the part of unions and corporations" to bring stability on the "wage-price front."[16] Following the 1970 mid-term elections, in which the Republicans lost nine seats in the House, Federal Reserve Chairman Arthur Burns, Under Secretary of the Treasury for Monetary Affairs Paul Volcker, and Treasury Secretary John Connally together represented a source of greater pressure for direct efforts to restrain the wage-price spiral.[17] In January 1971, having concluded that "We have to kick someone," Nixon mirrored the 1962 Kennedy steel confrontation in responding to Bethlehem Steel's announcement of a 12.5 percent increase in structural steel prices.[18] Denouncing the increase, Nixon called off negotiations designed to limit steel imports and restricted government purchases to "responsible" firms. Just as in 1966 and 1968, U.S. Steel stepped in to undercut Bethlehem, announcing a lesser 6.8 percent increase, leading the administration to laud its "restraint."[19] The administration followed this initiative with a February confrontation with construction unions, obtaining their agreement to work with a Construction Industry Stabilization Committee to maintain wage guidelines.[20] More broadly emulating Kennedy in January 1971, Nixon publicly affirmed "I am now a Keynesian."[21]

Eventually, even the self-proclaimed Friedmanesque Council Chairman Paul McCracken would concede the limits to gradualism. In its 1971 *Economic Report*, the Council admitted that progress in containing inflation had been "disappointingly slow."[22] While continuing to insist that "the primary instruments for achieving [price stability]" were "monetary and fiscal policies," the Council condemned "wage increases negotiated under major collective bargaining

---

[16] Nixon (1970, 617).
[17] Matusow (1998, 64–66).
[18] De Marchi (1975, 329); Matusow (1998, 94).
[19] Hall (1997, 80–81); Matusow (1998, 940).
[20] Matusow (1998, 95–96).
[21] Matusow (1998, 91).
[22] Council of Economic Advisers (1971, 49).

agreements" that had "continued to accelerate in 1970."[23] Council member Herbert Stein later compared administration policies over this period to that of "a Russian family fleeing over the snow in a horse-drawn troika pursued by wolves. Every once in a while they throw a baby out to slow down the wolves ... Every once in a while the administration would make another step in the direction of incomes policies, hoping to appease the critics while the [gradualist] demand-management policy would work."[24] Yet, into the summer of 1971, limits remained: while the administration continued to engage in exhortation, it refused to commit itself to formal guidelines or controls. In a June 1971 press conference, Secretary of the Treasury John Connally affirmed continued support for gradualism, setting out a set of "four no's," declaring that Nixon had decided "that No. 1, he is not going to initiate a wage-price board; No. 2, he is not going to impose mandatory price and wage controls; No. 3, he is not going to ask Congress for any tax relief and No. 4, he is not going to increase federal spending."[25]

However, in August 1971, domestic and international monetary tensions would reinforce each other in a way that spurred a more definitive administration move toward incomes policies. In late July, the United Steel Workers made up for what it saw as lost ground since the late 1960s – when it had yielded its cost-of-living adjustment (COLA) protection – by securing a 15 percent first-year wage increase, a reinstatement of COLA protection, and a commitment to a three-year 31 percent increase, all in the absence of significant administration criticisms.[26] U.S. Steel, emboldened, followed these increases the next day with an 8 percent price hike. On August 2, following the steel settlement, twelve Republican senators announced that they would introduce a bill to create a wage-price review board.[27] These domestic trends would in turn intersect with anxieties regarding the dollar's value. On August 6, the Subcommittee on International Exchange and Payments issued a report that highlighted the importance of wage-price stability to US competitiveness, arguing that "to avoid a steady deterioration of our ability to compete in international trade, implementation of

[23] Council of Economic Advisers (1971, 23, 58).
[24] Matusow (1998, 64–65).
[25] Matusow (1998, 107–109).
[26] Hoerr (1988, 111).
[27] Matusow (1998, 114).

a comprehensive domestic price-wage-incomes policy is required."[28] Reinforcing these arguments, the report also urged a dollar devaluation, arguing that "dollar overvaluation leads to the perpetuation of US deficits" and suggesting that the United States "may have no choice but to take unilateral action to go off gold and establish new dollar parities."[29] On August 12, when the British requested "cover" for $3 billion in dollar assets, this was widely interpreted as signaling an official run on gold – and Nixon later cited the British move as justification for subsequent US actions.[30] In this context, the shift to back incomes policies would not only be completed, but in fact would occur in a manner far beyond anything contemplated under Kennedy and Johnson, resulting in an across-the-board wage-freeze.

## The New Economic Policy: Freezing, Easing, and Refreezing

The second stage of Nixon's economic policy would be marked by shifts across tendencies to "freezing and easing." On August 13, meeting at Camp David, Nixon officials broke with gradualism and devised a "New Economic Policy," combining a ninety-day wage and price freeze, a fiscal stimulus, and the suspension of gold convertibility. Nixon harbored the greatest doubts regarding the freeze, expressing his concerns about "putting the economy in a strait jacket under the control of a bunch of damn bureaucrats for any length of time."[31] Recognizing that labor often opposed guidelines, Shultz assured Nixon that "a freeze will stop when labor blows it up with a strike. Don't worry about getting rid of it – labor will do that for you."[32] Nevertheless, given the disappointment with gradualism, the freeze was seen as necessary by all participants at the meeting. Indeed, as Herbert Stein later recalled, the freeze would be greeted as "the most popular economic action that anyone could remember."[33] In particular, the public responded positively to Treasury Secretary Connally's denunciations of "the capacity of big business and big labor to abuse

---

[28] US Congress. Joint Economic Committee (1971, 11).
[29] US Congress. Joint Economic Committee (1971, 13).
[30] Nixon (1978, 518).
[31] Matusow (1998, 150–151).
[32] Matusow (1998, 157).
[33] Matusow (1998, 159).

power in this country" and Nixon's mercantilist-styled arguments regarding the need to combat international speculation.[34]

Moreover, Shultz's prediction that the primary opposition to the freeze would come not from business but from labor would ultimately prove correct. Labor initially objected to the retroactive application of the freeze to already-negotiated contracts and to the simultaneous lack of controls on dividends, interest, or profits. In a more principled sense, labor would frame its opposition in libertarian terms, with AFL-CIO President George Meany warning Nixon in September 1971 that, "If you are going down the route of government control, we will fight you." In return for his support, the administration agreed to establish a postfreeze tripartite Pay Board, appointing Meany as a labor representative. In an October 7 nationwide address, Nixon more formally announced that the Phase II guidelines would be enforced by a Price Commission to contain price trends and a Pay Board to stabilize wage trends. Of these arrangements, Nixon elaborated that while the Price Commission and the Pay Board would each "seek voluntary cooperation from business and labor," he also stressed that each would ultimately possess "the authority of law to make their decisions stick."[35]

Still, labor's apprehensions remained. On November 8, the Pay Board met in an atmosphere marked by Meany's distrust of the public members to define a 5.5 percent wage guideline (later raised to 6.2 percent). Meany singled out two professional economists on the Pay Board for criticism, noting that Neil Jacoby had been "a conservative economist from the Council of Economic Advisers" under Eisenhower and criticizing former Kennedy Council member Kermit Gordon as "just as conservative as the industry men."[36] Tensions were more publicly on display at Nixon's November 1971 address to the AFL-CIO annual convention, at which Meany accused the administration of orchestrating a "crackdown" on labor.[37] Ultimately, Meany would resign from the Pay Board in March 1972, leading Joint Economic Committee Chairman William Proxmire to term him "the second most powerful man in the country," given his power over wages, and to accuse him of having undermined the national interest in price stability.[38] In

[34] Sobel (1980, 87–89).
[35] Nixon (1971).
[36] Robinson (1981, 312–313).
[37] Matusow (1998, 162).
[38] US Congress. Joint Economic Committee (1972, 251–252).

one exchange, Proxmire raised the plight of the "80 percent or more of Americans who are not organized." Demonstrating the erosion of broader notions of the public interest, Meany responded, "[t]hose 80 percent are your responsibility, Senator, not mine."[39]

While the administration maintained the Phase II guidelines through the fall 1972 elections, it would soon shift to a weaker, voluntary system. On January 11, 1973, announcing a "Phase III" system, it dismantled both the Price Commission and the Pay Board and made guidelines voluntary.[40] However, this move should also be viewed in the context of concerns for the 1974 mid-term elections, as 1973 would be a big "contract year," with many pending negotiations that would see labor seeking wage gains. If labor was to back the Republicans, removing any "Nixon controls" would be a necessity. Nevertheless, the administration's political calculations would soon be frustrated, as Phase III arrangements would prove quite unpopular – not least with key US allies. In an immediate sense, the capricious renunciation of heretofore successful Phase II controls was seen as reflecting a diminished US commitment to exchange rate stability, and a late-January 1973 dollar devaluation would be followed by the March 1973 collapse of the Bretton Woods fixed exchange rate system. Moreover, with the fall of the dollar, import prices would climb, first in food and later in energy. In June 1973, these inflationary pressures would spur Nixon to reprise his August 1971 triumph, announcing a sixty-day freeze on prices (but not wages – again bearing in mind labor opposition). Yet, this move had a more limited popularity both inside and outside the administration. Seeking to dissuade Nixon, Council Chairman Stein quoted the Greek philosopher Heraclitus to the effect that "You cannot step into the same river twice." Nixon replied that you could "if it were frozen." Treasury Secretary Shultz would submit his – rejected – resignation. Milton Friedman went so far as to term this second freeze "the worst mistake in American economic policy that has been made by an American president in the last 40 years."[41]

Taken as a whole, these shifts would prove damaging to the credibility of incomes policies. Once the second freeze came to an end in August, the administration commenced a Phase IV of gradual decontrol, to enable the United States "to return to the free market system

---

[39] US Congress. Joint Economic Committee (1972, 277).
[40] Nixon (1973).
[41] Matusow (1998, 228–231).

as soon as possible."[42] Looking back at the Nixon period, *Washington Post* reporter Hobart Rowan would write that, "the way Nixon ran the controls program from freeze to thaw, back to freeze again and a final dissolving, it is little wonder that the very idea of controls came to be tarnished."[43] Indeed, in having constructed the initial justification for the New Economic Policy in broadly Keynesian terms, the Nixon efforts had the effect of further discrediting Keynesian-styled incomes policies. In sum, on the brink of his resignation in the midst of the Watergate scandal, the Nixon administration had discredited both gradualism and incomes policies, widening the debate to encompass a possibility that had been ruled out-of-bounds in 1969 – that of unqualified fiscal or monetary restraint. However, while Nixon's successor would feint in that direction, Ford would revive a limited set of incomes policies before moving back toward a weak gradualism as a means to an – ultimately inadequate – recovery.

## 5.3 Ford's Stagflation: From "Public Enemy Number 1" to "Whip Inflation Now"

Over the Ford administration, macroeconomic policymaking shifted over two stages, as an initial use of austerity to end inflation would yield over early 1975 to a second phase marked by a renewed gradualism and effort to promote recovery from an increasingly severe recession. Yet, even in this later context of recession, concerns for inflation on the part of Treasury Secretary William E. Simon and CEA Chair Alan Greenspan revealed the difficulty inherent in seeking to address two concerns with a single, fiscal instrument. In the end, having failed to engineer a recovery sufficient to ensure reelection, the Ford administration would also fail to contain the sources of inflation, which would revive and accelerate under the Carter administration.

### Fighting Inflation: From 'Old Time Religion' to 'Whip Inflation Now'

Speaking to the wider frustration with Nixon administration's shifting approaches, Nixon CEA Chair Herbert Stein later endorsed an acceptance of austerity as the only surefire way to contain inflation.

---

[42] Nixon (1974, 122).
[43] Rowen (1994, 83).

Stein argued that "if you follow a policy of restraint ... you will get the inflation rate down. You will go through some period of excessive unemployment, but you will end up with no more unemployment than you would otherwise have had ... This is 'old time religion,' but I think it's the only effective medicine."[44] Upon assuming office, Ford declared inflation to be "Public Enemy Number One" in addressing a joint session of Congress on August 12, 1974. He immediately declared that "[w]age and price controls are out, period," and moved toward the advocacy of microeconomic reforms.[45] This stance accorded with the views expressed at a fall 1974 White House conference on inflation, which gathered not only economists and policymakers but also representatives of capital and labor, producing a series of reports proposing measures to address inflation. Many expressed outright opposition to incomes policies, emphasizing the need for restraint and revealing a new appreciation for legal-styled deregulation as a means to spur competition. Though one might expect labor to be most concerned with the effects of restraint, the labor report stated that "[n]o participant wishes to see the reimposition of wage-price controls ... for it is easy to police wage settlements, but next to impossible to track price-setting."[46] Similarly, business representatives "expressed their abhorrence of wage and price controls again and again."[47] Finally, key economists inveighed against incomes policies, as Walter Heller argued against "outmoded restrictions on the economy" and Paul Samuelson urged microeconomic "reform in energy, agriculture, and regulatory areas to ease inflation."[48]

Nevertheless, Ford shifted back to some scope for exhortation as the economy slowed toward the year's end, reconstructing Nixon's Cost of Living Council as the Council on Wage and Price Stability (COWPS) and devising the exhortatory, voluntary "Whip Inflation Now" (WIN) program – relying on buttons, bumper stickers, and appeals to the public good. Internally, this measure was opposed by Ford's Council Chairman Alan Greenspan, who later recalled his reaction, viewing WIN as "a low point of economic policymaking [that] made me glad

---

[44] Hargrove and Morley (1984, 402, 405).
[45] Ford (1974).
[46] The Conference on Inflation (1974, 311–312).
[47] The Conference on Inflation (1974, 452–453).
[48] Sobel (1980, 214–215).

I'd canceled the CEA's press briefings."⁴⁹ Looking back, Greenspan recalled that

> The very heavy rhetoric about some form of incomes policies in August and September of 1974 just disappeared overnight, as the WIN program disappeared over night. One of our problems ... [was] that you cannot turn on a dime. It's a long, agonizing process before you can get the whole executive system turning.⁵⁰

The abandonment of WIN reflected the extent to which policy had shifted to the problem of recession. Yet, Ford would also be constrained by a split within his administration, between inflation hawks and doves, as he sought to chart a middle course.

## Promoting Recovery, Carefully: The Limits to Fiscal Restraint

In his 1975 State of the Union address, Ford would declare that the "state of the union is not good," and depart from an anti-inflation stance to commence a qualified effort at promoting recovery. Ford argued that "[t]he moment has come to move in a new direction ... The emphasis of our economic efforts must now shift from inflation to jobs," and so proposed a one-year, one-time $16 billion tax cut – with $12 billion for consumers and $4 billion for business.⁵¹ Nevertheless, even as unemployment worsened, Ford faced opposition from within his own administration on his right flank. Treasury Secretary William Simon had not only opposed the tax cut, but also suggested to a reporter that if the deficit were to go above $40 billion, he would defect from the administration and throw his support to Ford's conservative rival Ronald Reagan.⁵² Influenced by Simon and CEA Chairman Alan Greenspan (who kept his objections private), Ford accepted the need for fiscal and monetary balance, on the grounds that while the "easiest solution to the unemployment problem would be for the federal government to go on a massive spending spree," this would ultimately result in only "short-term benefits."⁵³ In this light, when Congress raised his tax cut by 50 percent, to $22.8

---

⁴⁹ Greenspan (2007, 66).
⁵⁰ Hargrove and Morley (1984, 443–444).
⁵¹ Mieczkowki (2005, 154).
⁵² Mieczkowki (2005, 164).
⁵³ Ford (1979, 220–221).

billion cut in March 1975, this occasioned much debate within the White House, with Ford finally acquiescing even as he denounced the "many extraneous changes in our tax law" that Congress had added.[54]

While the recovery remained weak over 1975, Ford would resist further stimulus and argue in an October 6 address to the nation for a "dollar-for-dollar" approach to the budget, matching a $28 billion tax cut with a $28 billion cut in federal spending.[55] However, Ford would also be open to charges of engaging in political machinations, as the tax cuts would be granted in January 1976, but spending cuts would be delayed until September 1976 – too late to have a contractionary effect before voters went to the polls. Ultimately, while Ford's policies would be followed by reductions in the inflation rate – which had been essentially halved, from 11 percent in 1974 to 5.8 percent in 1976 – unemployment remained severe, having risen from 5.6 percent in 1974 to 8.5 percent in 1975, and remaining at 7.7 percent for 1976.[56] In February, with the primary campaign commencing, unemployment stood at 7.6 percent, and Ford's emerging Democratic rival Jimmy Carter was arguing for a monetary and fiscal stimulus.[57] In terms of electoral timing, Ford was particularly hurt by what Greenspan cast as a summer 1976 "pause" in recovery.[58] In the last month of the administration, inflation was reduced to 4.8 percent – but unemployment remained at 7.3 percent – an incomplete victory that the Carter administration would take for granted in its early stress on stimulus.[59]

Speaking to the eroding effectiveness of fiscal fine-tuning, Greenspan would argue to Ford that, even if they had sought a fiscal stimulus, "the level of economic activity wouldn't have been any better ... but you ... would have significantly increased the risk of inflation."[60] Ford later recalled agreeing with German Chancellor Helmut Schmidt that a fiscal stimulus might work "for a year or two, but catastrophe would be inevitable down the road."[61] Greenspan would later recall that

---

[54] Mieczkowki (2005, 172).
[55] Mieczkowki (2005, 175).
[56] Council of Economic Advisers (2012, 360, 392).
[57] Mieczkowki (2005, 175).
[58] Ford (1979, 428).
[59] Mieczkowki (2005, 194).
[60] Mieczkowki (2005, 190).
[61] Ford (1979, 220–221).

"when the time came in March 1975 for me to testify in Congress … I warned against panicky spending increases or tax cuts that would overstimulate the economy and trigger another inflationary spiral."[62] Having refrained from a more aggressive stimulus, this move was widely seen as having contributed to Ford's 1976 defeat. In short, the weak stimulus and limited restraint accomplished the worst of both worlds, as macroeconomic fine-tuning exhibited steadily diminishing returns – a trend that would continue under Carter, whose somewhat greater focus on inflation was less important than his inability, shared with Nixon and Ford, to satisfy two macroeconomic priorities with one instrument.

## 5.4 Carter's Stagflation: From "Behind the Game" to TIPs

During the Carter administration, macroeconomic policy shifted over two approaches to addressing inflationary concerns, leading to the final abandonment of efforts at fine-tuning the wage-price spiral – in a choice that was not an entirely deliberate one on Carter's part. First, as the Carter administration moved from an inaugural concern for ending recession to a new stress on limiting inflation, its Neoclassical CEA initially resisted the use of guidelines or controls in favor of austerity. This resistance briefly yielded in an effort to revive incomes policies in a more "microfoundation"-based way through the use of TIPs. However, where these worked not via communicative appeals but, rather, through mechanisms embedded in the tax code, to "tax away" inflationary wage gains, they can be seen as representing the application of coordinative logic to what might be better seen as an exhortative venture in legitimating wage-price restraint. Second, following the October 1978 abandonment of its TIPs proposal, the Carter administration would shift to an increasing acceptance of monetary and fiscal austerity as the sole means to limiting inflation. These efforts began with the November 1978 administration efforts to press the Federal Reserve to *tighten*, and culminated in the August 1979 appointment of Paul Volcker as Federal Reserve Chair – foreshadowing the shift to the Neoliberal order premised not on wage-price increases but rather asset-price appreciation.

---

[62] Greenspan (2007, 70).

## Promoting Recovery: From Macroeconomic Stimulus to TIPs

Before taking office, the Carter administration briefly considered seeking stand-by authority to employ wage and price controls. However, higher concerns for growth and labor's potential negative response to such a move led Carter in December 1976 to declare that he had "no intention of asking the Congress" for such authority.[63] Council Chairman Charles Schultze later recalled that "the theory was that we needed something to get us going," leading the administration to see a fiscal stimulus as far more necessary than any incomes policy. However, Schultze would later reflect that this stress on recovery was overdone, as the administration would confront the more enduring challenge of "revers[ing] ... a stubborn inherent inflation without stifling the economy."[64] Following this late start, Schultze recounted, the administration would always find itself "in terms of an anti-inflationary program, six months to a year behind the game."[65]

Over its first three months, the administration's miscalculation with respect to the strength of inflationary tailwinds could be seen in its reversal on the need for a stimulus, shifting by April 1977 to an anti-inflation initiative.[66] Having ruled out controls, guidelines, *and* fiscal restraint as means to limit revived inflation, Carter's first anti-inflation package relied primarily on exhortation. Schultze himself later conceded that the program "had all kinds of bits and pieces in it, none of which meant anything."[67] By the end of the year, the need for stronger action led to the development of a set of "deceleration" guidelines – to lower the *rate* of wage increases, rather than to reverse wage increases themselves.[68] Unveiling a second program in April 1978, a privately skeptical Carter declared himself "determined ... to take the lead in breaking the wage and price spiral by holding Federal pay increases down," by accepting "a limit of about 5½ percent this year, thereby setting the example for labor and industry."[69]

---

[63] Haas (1992, 87–95).
[64] Schultze (2003).
[65] Hargrove and Morley (1984, 479–480).
[66] The stimulus package included an increased standard deduction, an employer tax credit, and increased revenue sharing, amounting to $6 billion for 1977 and $17 billion for 1978. (Biven 2002, 77, 82–83).
[67] Biven (2002, 133).
[68] Biven (2002, 136–137).
[69] Revealing his own skepticism, Carter wrote in the margin of Schultze's January 1978 memo: "Charlie –The program seems (inevitably, I guess) very general in

Continuing the postwar trend, business would prove more receptive than labor, with key automobile, aluminum, and steel producers affirming their support. In contrast, inflation adviser Robert Strauss and Labor Secretary Ray Marshall stressed to Carter "that the unions are skeptical" and "unwilling to practice wage deceleration prior to any indication of a slowdown in price inflation."[70]

In October 1978, Carter advanced a third anti-inflation package. Positing alternatives of a "complicated scheme of Federal government wage and price controls" or a "deliberate recession," Carter framed as a middle ground "voluntary wage and price standards." Carter also suggested a new innovation, in incentivized TIPs, in which "workers who observe the standards would be eligible for a tax rebate if the inflation rate is more than 7 percent," providing "a real wage insurance policy against inflation which might be caused by others."[71] However, leaks and skepticism regarding TIPs, particularly its complexity, engendered a negative public reaction. Schultze later acknowledged that the Council had "a very lukewarm to negative attitude on the TIP."[72] Finally, speaking to the post-Watergate suspicion of authority, a US District Court would less than a year later rule against the administration's discretionary enforcement mechanisms, which United Auto Workers (UAW) President Douglas Fraser termed the "nail in the coffin" for the initiative.[73]

## Fighting Inflation: From TIPs to Renewed Restraint

Given the failure of its October initiative, as well as concerns for the dollar – which had lost nearly 18 percent of its value against the mark since the July 1978 G7 Bonn summit – the administration increasingly accepted the need for more decisive macroeconomic restraint, to limit inflation rather than restore growth.[74] Having agreed at Bonn to address anxieties regarding the dollar – and growing concerned himself for the interplay of depreciation and inflation – Carter had appointed the Institutionalist economist Alfred Kahn his "Inflation czar," a position

---

nature and mostly wishful thinking. However, I'll do all I can to help make it successful. J. C." Biven (2002, 136–137).

[70] Biven (2002, 138).
[71] Carter (1978, 1024).
[72] Hargrove and Morley (1984, 496–497).
[73] Shabecoff (1979, 4E).
[74] Biven (2002, 169).

that entailed efforts at jawboning on behalf of wage-price restraint.[75] Kahn was particularly concerned for the interplay of international and labor tensions in limiting the scope for wage-price accord, later recalling a conversation in which UAW leader Fraser had warned him, "If you make my workers pay a dollar for gasoline then I'm not going to stick to the wage standards."[76]

On November 1, the administration accordingly assembled a stronger package, employing $30 billion in foreign exchange to support the dollar and, in a coordinated move with the Federal Reserve, a 1 percent increase in the discount rate. Indeed, monetary austerity was seen as so crucial that administration officials actually pressed the Federal Reserve for *higher* interest rates. Schultze later recalled that "at the turn of the year 1978–79, Blumenthal and I carried on a leaked campaign in the press to try to pressure Miller into tightening up ... normally it's the other way around – and we got a very nasty note at one time in effect, saying, lay off."[77] Carter himself wrote to Schultze that "the little 2-week news media crusade to force Fed action is unnecessary and improper. In the future, remain silent on what the Fed might do unless I specifically approve any so-called leaks."[78] Even as the November shift foreshadowed increased reliance on the Federal Reserve, Federal Reserve Chairman G. William Miller was unprepared to impose significant restraint – having clashed with his colleagues at the Fed as he pursued a broadly accommodative monetary policy.

In this context, Carter would make one last attempt at employing presidential rhetoric in his "crisis of confidence" address – later rechristened by critics the "malaise" speech – delivered in the summer of 1979 following a week of meetings with varied state and societal agents at Camp David. This address can be seen as marking the limits of Carter's attempts at appealing to an egalitarian variety of liberalism, speaking to the effects of the Vietnam and Watergate

---

[75] Kahn recalled that his position involved efforts to "identify industries whose prices seemed to be behaving particularly badly, and inexplicably, and bring them in ... The quid pro quo under the whole President's anti-inflation program for business's standpoint was regulatory reform ..." Kahn (2003); on Carter's attitudes regarding depreciation, see Biven (2002, 170).
[76] Biven (2002, 165).
[77] Hargrove and Morley (1984, 486).
[78] Biven (2002, 144).

experiences on support for the common good, and the dangers of cynicism regarding the public interest. Carter argued that Vietnam and Watergate had eroded faith in the ability of "citizens to serve as the ultimate rulers and shapers of our democracy." Casting the current dilemma of governance as "a crisis of confidence ... that strikes at the very heart and soul and spirit of our national will," Carter argued that the nation could either move in the direction of increasing "fragmentation and self-interest," premised on the "right to grasp for ourselves some advantage over others," or it could embark upon a "path of common purpose and the restoration of American values."[79] Nevertheless, although the speech was initially well received, Carter failed to couple it with concrete policy proposals, instead following the speech by requesting his entire cabinet's resignation – a step that he later conceded had exacerbated a sense of crisis.[80]

In turn, the resignations also had more issue-specific consequences, ushering in a key personnel move that would have far-reaching implications. While retaining most of his cabinet, Carter dismissed Treasury Secretary Blumenthal and replaced him with Federal Reserve Chairman Miller. This created an unexpected opening at the Federal Reserve – one that would be filled, after a bit of a lag, by Paul Volcker. Volcker would later recall that "[t]o the people who cared about such things, the change that moved the Fed Chairman into the job of Treasury secretary left a vacancy at the top of the agency that would have to do something about inflation, if anybody could."[81] In the rush to find Miller's successor, Carter appointed Volcker, who had opposed monetarism when he was at the Nixon Treasury, but who now termed himself a "pragmatic monetarist," favoring a greater reliance on monetary restraint as a means of price stabilization. Despite an unsuccessful attempt by Carter's former adviser Bert Lance to warn that "[i]f [Carter] appoints Volcker, he will be mortgaging his re-election to the Federal Reserve," the appointment went through. Over the next year, the Federal Reserve would shift to impose a monetary austerity that would begin to limit inflationary pressures, but at the cost of undermining Carter's reelection prospects.[82]

---

[79] Carter (1979, 0715).
[80] Carter (1982, 121).
[81] Volcker and Gyohten (1992, 163).
[82] Greider (1987, 47).

## 5.5 The Social Context: Societal, Institutional, and Public Influences

To the extent that macroeconomic fine-tuning policy had lost its effectiveness and incomes policies had lost their legitimacy by the end of the 1970s, this reflected not simply shifts in adaptive or rational monetary expectations, but rather a broader change in public, sectoral, and institutional attitudes. First, to the extent that any attempt at imposing macroeconomic restraint or incomes policies could have success in restraining wage-price pressures, a key concern would be the credibility with which the public viewed fiscal, monetary, or regulatory commitments – and so broader trust in government. Here the decline since the early Keynesian era had been precipitous. This can be seen with respect to large-scale shifts in trust and attributions of responsibility for policy failure. While only 14 percent of the public had blamed government for inflation in 1959, 51 percent would blame government in 1978.[83] Similarly, while 73 percent of the public said that they could trust the government either "just about always" or "most of the time" in 1958, only 25 percent would still hold this view by 1979.[84] This erosion increased the "disconnect" between short-run institutional or macroeconomic commitments and public willingness to engage in wage restraint.

Second, although this context would on its own render it difficult to secure commitments from labor or firms with respect to price trends, the collapse in credibility had grown so great that these sectoral agents had since the 1970s increasingly renounced their own discretion, locking themselves in to institutional agreements that further insulated the wage-price spiral from market or macroeconomic pressures. In particular, postwar wage agreements between the United Steelworkers (USW) and the large steel companies, reached in tri-annual negotiations, often served as a bellwether for other industries. Into the 1970s, these would be removed even further from market or policy pressures where provisions for mandated cost of living adjustments (COLAs) reinforced wage-push inflation. For example, in 1974, the USW and steel firms had together come to view recurring strikes as a

---

[83] Gallup (1978).
[84] Trust the Federal Government, 1958–2004 *The American National Election Survey Guide to Public Opinion and Electoral Behavior* www.electionstudies.org/nesguide/text/tab5a_1.txt.

key source of import penetration, and so established an "Experimental Negotiating Agreement" (ENA) that locked in future productivity and COLAs. Under the ENA, labor and management agreed that wages would automatically increase by an annual rate of 3 percent – plus an added cost-of-living increase. In return, the USW pledged to submit any side issue disputes to binding arbitration. Into the early 1980s, fearing mediation, neither side sought arbitration, and steel labor costs increased in real terms by 38 percent from 1972 to 1982.[85] Significantly, one of the last examples of administration "jawboning" focused on steel came in an October 1977 study by the Council on Wage and Price Stability that condemned steel price increases.[86] Such trends could not have been addressed by fiscal or monetary fine tuning, but rather would have required an institutional reform of the ENA – which was abandoned only in 1984, following the Neoliberal order's imposition of massive restraint.

Third, inflationary pressures in the 1970s were further exacerbated by the post-1973 rise in uncontrolled global commodity and energy prices. For example, food prices would rise by 24 percent over the first three quarters of 1973, a development which was beyond the reach of the Nixon New Economic Policy and the Federal Reserve alike. Similarly, fall 1973 witnessed the first oil price shock, as the Organization of Petroleum Exporting Countries (OPEC) restricted the supply of oil and quadrupled its price.[87] Such developments themselves partly reflected the January 1973 dismantling of the Phase II guidelines, which had undermined international confidence in the dollar, followed within a month by the dollar's devaluation, and within three months by the collapse of the Bretton Woods fixed exchange rate regime itself.[88] Domestic and international trends in these ways were linked to the extent that international monetary expectations were shaped by US wage trends, as inflationary pressures were seen

[85] Hall (1997, 48–49).
[86] Ironically, by the end of 1978, increasing plant closings led the Carter administration to introduce a Trigger Price Mechanism (TPM), designed to *facilitate* price-fixing, treating import prices below certain levels as automatic evidence of foreign dumping. Hall (1997, 82–83).
[87] Although the 1976 presidential campaign would see some discussion of antitrust efforts and even a possible lawsuit against OPEC, foreign policy concerns for US relations with oil producing nations undermined such initiatives. See Geisst (2000, 258–259).
[88] Council of Economic Advisers (1974, 92); Matusow (1998, 228).

as presaging a weaker dollar – and a weaker dollar translated into higher import prices, and so renewed wage-price pressures. Council Chairman Herbert Stein admitted later that the administration had "underestimated the effect of depreciation of the dollar on the inflation rate in the U.S."[89]

Finally, even as these pressures only increased the challenges of ostensible fine-tuning, they did so in the context of not only an unwillingness on the part of fiscal policymakers to impose restraint – as noted throughout the above account – but also at the Federal Reserve, where Arthur Burns and his successor G. William Miller had shied away from imposing the ever-higher levels of monetary restraint that might have been required to contain inflation. These constraints were conceded by former Federal Reserve chairman Arthur Burns too in a late September 1979 address at the IMF/World Bank meetings on "the Anguish of Central Banking." To explain why central bankers had been "so ineffective in dealing with this worldwide problem," Burns offered an essentially social analysis, stressing the "philosophic and political currents that have been transforming economic life in the United States and elsewhere since the 1930s." Given this climate, Burns noted that if the Federal Reserve had suppressed inflation, this would have not only caused "severe difficulties [to] be quickly produced in the economy" but also frustrated the desire of the Congress and the electorate to maintain full employment.[90] In this light, Burns concluded that victory in the fight against inflation would not come "until new currents of thought create a political environment in which the difficult adjustments required to end inflation can be undertaken."[91]

To the extent that "new currents of thought" were needed, Burns was correct – though he likely did not appreciate the extent to which these would be advanced by the Federal Reserve itself. Tellingly, his talk irritated the new Federal Reserve Chairman Paul Volcker – who was in attendance and left, remarking, "I must be doing things wrong."[92] Within weeks, Volcker would advance a monetary policy shift against a backdrop of changes in principled beliefs, institutional alignments, and the market power of societal agents, setting the stage for the construction

---

[89] Hargrove and Morley (1984, 402); Matusow (1998, 238).
[90] Burns (1979).
[91] Burns (1979).
[92] Solomon (1995, 127).

of the Neoliberal order – one that would ensure that when monetary policy returned to an accommodative stance, it would be in the context of a repressed labor and an emboldened finance. Under these new arrangements, policy would not accommodate the wage-price spiral, but would support increasing asset-price bubbles.

## 5.6 Conclusions

Constructed against the backdrop of the Great Depression, the Keynesian order was marked by presidential appeals to a shared responsibility in wage-price restraint, providing a social foundation for stability that increased the scope for sustained growth. Nevertheless, it would prove over time to be a victim of its own successes, as stability spurred efforts to model relationships between variables – most importantly in the Phillips curve – in ways that removed them from the social contexts that made them possible. This would lead by the 1960s to the emergence of a Neoclassical Synthesis-styled overconfidence in the scope for removing incomes polices and misplaced certainty regarding the scope for macroeconomic stabilization, as policymakers increasingly overrated their ability to gradually restrain any wage-price spiral. Nevertheless, it would take several iterations of crisis to demonstrate the exhaustion of fine-tuning and late incomes policies. First, these dynamics could be seen across Nixon administration's New Economic Policy – which veered from freeze to guidelines to exhortation and back again – with Nixon's resignation yielding to Ford's definition of inflation as "public enemy number one." Second, where the Ford administration initially sought to address inflation primarily through austerity, its resolve would erode as slowing growth would see it deviate into the adoption of a "Whip Inflation Now" program – and would in turn yield to a lukewarm stimulus that was too weak to enable recovery and failed to address the underlying sources of inflation. Finally, the Carter administration's initial concern for recovery led it to underrate the latent inflationary momentum, and so it would attempt to make recourse to the TIPs of late 1978 – which were quickly abandoned in the context of constitutional objections and coalitional opposition. By the end of 1979, gradualism would be discredited across the Carter administration and Federal Reserve. In a larger sense, so had been the larger Neoclassical synthesis, as misplaced certainty yielded to uncertainty and broader calls for reform.

The arrival of Ronald Reagan and Paul Volcker would therefore be crucial in moving beyond the Keynesian order and constructing a Neoliberal alternative. However, the success of the Neoliberal order in breaking the market power of labor and establishing a foundation for financial growth would yield over subsequent decades to a mirror-image problem – with overconfidence in deregulation and monetary fine-tuning yielding by the early 2000s to the accommodation of unstable asset-price bubbles. While coalitional and institutional alignments would change from a labor-dominated support for the fiscal accommodation of wage-driven demand to the finance-driven monetary accommodation of asset-price bubbles, the social psychological shifts remained the same. In each case, misplaced certainty in fine-tuning obscured the imbalances of market power and speculative pressures that would culminate in revived crisis.

PART III

*The Construction, Conversion, and Crisis of the Neoliberal Order*

# 6 | Constructing the Neoliberal Order: Breaking Labor and Boosting Finance

In this present crisis, government is not the solution to our problem; government is the problem.
>   Ronald Reagan, First Inaugural Address, January 20, 1981

I must tell those who fail to report for duty this morning they are in violation of the law, and if they do not report for work within 48 hours, they have forfeited their jobs and will be terminated.
>   Ronald Reagan, Remarks on the Air Traffic Controllers Strike, August 3, 1981

## 6.1 Introduction/Overview

In the content of their ideas, Franklin Roosevelt and Ronald Reagan could hardly have been more different. However, each established orders that would endure over decades. Upon taking office in 1933, Roosevelt launched a Keynesian order premised on a "macro-morality" which highlighted the existence of uniquely public interests and sought to counter the tendency of individual choices to undermine the collective good. In terms of broad philosophical traditions, this enabled Roosevelt to recast the meaning of a long-standing Hamiltonian-Jeffersonian divide, reshaping the views of "big government" as meant not to support capital, but to strengthen the standing of labor and consumers. In contrast, Reagan constructed a Neoliberal order on a "micro-morality" in which the public good reflected the aggregate of private preferences, and private choices likewise advanced the public interest. This would lead in turn to a reconstruction of the meaning of Hamiltonian-Jeffersonian debates, enabling Reagan to redeploy a Jeffersonian libertarian rhetoric opposing "big government" and "big labor" as impediments to growth, while casting deregulation as a source of renewed entrepreneurial energy. Moreover, Reagan's efforts in advancing these views would derive a further popular accessibility as they came against the backdrop

135

of not the Depression and World War II – two crises that could be cast as "solved" by the state – but, instead, against the Vietnam and Watergate experiences, events that had been cast by Democrats and Republicans alike as undermining national confidence – and were less plausibly cast as governmental successes than as failures of the state.

In terms of rhetorical forms, despite their differences with respect to the content of their ideas, Roosevelt and Reagan gave them expression in similarly structured communicative appeals. Each president sought to construct the prevailing crisis as a serious material challenge, but one in which American values would prevail. In 1933, Roosevelt had argued that despite the difficult "conditions in our country today ... [t]his great Nation will endure as it has endured, will revive and will prosper."[1] In 1981, while Reagan would paint "a pretty grim picture," he would echo Roosevelt in insisting that "It is within our power to change this picture, and we can act with hope."[2] Moving to more specific economic concerns, each leader also infused economic debates with a principled import. For example, although Roosevelt condemned a "generation of self-seekers" and targeted the "money changers" who had "fled from their high seats," Reagan would decry "government by an elite group" and argued that "[i]n this present crisis, government is not the solution to our problem; government is the problem."[3] Similarly, responding to a strike called by the Professional Association of Air Traffic Controllers (PATCO) in August 1981, Reagan would cast the issue as not an economic but rather a moral one, emphasizing the principled concern that the strikers were "in violation of the law" – in a way that not only sought to moderate labor's market power but instead to break it.[4] Finally, just as Roosevelt had pragmatically ratcheted together egalitarian values with institutional changes in the conduct of fiscal and wage-price policy at the Office of Price Administration, leading to the eclipse of the Federal Reserve, Reagan's rhetoric would be aligned with the reemergence of an ascendant Federal Reserve – and Reagan would almost immediately dismantle the Council on Wage and Price Stability. In short, Roosevelt and Reagan mounted rhetorically similar appeals

---

[1] Roosevelt (1933a).
[2] Reagan (1981a).
[3] Reagan (1981a).
[4] Reagan (1981d).

to reconstruct the principled bases of economic models, in ways that would reshape institutional contexts, the coalitional balance of power, and wage-price and asset-price expectations.

In the first section of this chapter, I develop these themes, highlighting Reagan's communicative appeals for Neoliberal ends, as manifested in his inaugural address, national addresses on economic policy, and principled construction of the PATCO strike. In the second section, I pull back to address the role of Federal Reserve Chairman Paul Volcker in providing key institutional bases of the Neoliberal order, employing monetary policy to break the wage-price spiral but also to sustain financial values – setting the template for "too big to fail" in responding to the Mexican debt crisis of 1982 and in the rescue of Continent Illinois in 1984. In a third section, I examine early moves by Volcker's successor Alan Greenspan, who would mirror his predecessor in shifting from an initial attempt to restrain wage-price pressures to a stress on sustaining asset prices following the 1987 stock market crash. Even though the Taylor rule-styled refinement of Greenspan's fine-tuning would come later, the Neoliberal order's outlines would be set by the end of the decade.

## 6.2 Reagan: Constructing a Neoliberal Order

In establishing the principled bases of the Neoliberal order, Reagan offered – in rhetorical terms if not policy reality – a classically liberal, pre-Keynesian worldview, highlighting the scope for individual choice and its contributions to aggregate welfare. In holding this broad principled view, he drew most explicitly on the insights of Milton Friedman, who Attorney General Ed Meese later described as the "guru" of the administration.[5] To Reagan and Friedman, there existed no unique "macro" or aggregate perspective on economics. Indeed, Friedman would explicitly reject claims that "society has a duty" or that "government has a moral function," advancing instead a "moral view that suggests something wholly different: that 'a country' or a 'society' is a collection of individuals; that the basic entity is the individual or, more fundamentally, the family, and that only individuals can have moral obligations."[6] In economic terms, this harkened back to a pre-Keynesian

---

[5] Ebenstein (2007, 205, 208).
[6] Friedman (1987, 104–105).

opposition to deficit spending or monetary stimulus on "Ricardian" grounds that rational agents would anticipate the future costs of such measures and save accordingly, and to an associated view of inflation as "always and everywhere" a monetary phenomenon.[7] With respect to regulation, Friedman would oppose incomes policies in particular as infringements on choice, casting "the violation of legally imposed price and wage controls" as "both privately and socially beneficial."[8]

Given these principled backdrops, in terms of fiscal, regulatory, and monetary policies, Reagan would pursue an agenda marked by support for across-the-board marginal tax cuts and the preferential treatment of capital gains, the removal of Depression-era financial regulations, and a (final) end to the use of incomes policies. These priorities would be most prominently addressed in a February 18 nationally televised address to Congress, as Reagan urged a reduction in spending and tax rates, deregulation, and support for Federal Reserve monetary restraint. First, on fiscal priorities, the Reagan administration's main goal was to secure passage of a series of across-the-board cuts to marginal rates, to be phased in at 5 (reduced from an initially proposed 10 percent), 10 percent, and yet again at 10 percent over its first three successive years – a tax reduction approach that would also be applied to the capital gains tax, with the goal of enabling the "eventual elimination of the present differential between the tax on earned and unearned income."[9] Indeed, the cuts in income tax rates that the Reagan administration would obtain would be outdone by the still larger cuts in taxes on capital gains. In 1978, Congress had cut the top rate on capital gains from 49 percent to 28 percent, and the Reagan tax cuts would eventually lower this rate to 20 percent.[10] In justifying these cuts, Reagan

---

[7] Although Reagan and Friedman would each take principled stances in public settings, each recognized that compromises would always be necessary. For example, Reagan's "revolution" would remain incomplete to the extent that his promise of a balanced budget was never redeemed – something that his more committed aides such as Budget Director David Stockman (1986) would lament as reflecting a loss of will, or "the triumph of politics." Likewise, Friedman would affirm the need to avoid too much nuance in popular writing, noting that the "circumlocutions that may be appropriate for a scientific audience will lose ... your popular audience," elaborating that "in respect to popular writing ... you're trying to convey certain ideas to people, and you don't want excessive qualifications to get in the way" (Ebenstein 2007, 182).
[8] Friedman (1966, 19).
[9] Reagan (1981c).
[10] Phillips (1991, 78–79).

would advance a supply-side argument that reductions in tax rates could induce new investment and wealth creation. While superficially similar to the Keynesian case for a stimulus, the key difference is that Keynesians would favor targeted tax cuts, aimed toward the middle or lower tiers on the distribution of income – where the marginal propensity to consume was higher. In contrast, where the supply-side perspective stresses the importance of investment rather than consumption, tax cuts are better shifted toward the upper end of the income scale, where more money is available to invest. To be sure, Reagan would attempt to blur the distinction – later arguing that Kennedy "cut those tax rates, and the government ended up getting more revenues."[11] Moreover, although cuts to social spending would be forthcoming, these would not be sufficient to reduce the ensuing deficits. Indeed, where the administration proposed $47 billion in new spending cuts, the loss of revenues from the tax cuts would be $280 billion – and Congress would in the end only accept $35 billion in cuts.[12]

Moving from fiscal to regulatory policies, the Neoliberal shift would see improved treatment of capital coupled with a stress on reducing the market power of labor. In terms of capital, the Carter administration had foreshadowed this shift in the decontrol of interest rates, reversing New Deal–era limits on what could be charged across financial markets in the Depository Institutions Deregulation and Monetary Control Act in 1980. This act set the stage for the abolition of the Depression-era "Regulation Q" interest rate controls which had made banking more akin to a public utility than a speculative enterprise. In contrast to the postwar notion of a "3-6-3" rule – of collecting deposits at 3 percent, lending them out at 6 percent, and taking off for the gold course at 3 o'clock in the afternoon – the early Neoliberal era saw the shift to a more competitive financial system – with higher real interest rates combining with lower taxes on capital gains to increase the relative gains to unearned income.

Paralleling this easing of restraints on capital, Reagan moved to limit the market power of labor. In his first press conference, he announced "major steps toward the elimination of the Council on Wage and Price Stability" on grounds that the council had been "totally ineffective in controlling inflation," and had "imposed unnecessary burdens on labor

---

[11] Reagan (1981f).
[12] Willentz (2008, 141–143).

and business."[13] However, while Reagan's move saw the administration renounce formal institutional efforts at shaping wage and price expectations, Reagan's August 1981 firing of striking PATCO workers embodied a more direct confrontation with labor that would reshape wage and price expectations in a lasting way. Employing charged rhetoric, Reagan constructed the PATCO strike as less an economic issue than a legal one – of federal workers breaking the law in a prohibited strike.[14] Given this backdrop, when Reagan ventured into the White House Rose Garden on the morning of August 3, 1981 to condemn the strike, he would note the gains that PATCO stood to reap relative to other workers, but most insistently stressed the principle of respect for the law. While Reagan affirmed "the right of workers in the private sector to strike," he argued that this right did not extend to government employees who provided the "protective services which are government's reason for being." Reagan went on to read the oath taken by PATCO workers renouncing "any strike against the Government of the United States," and concluded with an ultimatum that PATCO employees must return or be dismissed. When asked why he had opted for such a punitive stance, Reagan replied that "[t]hey are violating the law."[15]

Having infused the debate with sentiment, Reagan's rhetoric gave new meaning to the PATCO strike – as less a distributional dispute than a principled contest. The public would subsequently prove inclined to support Reagan, with support in calls to the White House favoring Reagan by a 13-1 margin.[16] Union leaders in Chicago for the annual AFL-CIO Executive Council meetings were particularly frustrated, as PATCO had not coordinated with them, and as they recognized the difficulty of fighting a popular president on such a principled front. United Auto Workers (UAW) leader Doug Fraser recalled that the assembled leaders feared the PATCO strike "could do massive damage to the

[13] Reagan (1981b).
[14] PATCO was something of an easy target of opportunity, particularly as it had poor relations with the rest of the labor movement. When PATCO was established in the late 1960s, it sought to avoid the stigma of being a union, using the term "professional" to distinguish its members from workers and the term "organization" to set itself apart from unions. In 1980, PATCO had even endorsed Reagan – a move which contributed to both its prestrike boldness and poststrike alienation from the labor movement.
[15] Reagan (1981e).
[16] McCartin (2011, 293).

labor movement."[17] Their fears were well-founded to the extent that the PATCO strike reshaped labor norms in a way that altered the balance of power between labor and employers – rendering employers much more willing to hire replacement workers. Given this new calculus, striking became a much riskier proposition. Over the next decade labor would be weakened over a series of major strikes – marked by wage givebacks and other concessions – by workers at the Arizona mining giant Phelps Dodge in 1983, at Continental Airlines in 1984, at the *Chicago Tribune* in 1985, and at Trans World Airlines (TWA) in 1986.[18] Put in historical relief, the number of major work stoppages involving at least 1,000 workers had averaged more than 286 annually from 1960 to 1980. Following the PATCO strike, over the 1980s, the annual average plummeted to eighty-three. By the 2000s, it would fall to twenty.[19] Volcker would later remark that the PATCO dismissals had been a "watershed" moment, having "a profound effect on the aggressiveness of labor at that time."[20] Similarly, Alan Greenspan argued that the resulting "increased flexibility contributed to the ability of the economy to operate with both low unemployment and low inflation."[21]

While Volcker supported Reagan's stance in the PATCO dispute, Reagan in turn support the Federal Reserve's sustained restraint. In his February 1981 congressional address, Reagan affirmed specifically that "to curb inflation we need to slow the growth in our money supply."[22] Characterizing Reagan's view of monetary policy, Budget Director David Stockman noted that he used two basic metaphors: of "zooming" the money supply and "pulling the string." Stockman recalled that Reagan would trace the money-supply growth "all the way back to the sixties," showing how the "money supply 'zoomed' in every election year ... and then, after the election, the Fed 'pulled the string' and the economy went into recession."[23] In this light, to deflect appeals for a monetary easing in his early term, Reagan would argue

[17] McCartin (2011, 290–291).
[18] McCartin (2011, 348–349).
[19] The Reagan administration also shifted statistical procedures in ways that limited public awareness of labor concerns, instructing the Bureau of Labor Statistics, which had tracked strikes involving as few as six workers, to limit itself to strikes involving 1,000 workers. McCartin (2011, 351).
[20] Volcker (2000).
[21] Greenspan (2003).
[22] Reagan (1981c).
[23] Greider (1987, 379).

that, "[t]his was done ... in '70 [and] ... up went inflation and up went unemployment ... Then, for the '72 election, the same thing had happened ... Then in '74 we had a deeper recession, where unemployment was greater, inflation was greater" – concluding that the principled case was for monetary restraint as a means to ensure continued low inflation, rather than manipulate short-run trade-offs that would only deteriorate in the longer run.[24] Given this support, Volcker would be able to sustain monetary restraint as a means to contain labor for nearly three years – though he would also shift in late 1982 given a need to accommodate finance.

## 6.3 The Federal Reserve's Neoliberal Switch: From Wage- to Asset-Price Accommodation

While Reagan's presidential rhetoric provided the key principled basis for a shift from a Keynesian to a Neoliberal order, his rhetorical efforts were augmented by Paul Volcker's parallel efforts at the Federal Reserve to not only alter monetary policy incentives, but also redefine the conventions governing wage and asset-price expectations. Over the first three years of his term, Volcker would succeed in using a monetary rule to push interest rates up – and so spark a prolonged downturn over two recessions spanning 1979–1982. Having driven the economy into recession, the Volcker Federal Reserve would even use the threat of sustained restraint to pressure the Reagan administration to limit its own fiscal excesses, bringing the budget closer to balance. However, sustained restraint would also cause problems in the financial realm, contributing to the onset of a global debt crisis, and so Volcker would move after his first three years to shift his focus from eradicating the wage-price spirals of the 1970s to sustaining the asset-price bubbles, "mopping up" after crises in a way that would recur over the next several decades.

### Volcker's Initial Neoliberalism: Repudiating Labor and Fiscal Fine-Tuning

When appointed to head the Federal Reserve by Jimmy Carter in late 1979, Paul Volcker was far from a committed monetarist or

---

[24] Reagan (1981g).

free-market adherent. Having been a key figure in the international monetary diplomacy at the Nixon Treasury, Volcker recognized the extent to which inflationary wage-price settlements had destabilized international currency trends. Given this background, he saw a primary objective as restraining the continued abuses of labor power that had driven self-reinforcing wage-price spirals. In congressional testimony, Volcker stressed the magnitude of the challenge of ratcheting back these expectations, noting that:

> An entire generation of young adults has grown up since the mid-1960s knowing only ... an inflation that has seemed to accelerate inexorably [and] ... feeds in part on itself. So part of the job of returning to a more stable and more productive economy must be to break the grip of inflationary expectations.[25]

Yet, Volcker initially hoped to "break the grip of inflationary expectations" in a way that would require only minimal austerity. To this end, Volcker entertained the possibility of a "grand bargain" with labor. As Carter adviser Alfred Kahn later recalled, an accord was considered in which labor would accept lower wages in return for a less restrictive Federal Reserve policy, as Volcker suggested to "[AFL-CIO President] Lane Kirkland ... 'Look, you give me six percent wages and I'll give you six percent interest rates.'" The result could have been to avoid the high interest rates and unemployment that would follow over the recession of 1981–1982. In this light, Kahn later expressed frustration that while the statement "points to an economic reality," administration officials "could never get anybody in organized labor to recognize the association."[26] Similarly, in the aftermath of the New Economic Policy, Whip Inflation Now (WIN), and Tax-Based Incomes Policies (TIPs), Volcker feared that incomes policies had become so discredited that to propose their reestablishment risked emboldening workers and firms to push for *higher* wages and prices. In congressional testimony, Volcker suggested that support for incomes policies might be "interpreted as waving an ineffectual wand," concluding, "[w]ith some

---

[25] Highlighting the similarly psychological nature of currency trends, Volcker argued that "We have recently seen clear evidence of the pervasive influence of inflationary expectations on the orderly functioning of financial and commodity markets, and on the value of the dollar internationally." Quoted in Van Overtveldt (2009, 40).
[26] Kahn (2003, 96–97).

reluctance, I do not think that's a practical or workable approach in the particular situation that we find ourselves in now."[27] To be sure, Volcker would remain attentive to the trend in wage settlements. Into late 1982, Volcker stressed the importance of "recent negotiations completed or in progress that seem to point toward some significant moderation"[28] William Greider later noted that Volcker "carried in his pocket a little card on which he kept track of his latest wage settlements by major labor unions" and often "called various people around the country and took soundings on the status of current contract negotiations" in an effort to retain a sense of labor sentiment.[29]

In this light, Volcker did not view inflation as "always and everywhere" a monetary phenomenon so much as he sought to pragmatically reshape market expectations to follow the money supply – casting his approach as a "practical monetarism."[30] In a theoretical sense, Volcker rejected any "simple causal explanation running from monetary behavior to price behavior" in favor of acknowledging a wide variety of factors – economic, social, and political – that were "not easily, or even practically, subject to central bank control."[31] However, Volcker still saw a role for "monetary targeting" as "an instrument for expressing policy intentions, for setting some guidelines for action, and for ultimately measuring performance."[32] This can be seen as a pragmatic approach to monetarism, in which Volcker was "thinking operationally, not theoretically."[33]

The specific operational means by which Volcker would engineer this shift would be through a change in Federal Reserve procedures, to target the money supply rather than interest rates – an approach that would hold for roughly three years. In early October 1979 – following his return from the 1979 World Bank/IMF Meetings at which Arthur Burns had addressed "the anguish of central banking," Volcker would suggest to the Federal Open Market Committee (FOMC) that

---

[27] US Congress. Joint Economic Committee (1982, 179–180).
[28] US Congress. Joint Economic Committee (1982, 154).
[29] Greider (1987, 429).
[30] Mehrling (2007, 177); see also Volcker (1978).
[31] Volcker (1978, 330–331).
[32] Volcker (1978, 332).
[33] Indeed, in theoretical terms, Volcker took issue with a basic monetarist precept, that the velocity of money – or the frequency with which it is spent – is a constant. Solomon (1995, 137).

"the traditional method of making small moves has in some sense, though not completely, run out of psychological gas," elaborating that "I am not saying that that reasoning is correct but I think it is the reasoning in the market psychologically."[34] To try to shock markets and reshape their expectations – given that "[s]ome board members were reluctant to take overt moves to raise interest rates" – Volcker came to see a Friedman-styled shift to targeting the money supply as an operational "way to get more unanimity."[35] He hoped that once the Federal Reserve had changed its operating techniques, it "would find it difficult to back off even if our decisions led to painfully high interest rates." This shift further provided a means to reshape public expectations, Volcker argued, on the grounds that markets would always "seize upon markers of one kind or another," giving the Federal Reserve the opportunity to establish "some rule or indicator to supply discipline."[36] Volcker later recalled that he sought to "get out the message that when we say we're going to control money, we mean we're going to deal with inflation, then we would have a chance of affecting … behavior."[37]

Moreover, the institutional adoption of a monetarist approach on the FOMC provided political cover for the ensuing increase in interest rates and unemployment. Volcker's Carter administration colleague Anthony Solomon would later recall that "Volcker valued the political shield aspect very highly," as the shift would enable him to argue that "We're not controlling interest rates – we're just controlling the money supply."[38] In this context, the Carter administration acquiesced to Volcker's shift, with Schultze later noting the importance of Volcker's monetarist rationale in limiting political criticisms, suggesting that

if the Fed had gone about doing it the way it used to do every month picking the federal funds target, then, in the eyes of the public, the Fed would have been driving those rates up. And the genius of what Volcker did, during the period when you had to get the public used to this, was to adopt a system which came to the same thing, but in which he said we are not raising interest rates … the markets are raising interest rates.[39]

[34] Federal Open Market Committee Meeting (1979, 8).
[35] Solomon (1995, 139).
[36] Solomon (1995, 140).
[37] Volcker and Gyohten (1992, 164–167).
[38] Solomon (1995, 139).
[39] Biven (2002, 242).

In formal terms, the Federal Reserve's key step was taken on October 6, 1979, when it announced an increase in the discount rate from 11 to 12 percent, an increase on the reserve requirement on "managed liabilities," and most importantly a "greater emphasis on the day-to-day operations on the supply of bank reserves and less emphasis on containing short-term fluctuations in the Federal funds rate," conceding that "wider day-to-day or week-to-week fluctuations in the Federal Funds rate may occur."[40] Nevertheless – even as subsequent accounts have stressed the decisiveness of the Volcker shift – commercial banks would continue to expand consumer lending at an annual rate of 14 percent, seen as a key source of excess demand.[41] In this light, even Volcker briefly backpedalled toward controls, supporting – albeit reluctantly – the Carter administration's mid-1980 attempt to impose controls on the use of consumer credit as a means to restrain demand-driven inflation. Although Volcker "didn't like the idea," he thought, "we were putting the country through hell, interest rates are rising way up, the budget is being redone, and the President wants us to do this, and the President has been broadly supportive of what we are trying to do."[42] Indeed, these controls were considered *too* effective. Kahn later recalled that "Nobody contemplated that the response would be so enormous … Some people sent me credit cards, wrote irate letters to the effect that Sears Roebuck was soliciting credit card accounts. They said that's unpatriotic."[43] The result was to plunge the economy into a recession and contract the money supply. Ironically, this would lead monetarists to press the Federal Reserve to ease up – to keep things constant – and so Volcker would prematurely ease, reflecting that "we really got behind the eight ball." This would cost his monetarist experiment, he argued, "eight months or so," in terms of reshaping expectations.[44]

---

[40] "Text of Fed's Announcement on Measures to Control Inflation," *New York Times* (October 8, 1979), D6.
[41] Greider (1987, 140).
[42] Mehrling (2007, 181).
[43] Interestingly, paralleling Kennedy-era debates, a split within the administration pitted Neoclassical CEA officials such as Schultze against Institutionally oriented Keynesians such as Alfred Kahn. Schultze dismissed the controls as "a comedy of errors" and criticized "the White House political people" who held "that if we were going to do all these 'anti-liberal' things, like raise the discount rate … we've got to do something the 'liberals' want … So let's have credit controls." In contrast, Kahn later recalled that he had been "the only one among the economic advisers … who was attracted by the notion that capital markets did not work perfectly" Biven (2002, 247–249).
[44] Mehrling (2007, 182).

Following this misstep, Volcker – with the support of the newly installed Reagan administration – would sustain the tightening of the money supply for the next two-and-a-half years. From 1979 to 1982, the federal funds rate – the main overnight rate controlled by the Federal Reserve – would rise from 7.9 percent in 1978 to 11.9 percent in Volcker's first year, to peak at 16.4 percent in 1982 – only falling back into single digits in 1984.[45] This increase would have been unimaginable if it had been pursued through discrete votes over quarter-point rises – particularly as it tracked fairly closely a similarly dramatic increase in unemployment – from 5.8 percent in 1979 to 9.7 percent in 1982.[46] Indeed, at the depths of the recession, in February 1982, the Federal Reserve would not only maintain its tightening – promising "no further growth" in the money supply – but Volcker would in fact arrange a February 1982 meeting with Reagan to stress the need for *fiscal* restraint – suggesting to Reagan that the administration's deficits precluded any monetary easing.[47] In a press conference given a year to the day after the introduction of his economic plan, Reagan would concede the need for a fiscal correction. Having met with Volcker. Reagan affirmed that he himself was "sensitive to the need for a responsible fiscal policy to complement a firm, anti-inflationary monetary policy."[48] This Reagan-Volcker meeting anticipated a dynamic that would emerge over the next two decades, as the Federal Reserve used the threat of monetary tightening to secure fiscal restraint. Even as Reagan had cut marginal taxes only a few months earlier, the emergent deficits had led to renewed pressures for restraint, and so Reagan pledged to "devote the resources of my Presidency to keeping deficits down over the next several years."[49] Reagan would push through the Tax Equity and Fiscal Responsibility Act of 1982, which provided for a targeted set of tax increases that would restore one-third of the revenues lost in the supply-side reductions of the year before.[50]

[45] Council of Economic Advisers (2007, 316).
[46] Council of Economic Advisers (2007, 281).
[47] Silber (2012, 213).
[48] Reagan (1982); Cannon (1991, 232–234).
[49] Reagan (1982).
[50] A tax study by Tempalski (2006, 17) estimated that while the Economic Recovery Tax Act of 1981 had lost revenues amounting to 2.89 percent of GDP over its first four years, the Tax Equity and Fiscal Responsibility Act of 1982 would restore revenues of 0.98 percent of GDP over its first four years. See also Reeves (2005, 118–120).

However, Volcker's policy pressures would also produce blowback from the administration. Even as Reagan stressed his support for Federal Reserve restraint, Treasury Secretary Donald Regan would criticize the Federal Reserve in February 1982 for "slamming the breaks" on the economy. Behind the scenes, Reagan's Chief of Staff Jim Baker – who was seen as too pragmatic by many monetarists – was concerned for the economy's implications for Republican prospects in midterm elections.[51] Placing direct pressure on Volcker, Carter and Reagan appointees on the FOMC increasingly urged an easing. For example, Carter appointee Nancy Teeters argued that the Federal Reserve had pushed "the whole economy not just into recession, but into depression," declaring that she had "had it with the monetary experiment" and that it was "time to put the economy back together."[52] However, it would be less Reagan's acquiescence to budgetary restraint or pressures from within the FOMC that would force Volcker to relent than an erosion of the global financial system that compelled a reassertion of discretionary control. While the Volcker Federal Reserve had for its first three years sought to restrain wage-price increases, it would – beginning in mid-1982 – increasingly seek to accommodate or promote asset-price increases.

## Volcker's Iterative Neoliberalism: Reviving Finance and Monetary Fine-Tuning

Despite the costs of recession, the Federal Reserve could point to an enduring accomplishment, having broken the wage-price spirals that had built over the past decade-and-a-half. Inflation, which had peaked at 13.3 percent in 1979 – and remained at 12.5 percent in 1980 – would fall to 3.8 percent in 1982. In mid-1982, this success increased the space for an easing at the Federal Reserve. As Volcker would later put it, while "early and mid-1982 was a tense period," a scope for easing would develop as "it was some time in July that the money supply suddenly came within our target band." Volcker recalled viewing these circumstances as providing a "chance to ease credibly." When the Federal Reserve "took the first small easing step ... that was all the

---

[51] On intra-administration debates over the Federal Reserve, see Cannon (1991, 233–234).
[52] Meltzer (2009, 1107).

market needed ... the stock market took off [and] the bond market took off."[53] In this light, the Federal Reserve "came to the conclusion that it was not very reliable to put so much weight on the money supply anymore, so we backed off that approach."[54] Practical monetarism had come to a practical ending.

However, the easing also reflected concerns for financial strains. To the extent that the high interest rates of 1979–1982 led to reduced commodity prices and high debt service costs, they contributed to the interlocking global debt crisis and domestic banking crises of 1982. First, these emerged from the July 1982 failure of a small Oklahoma bank, Penn Square, which had its roots in the collapse of energy prices. While Volcker lent $20 million to Penn Square, this aid proved insufficient to stabilize the bank – and Federal Deposit Insurance Corporation (FDIC) Chairman William Isaac foreshadowed a later stance taken by FDIC Chair Sheila Bair in 2008, refusing to provide additional support to Penn Square, as such a move might court a moral hazard and drain FDIC resources. In the debate between Volcker and Isaac, Treasury Secretary Donald Regan ultimately sided with the FDIC, and the bank was shut down.[55] Yet, despite having come out on the losing side, the Penn Square collapse reveals that – even as Volcker broke the wage-price spiral – he would embrace the Federal Reserve's role as lender of last resort, arguing at the October 1982 FOMC meeting that "[i]f it gets bad enough, we can't stay on the side or have a major liquidity crisis ... We are not out to see the economy destroyed in the interest of not bailing somebody out."[56]

Second, in the international context, Penn Square was paralleled by the near-default of Mexico in 1982. Since the February 1982 peso devaluation, Volcker had been worried about Mexico's ability to service its debts – particularly given its reliance on short-run financing. To buy time, Volcker provided ill-conceived "window dressing" by swapping pesos for dollars with the Bank of Mexico at the end of April and June.[57] The result was only to delay the day of reckoning. Volcker's anxieties were increased when, on August 9, the head of Continental Illinois – the seventh largest bank in America – contacted him to warn

[53] Mehrling (2007, 183).
[54] Mehrling (2007, 183).
[55] Meltzer (2009, 1105–1106).
[56] Meltzer (2009, 1105).
[57] Silber (2012, 221).

about losses stemming from Penn Square and concerns about Latin American defaults. The next day, Mexican Finance Minister Jesús Silva Herzog flew to Washington to inform US and IMF officials that Mexico had almost exhausted its reserves. Volcker's concern reflected the extent to which the largest US banks had made $60 billion in loans to Mexico, amounting to approximately 45 percent of their capital.[58] Initial responses were marked by a "muddling through" approach, as authorities sought to cajole new money from the banks and achieve rescheduling agreements that would avoid the appearance of default.

Third and finally, in 1984, the Federal Reserve would continue in this vein by rescuing the long-on-the-brink Continental Illinois. Dependent on $8 billion in revolving daily credit, Continental was initially kept afloat with a Federal Reserve Bank of Chicago $3.6 billion loan. Yet, accelerating withdrawals would lead Volcker to worry about systemic stability. When an attempt to motivate a "bail-in" of leading bankers would fail – foreshadowing the difficulties of "Lehman Weekend" in September 2008 – the Federal Reserve would support a public rescue of Continental.[59] Taken as a whole, spanning the failure to aid Penn Square and the embrace of a "too big to fail" view of Continental, Volcker set an enduring Neoliberal template for accommodating rather than containing asset-price inflation.

Moving forward, this willingness to depart from the austere approach that had broken the wage-price spiral would grow more apparent over the mid-1980s, as administration and Federal Reserve officials proved willing to intervene to stabilize currency markets and address global debt issues.[60] For example, Volcker would argue for cooperative currency interventions – most importantly to bring down the "superdollar" of the early 1980s. He justified this stance, arguing that the "case for an open economic order rests ... on the idea that the world will be better off if international trade and investment follow patterns of comparative advantage." Where currency values

---

[58] Volcker and Gyohten (1992, 198–200).
[59] Silber (2012, 242–243).
[60] Speaking to the earlier attitude, for example, Reagan's first Treasury Secretary Donald Regan initially renounced any concern for the dollar's value, renouncing intervention – save in "disorderly" conditions – and asserting that "[I]f it is a strong dollar, we are not going to intervene to weaken it. If it is a weak dollar, we are not going to intervene to make it stronger. If it is a disorderly market in the dollar, we will intervene" James (1996, 425).

swung between extremes, Volcker argued that it was "hard to see how business can effectively calculate where lasting comparative advantage lies".[61] Reflecting these views, the Group of 5 (G5) finance ministers reached the Plaza Accord of 1985, which called for the orderly appreciation of other currencies against the dollar to accomplish a de facto depreciation. This stance was later reversed as the Louvre Accord of February 1987 saw joint efforts to *strengthen* the dollar, reflecting concerns that markets had swung too far in the weakening direction. Similarly highlighting the scope for international plans and accords, the "muddling through" approach to the debt crisis would yield to the 1985 Baker Plan to promote new lending and the 1989 Brady Plan for debt relief – with "Brady Bonds" providing an outlet for the "emerging markets" enthusiasms of the 1990s.

Successes in defeating inflation aside, ongoing disputes over such policies would work to hasten Volcker's exit. First, his Carter-appointed status remained a source of suspicion among Reagan officials, reinforced by irritation over Volcker's independent streak.[62] Reagan's Chief of Staff Donald Regan had memorably argued against Volcker's first reappointment in 1983 on grounds that "He won't take orders."[63] Second, his stress on fiscal balance – dating back to his February 1982 meeting with Reagan – was not always appreciated as the deficit grew into a perennial problem. Third, Volcker's predilection for tighter money would spur tensions at the FOMC that undercut his own desire to stay. In February 1986, Volcker had lost a vote over a half-point discount rate cut on a 4-3 split, with Reagan appointees voting as a bloc. While Volcker briefly submitted his resignation to Treasury Secretary Baker, a new vote would paper over immediate tensions – though Volcker's time as chair was numbered, going forward.[64] Finally, in early 1987 – highlighting Volcker's emergent wariness of financial market power – Volcker would lose a Board struggle over the weakening of Glass-Steagall limitations on commercial bank underwriting of debt

---

[61] Volcker and Gyohten (1992, 293).
[62] Recognizing administration skepticism, Volcker had told Reagan in June 1983 that, if reappointed, he would "expect to stay for only the next eighteen months to two years" – Volcker would stay through June 1987. Silber (2012, 232).
[63] Hirsh (2010, 80).
[64] On Volcker's attempted resignation, see Greider (1987, 699–701); Silber (2012, 255–258).

issues. Citicorp Vice Chairman Thomas Theobald argued to the Federal Reserve Board that "the world has changed a lot" since the 1930s, citing "outside checks" on financial abuses in "a very effective" Securities and Exchange Commission and "very sophisticated" credit rating agencies, concluding that "we don't have to worry a bit" about conflicts of interests vis-à-vis corporate and commercial customers. Volcker would reply that "I guess I worry a little bit" about such conflicts, and suggested that this call was more of a legislative than a regulatory matter. However, the loss of this vote – in contrast to the discount rate clash from the year before – would not produce a resignation threat, as Volcker had already decided to depart, leaving in August 1987.[65]

While his successor Alan Greenspan shared Volcker's concern for wage restraint and asset price stability, he would be favored by the Reagan administration because of a much greater enthusiasm for deregulation. However, relations between Greenspan and Reagan's successors in the George H. W. Bush administration would soon deteriorate. Most importantly, Bush – lacking the credibility that Reagan had with supply-siders and tax cutters – had felt compelled to "double down" on a pledge to renounce tax increases in the 1988 campaign. In contrast, amidst a slight increase in inflation over the late 1980s, Greenspan would amplify Volcker's early-1980s stress on fiscal restraint, using monetary restraint to motivate fiscal balance, in a way that would lead to a rupture between the Federal Reserve and the Bush administration.

## 6.4 Greenspan's Institutional Agenda: Displacing Fiscal Policy

Looking back on his early years at the Federal Reserve, Greenspan recalled that struggles to limit inflation remained at the forefront of his concern, arguing that "the trauma of the 1970s was still so vivid throughout the 1980s that preventing a return to accelerating prices was the unvarying focus of our efforts during those years."[66] In this light, while the mid-1980s had seen a slight loosening of monetary policy, the Volcker Federal Reserve began tightening again in the spring of

---

[65] On the debate over the weakening of Glass-Steagall, see Hirsh (2010, 81–82); Silber (2012, 259–260).
[66] Greenspan (2004a).

1987, seeking, as Greenspan put it, to "lean against increasing inflationary pressures."[67] Upon taking control, Greenspan continued in this vein. While his first FOMC meeting had seen Greenspan simply seek to gather information in an effort to build consensus, he would continue to tighten as he pushed through a half-point rate increase at his second FOMC meeting.[68]

Yet, wage-price concerns would soon yield again to asset-price matters with the onset of the "Black Monday" crash of late 1987. On October 19, 1987, amid concerns for US fiscal position and dollar's value, the stock market would plunge by 508 points, losing 22 percent of its value in a single day.[69] Greenspan himself spent that afternoon in flight to Dallas, to address the American Bankers Association. When Greenspan landed, he asked an aide about the market close, and interpreted the response, "five-oh-eight," as news of a recovery – in a five point decline – only to be taken aback when informed of the magnitude of the market's true – five hundred point – decline.[70] While commentators suggested that this potentially marked the end of the Neoliberal era, the 1987 crash had little in the way of an enduring economic impact, mattering mostly as it provided the template for subsequent crisis-management efforts. Early on October 20, Greenspan would issue a brief statement affirming that the Federal Reserve recognized its role "as a source of liquidity to support the economic and financial system." Reagan's Chief of Staff Howard Baker would meet Greenspan at the White House that afternoon, characterizing the statement as "the best lines I've read since Shakespeare."[71] However, Greenspan would later share credit for the rescue with New York Federal Reserve President Gerry Corrigan for having engaged in the "jawboning" of banks and reminding them to consider their "overall interests."[72] While the overconfidence of the 2000s "Great Moderation" had not yet taken hold, there would emerge a widespread sense that monetary policy had saved the day – and so Black Monday produced no major institutional or policy change, save to reinforce the Federal Reserve's rising influence.

---

[67] Greenspan (2004a).
[68] Greenspan (2007, 103–104).
[69] Solomon (1995, 19–20).
[70] Greenspan (2007, 104–105).
[71] Solomon (1995, 61).
[72] Greenspan (2007, 108).

However, the aftermath of the crisis did embolden the Federal Reserve in one key way – to compensate for the absence of a suitably restrictive fiscal policy. Greenspan would use the threat of monetary tightening to push more aggressively for fiscal restraint. While the Reagan administration was heading for the exits in early 1988, tensions with the George H. W. Bush campaign would intensify, particularly as Greenspan had resumed tightening in March 1988. Bush pushed back in public, warning that he "wouldn't want to see them step over some [line] that would ratchet down, tighten down on the economic growth."[73] More significantly for future relations, Bush would issue a Clint Eastwood–styled "read my lips – no new taxes" pledge at the Republican National Convention in mid-1988, limiting his scope for efforts on the deficit. While his more pragmatically oriented advisers such as eventual Budget Director Richard Darman opposed the pledge, they were overruled on grounds that electoral priorities trumped policy concerns. Likewise, as Greenspan put it, the pledge "was a memorable line, but at some point he was going to have to tackle the deficit – and he'd tied one hand behind his back."[74] On taking office, Darman recalled his early meetings with Greenspan as focused on the need for deficit reduction. Darman recalled Greenspan's "polite implication... that he would not allow higher money supply growth or higher real economic growth without our first achieving a legislative solution to the deficit problem."[75] In this light, when Bush himself belatedly recognized that the pledge had been a case of "rhetorical overkill," his mid-1990 acceptance of a tax increase would alienate his Republican base. Ironically, Bush would then be forced to rely on *Democratic* support in getting the increase passed in the Omnibus Budget Reconciliation Act of 1990.[76] Characterizing his tensions with the Bush administration, Greenspan later recalled that he had believed that they should have addressed the deficit "right away, while the economy was still strong enough to absorb the shock of cuts in federal spending." Unfortunately, Greenspan recalled that "I quickly found myself in the same public conflict with President Bush that we'd had during the campaign ... and as a result we ended up with a terrible

---

[73] Greenspan (2007, 111).
[74] Greenspan (2007, 112).
[75] Darman (1996, 202).
[76] Bush and Scowcroft (1998, 379–380).

relationship" – one revealed in Bush's later remark that "I reappointed him and he disappointed me."[77]

Yet, this willingness to take on a Republican president bolstered Greenspan's credibility in a way that enabled him to work out an implicit fiscal-monetary accord with the subsequent Clinton administration. Indeed, speaking to an emergent macroeconomic policy consensus, Greenspan would later reflect on the convergence between his and Clinton's views, noting that during the 1970s, "a great ideological chasm in economics had divided Republicans from Democrats." In contrast, the 1990s saw "a consensus" in which "no longer could Alan Greenspan be so easily distinguished from Bill Clinton ... as Clinton's plans ... even resembled President Ford's in the 1976 Republican platform."[78] Over the next decade, however, the consensus would harden to the point that it obscured new problems – with success in defeating inflation obscuring new limits to macroeconomic fine-tuning where market power or psychology might take on lives of their own.

## 6.5 Conclusions

In addressing the construction of the Neoliberal order, the most important initial step was with respect to the rhetorical transformation of principled ideas. Echoing Franklin Roosevelt in form but not content, Ronald Reagan shifted the burden of proof in public debate from the Keynesian presumption that government could advance a "common cause" to a view of government as "the problem." Having accomplished this fast thinking principled shift, Reagan would introduce more refined elaborations with respect to fiscal, regulatory, and monetary policies. First, Reagan would advance a supply-side critique of Keynesian demand stimulus, arguing for cuts in marginal tax rates to spur investment. Second, Reagan would not only critique Keynesian efforts at wage-price regulation, but would embark on a revived antitrust-styled effort to break the market power of unions in the dismissal of striking PATCO workers. Third, Reagan would support Paul Volcker's monetarist initiative. While these efforts would set off a major economic downturn, they would also provide a foundation for prolonged wage restraint, breaking the back of the wage-price spiral.

[77] Greenspan (2007, 113, 122).
[78] Woodward (1994, 71).

Having repudiated the old Keynesian order, Reagan and Volcker would in turn provide key foundations for the Neoliberal alternative, bolstering the standing of finance. First, Reagan's tax cuts entailed not only a reduction in marginal rates on income, but also an inversion of the relationship between earned and unearned income, reducing rates on capital gains and investment income. Second, even as Volcker broke the wage-price spiral, he would ease over the course of 1982 to stabilize the financial system, given threats from the Latin American debt crisis and Continental Illinois. Third, these improvised supports would be supplanted by a further set of accords and plans meant to stabilize the financial and monetary orders, across the Plaza and Louvre Accords and Baker and Brady Plans.

Yet, just as the Keynesian order had been marked by a shift in authority to a Council of Economic Advisers that would exhibit a misplaced confidence in fiscal fine-tuning, the Neoliberal order would enable a shift to a Federal Reserve that would evince a parallel overconfidence in monetary fine-tuning. In turn, just as the Keynesian order had been undermined by a lack of attention to rising labor power and wage-price spirals, the Neoliberal order would be undermined by a failure to recognize shifts in financial power and asset-price bubbles. In each case, intellectual stability obscured new sources of economic instability.

# 7 Converting the Neoliberal Order: Toward the New Keynesianism

> We know big Government does not have all the answers ... The era of big Government is over.
>
> Bill Clinton, State of the Union Address, 1996[1]

## 7.1 Introduction/Overview

In refining the Progressive order, Woodrow Wilson favored "the limitation of governmental power" in a way that set the stage for monetary fine-tuning at the Federal Reserve.[2] Similarly, as the Keynesian order matured amid calls for an "end of ideology," John F. Kennedy abstracted away from the "grand warfare of rival ideologies" in favor of a Neoclassical Synthesis.[3] With the rise of the Neoliberal order, Bill Clinton presided over a parallel intellectual conversion, arguing that the "era of big Government is over" while embracing reliance on the Federal Reserve's New Keynesian monetary activism. To be sure, when Clinton came to power, he initially aspired to fiscal activism, seeking new investments in education and health care. However, given rising fiscal deficits and the threat of Federal Reserve austerity, Clinton would curtail this agenda, embracing fiscal restraint while appointing to the Federal Reserve Board New Keynesian economists such as Janet Yellen and Alan Blinder who would in turn promote a Taylor rule-styled fine-tuning of interest rates. By the end of the decade, given the success of these efforts, economic policy debates would be reduced to intellectual questions of macroeconomic fine-tuning and deregulation – obscuring more explicitly political questions of market power and psychology.[4]

---

[1] Clinton (1996).
[2] Cooper (2009, 163–164).
[3] Kennedy (1962a).
[4] Speaking to the narrowing of economic visions, Paul Krugman (1994, 121) lauded the Federal Reserve under Volcker for "fighting inflation the only

Tracing this intellectual conversion, I address in the first section of this chapter the Clinton administration's shift from promoting public investment to budgetary restraint as a means to increased financial credibility and availability of credit. In the second section, I pull back to describe how the Clinton administration would press Greenspan in more coordinative contexts, advancing a more growth-oriented approach on the Federal Reserve Board through the appointments of New Keynesian economists Alan Blinder and Janet Yellen. In the third section, I address the consolidation of New Keynesian consensus across successive debates: as the shift from the early 1994 Federal Reserve tightening to its late 1995 easing fueled confidence in Greenspan's ability to engineer "soft landings" of the business cycle; as the successful resolution of the financial crises of 1997–1999 and eased concerns regarding deregulation. Taken as a whole, these shifts would enhance the scope for fine-tuning and deregulation, albeit at the cost of obscuring shifts in market power and psychology.

## 7.2 Clinton's New Keynesian Turns: Fiscal Restraint and Monetary Fine-Tuning

The Clinton years would be marked by the intellectual conversion of the Neoliberal order, as the administration moved away from a stress on public investment and fiscal activism to favor instead budgetary restraint, deregulation, and New Keynesian monetary fine-tuning. Initially, in his 1992 campaign, Bill Clinton had argued *not* for deficit reduction, but instead advanced a "Putting People First" agenda that stressed the need for a targeted middle-class tax cut and $60 billion in new investment spending on education and infrastructure.[5] Yet, over the transition, Clinton's agenda would shift, reflecting both new fiscal developments and debate within the administration. First, just two weeks before Clinton's inauguration, the Bush administration issued new deficit figures, estimating that by 1997 the budget shortfall would be one-third higher than previously anticipated. Second, even

---

reliable way we know: by tightening up on monetary policy" – abstracting away from the prior use of incomes policies, and political moves like the breaking of labor power.

[5] It is worth noting that in terms of his background as governor of Arkansas, Clinton had not previously been allied with Labor or the Democratic left, and even had chaired the avowedly moderate Democratic Leadership Council.

as Clinton's campaign staff favored new spending, political appointees such as Treasury Secretary Lloyd Bentsen and outside voices such as Federal Reserve Chairman Alan Greenspan would stress the extent to which inflation fears were keeping long-term interest rates high, arguing that where fiscal restraint might lower inflation fears, this could make available new private investment in excess of official capacities. In an early meeting with Clinton, Greenspan argued that long-term interest rates reflected an "inflation premium," and that just as the "double- digit inflation of the late 1970s had been induced by the budget deficits from the Vietnam War ... investors were now wary and demanding a higher long-term return because of the expectations on the federal deficit."[6] In this context, Clinton would abandon his promised middle-class tax cut – and seeing congressional Republicans defeat his proposed $16 billion stimulus – would make a tax *increase* his top priority, as a means to deficit reduction. Over these early months, Clinton officials accordingly coordinated with Greenspan, adopting his recommendation of $130 billion in spending reductions as a benchmark for their own budgetary blueprint.[7] Greenspan later recalled that "I advised Bentsen on how deeply I thought the deficit would have to be cut in order to convince Wall Street and thereby bring down long-term interest rates. 'Not less than $130 billion a year by 1997' was his shorthand description of what I said ... Within the White House, $130 billion became known as the 'magic number.'"[8] Eventually, the administration would actually push for $140 billion, and Bentsen would inform Clinton that they had reached a "gentleman's agreement" with Greenspan.[9]

To be sure, Clinton himself at times expressed frustration at this shift in his administration's agenda, objecting at one point that "the success

---

[6] Looking back in his memoirs, Greenspan recalled of his meeting with Clinton that "I was ready with a pitch. Short-term interest rates were rock-bottom low – we'd cut them to 3 percent ... But long-term interest rates were still stubbornly high ... They reflected an expectation of ongoing inflation for which investors had come to require an extra margin of interest to offset the added uncertainty and risk. Improve investors' expectations, I told Clinton, and long-term rates could fall ... All told, the latter part of the 1990s could look awfully good. I was not oblivious of the fact that 1996 would be a presidential election year ... To my delight, Clinton seemed fully engaged." Quotes in text from Woodward (1994, 48); See also Clinton (2004, 451).
[7] Greenspan (2007, 147).
[8] Greenspan (2007, 147).
[9] Woodward (2000, 100).

of the program and my reelection hinges on the Federal Reserve and a bunch of fucking bond traders"[10] Even a month into his term, Clinton's ultimate principled direction remained in flux. On February 15, only two nights before a formal address presenting his economic plan to Congress, Clinton made a televised address from the Oval Office, rejecting Reagan's claims that "Government is the problem."[11] Instead, Clinton stressed the need for "fairness to the middle class" rather than the Reagan priority of "keeping taxes low on the wealthy."[12] However, the next day, the stock market suffered its largest single-day decline in more than a year, and White House speechwriters – prodded by Hillary Clinton – quickly recast Clinton's address to Congress scheduled for the next evening.[13] This appeal would adopt a more measured tone, as Clinton made explicit concessions to the Neoliberal order, arguing that his budget enabled shifts "from consumption to investment" and would reduce the deficit "honestly and credibly."[14] Indeed, the administration had arranged for a public show of support from Greenspan himself, who had accepted an invitation to sit in the balcony next to Hillary Clinton during Clinton's address. Providing more concrete support, Greenspan would testify before Congress that Clinton was "to be commended for placing on the table" a plan that was "serious" and "plausible."[15] While the budget would receive no votes from Republicans in Congress, Greenspan's support was key to public credibility. Moreover, the promise of Bentsen's "gentleman's agreement" suggested that a balanced budget might result in at least a *quid pro quo*, in which not only long-term but also short-term rates might fall.

Yet, only a year into the Clinton administration, Greenspan would move in a tightening direction, visiting the White House on January 21, 1994 to prepare the ground for a resumption of rate increase. Greenspan informed Clinton that "We've got a dilemma, and you should understand ... We haven't made a decision, but the choices are, we sit and wait and then likely we'll have to raise short-term interest rates more. Or we could take some small increases now." Clinton replied that while he wanted "to keep interest rates low," he understood

---

[10] Woodward (1994, 84).
[11] Clinton (1993a).
[12] Clinton (1993a).
[13] Harris (2006, 30).
[14] Clinton (1993b).
[15] Woodward (1994, 143–144).

what Greenspan "may have to do."[16] Over the next year and a half, Greenspan would nearly double interest rates, from 3 percent in early 1994 to 6 percent by the end of 1995, arguing for the need to contain both wage and asset-price instability. First, to the extent that the financial system was on increasingly solid ground, Greenspan turned to the possibility that sustained growth might fuel wage-price pressures.[17] Second, this preemptive tightening was not simply meant to stabilize inflation, but also what appeared to be a growing stock-market boom – as Greenspan suggested that "[i]f we have the capability of having a Sword of Damocles over the market we can prevent it from running away."[18] Clinton privately disagreed with Greenspan's tightening, suggesting in late 1994 that Greenspan was too focused on maintaining a "natural" unemployment rate of 6 percent, beneath which inflation might begin to accelerate. Stressing the scope for continued easing, Clinton pointed to "global price competition and the decline of unions to argue that unemployment could go lower without touching off inflation." Yet, even though Clinton thought "stale economic theory was punishing minimum wage workers," he "lobbied Greenspan carefully because of the Fed's insulated power."[19]

This abandonment of communicative engagement would carry a price. To the extent that Clinton had abandoned his principled embrace of public investment, this would limit his ability to offer a public justification for his economic policies. Unfortunately for Democratic candidates in Congress, economic results did not "speak for themselves." Even as GDP growth would increase by 3.9 percent in 1994 and unemployment would fall to 5.7 percent just before the 1994 midterm elections, technocratic arguments for fiscal restraint carried little communicative weight. This communicative gap would be exploited by Republicans in congress – most importantly by House Republican leader Newt Gingrich, who stressed in sessions with his colleagues the importance of language as a "key mechanism of control," and distributed a memo describing language "to define our opponents." Gingrich contrasted positive options like "opportunity," "reform," and "freedom," with contrasting terms like "crisis," "welfare," and "taxes"

---

[16] Woodward (2000, 116).
[17] Woodward (2000, 118).
[18] Federal Open Market Committee (1994, 47–48).
[19] Branch (2009, 215).

in defining the Democratic position. These efforts culminated in the 1994 "Contract with America" Republican platform which set forth a broad agenda and pledges for specific votes to be held in the House. As House Speaker, Gingrich further framed his role as a transformative one, setting out to change nothing less than "the whole language of politics."[20]

Nevertheless, following the November 1994 loss of Congress to the Republicans, Clinton would "double down" on his commitment to financial credibility. First, this could be seen almost immediately, as the Mexican peso crisis hit in December 1994. The collapse of the peso was particularly damaging as the prevailing enthusiasm for "emerging markets" during this period fed concerns that investors might reverse themselves throughout Latin America, engendering a "Tequila Effect" of capital flight. Greenspan later recalled that "None of us had forgotten the Latin American debt crisis of 1982" and those memories fueled concerns that the crisis "could spread to other nations."[21] Given Greenspan's support, even as Gingrich had engaged in the political demonization of Clinton, he would back the administration in seeking congressional support for the peso. However, in a strange confluence of forces, the administration's attempted initiative would be thwarted by both liberal Democrats and conservative Republicans. Looking back, Clinton recalled that "congressional Democrats [thought] … the bailout proved that NAFTA was ill advised in the first place" and "newly elected Republicans, especially in the House, didn't share the Speaker's enthusiasm for international affairs." Within his administration, Clinton elaborated that "I thought the decision was clear-cut, but [those] … who wanted to speed my political recovery after the crushing midterm defeat thought I was nuts."[22] Eventually, the administration used its executive authority and employed the Treasury's Exchange Stabilization Fund to enable a Mexican rescue. Moving forward, this experience would also have an enduring impact on officials such as Greenspan and future treasury secretaries Rubin and Geithner, as they would often dismiss opposition to market accommodation as reflecting populist excess. Geithner later recalled that "the politics of the things we did in the past financial crises in Mexico and Asia had a powerful effect on me. The surveys were 9-to-1 against almost

[20] Drew (1996, 14).
[21] Greenspan (2007, 157).
[22] Clinton (2004, 641–642).

everything that helped contain the damage. And I watched exceptionally capable people just get killed in the court of public opinion."[23]

Second, Clinton would overrule many of his advisors to offer an alternative to Republican proposals for a balanced budget – countering his advisers who favored letting the Republicans show their excesses. Clinton reacted in one meeting by responding to such arguments, "That's fine. When people say 'Where's your plan?' I'll say, 'Oh, I'm just president of the United States. You want me to have a plan?'"[24] In a May 1995 radio interview with New Hampshire public radio, Clinton would in effect perform an "end run" around his own staff, suggesting that balancing the budget "clearly can be done in less than 10 years."[25] On June 13, Clinton formalized this view in a nationally televised address, one which gave rise to what would be termed his "triangulation" approach to balancing congressional extremes of liberal Democrats and conservative Republicans – leading Democratic allies such as Congresswoman Patricia Schroeder to accuse Clinton of "thinking about himself and presidential politics" rather than the larger party.[26] Nevertheless, Clinton would later prove fortunate in his enemies, as Republicans over winter 1995–1996 would shut down the federal government in an effort to force Clinton to accept their plan. In this context, the focus of public debate would shift from the substance of fiscal disputes to the tactical abuses of the shutdown. Particularly damaging to Republicans would be Gingrich's admission that he had been partly motivated by a presidential snub on the Air Force One flight to the funeral of Israeli Prime Minister Yitzhak Rabin – conceding that "It's petty, but I think it's human."[27] To the extent that Republicans were seen as having surrendered principle for pique, their support would collapse.

Moving forward, Clinton would advance his shift toward the role of Neoliberal reformer in his 1996 State of the Union address, reaffirming his claims to a middle ground in which fiscal restraint could enable a greater supply of private credit. In terms of economic reasoning, he argued that "we have all begun to see the benefits of deficit reduction. Lower interest rates have made it easier for businesses to borrow and to invest and to create new jobs." However, the most enduring

---

[23] Gross (2009).
[24] Harris (2006, 182).
[25] Clinton (1995); Harris (2006, 183).
[26] Harris (2006, 185).
[27] Harris (2006, 217).

lines would embody a principled concession, as Clinton affirmed that "era of big Government is over."[28] Little more than a year later, in his second inaugural address, Clinton offered what might be seen as a long-distance compromise with Reagan, affirming that "Government is not the problem, and Government is not the solution," embodying the notion of what would be termed a "third way" between statist and free market excesses.[29]

However, in more formal terms, much policy debate was also occurring out of public sight – in the meetings of the Federal Open Market Committee (FOMC). To be sure, even as Clinton would seek to influence monetary policy debates through appointments to the FOMC, the administration was initially highly averse to any sort of public conflict, to the point that when White House Chief of Staff Leon Panetta was asked in a June 12, 1995 appearance on *Meet the Press* whether he believed the Federal Reserve should cut interest rates, he answered that "it would be nice to get whatever kind of cooperation we can get to get this economy going." When asked whether he was "jawboning" the Fed, Panetta replied coyly, "Is that what it's called?" Within the administration, Treasury Secretary Robert Rubin immediately issued a disclaimer, castigating the chief of staff as "careless" and affirming that "policy with respect to the Federal Reserve has been consistent from the beginning of the administration – and that is not to comment."[30] Ironically, Panetta could not have known that the Federal Reserve's last interest rate increase had come in a half-point hike on February 1– and that its easing would begin less than a month later. More important still, these "behind the scenes" shifts reflected less principled debate than intellectual struggles among a new generation of economists – who would revive the fiscal fine-tuning of the Neoclassical Synthesis as the monetary fine-tuning of a New Keynesian school.

## 7.3 Intellectual Conversion and Displacement: New Keynesian Monetary Fine-Tuning

In the construction of the Neoliberal order, Reagan-era principled libertarianism had found intellectual expression in "New Classical"

---

[28] Clinton (1996).
[29] Clinton (1997).
[30] Woodward (2000, 147–148).

theoretical assumptions. These stressed the absolute, unqualified efficiency with which market agents used information, and so limited the scope for discretionary macroeconomic interventions. More specifically, New Classical analyses suggested that there existed little space for macroeconomic policy to have "real" economic effects, as rational agents could be expected to preempt any fiscal or monetary stimulus, leaving the economy unchanged save for higher "nominal" wages or prices. In the context of an early 1980s triumphalism, New Classical advocates such as Robert Lucas cast Keynesianism as a fading view, arguing that "one cannot find good, under-forty economists who identify their work as 'Keynesian' " and that economists "even take offense if referred to as 'Keynesians.' "[31] Yet, this dismissal turned out to be premature. Indeed, once labor had been "broken" via the temporary renunciation of wage-price fine-tuning and Professional Air Traffic Controllers Association (PATCO) dismissals, new forms of fine-tuning would be needed to stabilize financial markets. Highlighting New Classical limits, Clinton Federal Reserve Board appointee Alan Blinder would argue that "the ascendancy of [N]ew [C]lassicism in academia" represented a "triumph of a priori theorizing over empiricism," but not any sort of "Kuhnian scientific revolution."[32]

Characterizing New Keynesian views – and revealing its bipartisan appeal – subsequent George W. Bush administration Council of Economic Advisers Chair N. Gregory Mankiw argued that "New Keynesians are the keepers of the faith that policymakers face a *short-run tradeoff* between inflation and unemployment." Stressing "how misleading the labels have become," Mankiw elaborated that while Classical economists "deny the existence of any trade-off over any time horizon," prior generations of "Old classical economists, such as David Hume, asserted that money was neutral in the long run but not in the short run," which "is exactly the position held by the New Keynesians."[33] In terms of policy implications, Mankiw would note that "New Keynesians accept the view of the world summarized by the Neoclassical Synthesis: the economy can deviate in the short term from its equilibrium level, and monetary and fiscal policy have important influences on real economic activity." In theoretical terms,

---

[31] Lucas (1980, 18–19).
[32] Blinder (1998, 278).
[33] Mankiw (1992, 449).

they are saying that the Neoclassical Synthesis is "not as flawed" as its critics suggest and so have set out to "fix those theoretical problems" and provide "better microeconomic foundations." Parallels with Samuelson and Solow even extended to Mankiw's renunciation of a "Galbraithian" stress on controls, on grounds that "When the government gets in the business of setting wages and prices it is not very good at it. The setting of wages and prices should be left to free markets."[34] In this way, the 1960s Neoclassical Synthesis and 1990s New Keynesianism may have rested on different foundations, but they would enable similar conclusions regarding macroeconomic fine-tuning. Indeed, New Keynesianism would even see the Phillips Curve reincarnated in loose fashion, as Stanford economist John Taylor argued that monetary policymakers should strike a balance between promoting growth and price stability, positing a "Taylor rule" that would place "a positive weight on both the price level and real output in the interest-rate rule."[35] In simpler terms, Taylor defined a rule describing how central bankers "should set the short-term interest rate," as they would "raise the interest rate when inflation increases and lower it when GDP declines."[36] Even if the theoretical underpinning were more dynamic than had been the case in early constructions of the Phillips curve, the policy implications were quite similar.

In this light, even as it renounced public efforts to pressure the Federal Reserve, the Clinton administration would play a key role in behind-the-scenes efforts to place sympathetic economists on the Federal Reserve Board, leading off in mid-1994 with New Keynesians Alan Blinder and Janet Yellen. First, Blinder would be appointed to replace outgoing Vice Chairman David Mullins in June 1994. However, he would ultimately have an unhappy term, conflicting with Greenspan and even engaging in a degree of public debate over the limits to noninflationary growth. Even before Blinder arrived, Greenspan considered his past record to have revealed an inappropriate lack of concern for inflation. When Mullins suggested that "It's not like he's a Communist or something. It's just in his early publications he's notably soft on inflation," Greenspan would reply that "I would have preferred he were a communist."[37] Blinder would subsequently irritate Greenspan

---

[34] Snowdon and Vane (1995, 53–54).
[35] Taylor (1993, 201–202).
[36] Taylor (2009, 67).
[37] Woodward (2000, 126–127).

by publically advancing New Keynesian challenges, particularly in an August 1994 Jackson Hole address at which he urged an equal focus on inflation *and* unemployment – which was seen as reflecting a "split" within the Federal Reserve.[38] Clinton's August 1994 appointment of Berkeley economist Janet Yellen would have a more lasting import, as Yellen would successfully advocate for the merit of the Taylor rule and a balanced approach to addressing unemployment and inflation. In a 1996 address to the National Association of Business Economists, Yellen explicitly held forth that the Taylor rule indicated a way in which the Federal Reserve could reconcile "multiple objectives simultaneously." While acknowledging that the "Fed has only one tool – the Federal funds rate" – Yellen held that "there is no conflict whatever between pursuing price stability as the primary long-term goal" while also promoting "the economy's real economic performance." Yellen continued that this could require that "the real federal funds rate will be above its long-run equilibrium level when the trend inflation rate exceeds its long-run target." However, it would also entail an acceptance of "more temporary inflation … to prevent output from falling further below its potential in the short run."[39]

In mid-1994, the two Clinton appointees took their seats at the table in the midst of the tightening phase at the Federal Reserve. While neither Blinder nor Yellen publically broke with Greenspan, they did wage behind-the-scenes struggles over the announcements accompanying the rate increases, and as the restrictive approach continued into

---

[38] Morgan (2004, 1034); Woodward (2000, 132).
[39] More explicitly describing the Taylor rule, Yellen (1996, 4–6) would argue that "The existence of policy trade-offs requires a strategy for managing them. John Taylor, of Stanford University, has designed a policy rule of thumb that neatly illustrates how a central bank can pursue stabilization policy without losing its focus on the long-term price stability goal. According to the Taylor rule, the Fed's key instrument, the federal funds rate, should respond to gaps between actual and ideal performance on each of the Fed's dual objectives-price stability and output stability. The Taylor rule calls for the Fed to adjust the real federal funds rate above his estimated 2 percent 'neutral' or 'equilibrium' level, by an amount which depends on the deviation between actual and potential output and the deviation between actual and target inflation." Foreshadowing future issues, Taylor (1993, 201–202) conceded that his rule did not encompass the use of monetary policy to address asset-price fluctuations, asserting that "this rule fits the actual policy performance during the last few years [1987–1992] remarkably well," but acknowledging "a significant deviation in 1987 when the Fed reacted to the crash in the stock market by easing interest rates."

1995 would grow increasingly uncomfortable regarding the potential costs for real growth. As interest rates were raised into 1995, Yellen increasingly opposed the tightening – "want[ing] to scream out, There's a lag here, folks! Rate increases take a year or more to have a real impact."[40] For a time, Blinder and Yellen even considered making a joint protest, though they dropped the idea in part on grounds that it might appear too political. Nevertheless, even as they would compromise on rate levels, Blinder and Yellen set the stage for a new conventional wisdom, providing an intellectual justification for the fine-tuning of interest rates. Following what would be the last rate increase – on February 1 – Greenspan would echo Blinder, Yellen, and the Taylor rule by arguing in congressional testimony that the Federal Reserve had been seeking to "head off inflation pressures not yet evident in the data," but also conceding that there might "come a time when we hold our policy stance unchanged or even ease despite adverse price data."[41] Put bluntly, the Federal Reserve might cut rates in the face of inflation if it thought that the underlying trend was to slowing growth – a view that Blinder saw as reflecting his own discrete pressures in debate. Having ceased raising rates in February 1995, the Federal Reserve would propose its first cut of the Clinton era in July 1995 – albeit holding off on another until December 1995. Looking back, Greenspan would term the soft landing "one of the Fed's proudest accomplishments" during his term as chair.[42] In short, fine-tuning was back – though debate over its scope would continue.

## 7.4 Three Debates: Traumatized Workers; Irrational Exuberance; Regulatory Rollback

This success in enabling growth would foreshadow increasing confidence at the Federal Reserve, which would be amplified across three subsequent sets of crisis and debate: First, the shift from the 1994 tightening to the late 1995 "soft landing" spurred debate over new labor attitudes, technological developments, and the increased scope for accommodating growth. Second, the financial crises of 1997–1999 intensified debate over the precrisis need for monetary policy to

---

[40] Woodward (2000, 144–146).
[41] Woodward (2000, 146).
[42] Greenspan (2007, 155–156).

contain asset-price bubbles or the postcrisis acceptability of simply "mopping up" by providing lender of last resort assistance. Third and finally, successes in fine-tuning and lender of last resort efforts together over 1999–2000 raised concerns regarding the need for regulation, as greater monetary policy acumen seemed to enhance the case for deregulation.

## The Scope for Monetary Policy Accommodation – Technology and Trauma

The policy successes of the mid-1990s – as unemployment fell toward 5 percent – would lead to an intensification of debate over the limits to growth and the lower bound that unemployment might hit before reigniting inflation. First, at the December 1995 FOMC meeting, Greenspan raised "the big picture of technological change" as an explanation for why "at least for a while, time-honored rules of thumb might not apply."[43] Pressing the issue at the September 24, 1996 FOMC meeting, Greenspan argued that "the rate of increase in productivity is a lot higher than is shown by the conventional numbers."[44] This mattered to the extent that it helped "to explain the extraordinary [restrained] behavior of prices when wage increases are very clearly accelerating." Greenspan argued that "we can explain it only if productivity is indeed rising a lot faster than our statistics indicate."[45] Looking back, Greenspan later argued that rising productivity meant that, even given the approach to a below-5 percent unemployment in September 1996, "raising interest rates would be a mistake." While "always wary of inflation," he later argued that he had felt "that the risk was much lower than many of my colleagues thought," because increasing productivity had altered the implications of wage increases.[46] Put differently, where workers provided their employers with a higher productivity, this would undercut any pressure wages might place on prices.

Second, Greenspan posited that worker attitudes had evolved since the 1970s, arguing that "traumatized workers" may be more concerned for possible job losses than wages, providing a crucial source of

[43] Greenspan (2007, 167).
[44] Federal Open Market Committee (1996, 27).
[45] Federal Open Market Committee (1996, 28).
[46] Greenspan (2007, 171).

wage-price restraint.[47] At the December 1995 FOMC meeting, he elaborated that "a very significant increase in the sense of job insecurity" and a broader "trade-off between job insecurity and wage increases ... increasingly explains why wage patterns have been as restrained as they have been."[48] This argument might also be seen as of a piece with institutional arguments regarding the post-PATCO reduction in labor militancy. However, Greenspan also encountered difficulties in making these quasi-sociological arguments – which he employed to resist pressures for preemptive tightening – as they conflicted with his colleagues' own rationalist worldviews. To overcome FOMC objections, he was forced to rely on support from Yellen in "translating" his views into acceptable economic language. As Bob Woodward later recounted, "Yellen thought Greenspan spoke a language different from what was taught in graduate school ... the chairman's language was highly idiosyncratic ... At the FOMC, Yellen noticed that the Ph.D.'s on the committee, or some members of the staff, would be nearly rolling their eyes as the chairman voiced his views ... Nobody challenged him or dared say anything, but it weakened his hold on the committee." In this context, Yellen sought to help the chairman, as she "told Greenspan that she might be able to find a theoretical underpinning for his job insecurity thesis" as she proceeded to draft "a 13-page memo that ... concluded that since workers had been paid more in the earlier years of the 1990s, the higher pay had induced them to feel greater attachment to their jobs and to be more productive." Greenspan himself later thanked Yellen for providing "an economically conventional way of saying what he wanted to say."[49]

### The Scope for Monetary Policy Accommodation – From Leaning to Cleaning

However, efforts to balance inflation and unemployment might in turn be complicated to the extent that the Greenspan Federal Reserve placed – into the mid-1990s – a stress on a third goal, of containing asset-price pressures. This might have been addressed via regulatory means, but Greenspan was wary of regulatory responses to asset-price

---

[47] Woodward (2000, 168).
[48] Federal Open Market Committee (1995, 36).
[49] Woodward (2000, 169).

bubbles. For example, while Greenspan conceded the potential for "increasing margin requirements" and guaranteed that "if you want to get rid of the bubble, whatever it is, that will do it," he also argued to his colleagues on the FOMC that "I am not sure what else it will do" – suggesting that regulation might risk inefficiencies of its own.[50] Instead, in an initial attempt to address asset bubbles, Greenspan would seek to "talk down" asset prices. In a December 1996 address at the American Enterprise Institute, Greenspan argued that while "sustained low inflation implies less uncertainty about the future," it was possible over time that such reductions in uncertainty might fuel an "irrational exuberance." While citing the 1987 stock crash as "a collapsing financial asset bubble" that "had few negative consequences for the economy," Greenspan warned against complacency and concluded that "evaluating shifts in balance sheets generally, and in asset prices particularly, must be an integral part of the development of monetary policy."[51] Greenspan would reaffirm these concerns in a February 1997 FOMC meeting as he noted that the Dow was approaching 7,000 and suggested that "we might need an interest rate increase to try to rein in the bull."[52] On February 26, Greenspan engaged in a further bit of moral suasion in testimony before the Senate Banking committee, urging "caution ... with regard to the sharp rise in equity prices during the last two years."[53] Yet, revealing his underlying discomfort, when Greenspan was asked a week later before House Banking Committee whether he was "jawboning" the market, he would reply that was "not what I was intending to do ... It can't be done."[54] On March 25, the Federal Reserve would seek to address the rising market with a more traditional rate hike, in a signal to asset markets.[55]

Yet, this restraining move would prove the last for a while, as Greenspan's tightening was disrupted in mid-1997 when Thailand, the Philippines, Indonesia, and Malaysia abandoned exchange-rate pegs

[50] Federal Open Market Committee Transcript (1996).
[51] Greenspan (1996).
[52] Greenspan (2007, 178).
[53] Greenspan (1997a).
[54] Woodward (2000, 182).
[55] Highlighting the limits to Greenspan's moral suasion, Federal Reserve Governor Lawrence Meyer would later point to research suggesting that "while 'central bank talk' about the outlook and monetary policy prospects had a significant effect on interest rates, the Chairman's comments on the stock market had very little effect on stock prices." Meyer (2004, 144).

and their currencies collapsed. While later years would see policymakers speak of the need for an economic "Powell Doctrine" of sorts – justifying massive interventions to stabilize markets – the Mexican precedent had created some concern within the White House that too-ready a recourse to currency interventions might fuel a congressional backlash. Indeed, in the midst of the Asian crisis, Bill Clinton stressed his fear of getting the "black helicopter crowd stirred up" lest he move too aggressively.[56] US policymakers would more seriously engage the Asian crises when instability spread to South Korea in November. Given South Korea's greater importance as the world's eleventh-largest economy and the security concerns on the Korean peninsula, this would motivate rapid support for a Mexico-styled bailout. Yet, this Korean assistance would exhibit at most limited success, necessitating more direct "arm-twisting" of private actors by Rubin, Greenspan, and New York Federal Reserve President Bill McDonough in December 1997, leading them to reschedule $22 billion in loans and so keep funds flowing into Korea.[57]

In 1998, global instability continued to increase, as a Russian default sparked a global economic collapse and, over the final week of August, prompted a 12 percent collapse on Wall Street. In September 1998, these shocks would lead to the collapse of the hedge fund Long Term Capital Management (LTCM), promoting the Federal Reserve to not only organize a "bail-in," but also push through three quarter-point rate cuts from September to October 1998, bringing the Fed funds rate down to 4.5 percent.[58] Justifying this easing, the Federal Reserve Board would argue in its 1998 *Annual Report* that it had sought to "balance two major risks to the economic expansion." On the one hand, fearing an overheating, "with the domestic economy displaying considerable momentum and labor markets tight," the FOMC sought to prevent the "emergence of imbalances that would lead to higher inflation." On the other hand, fearing an economic collapse, the FOMC was concerned that "troubles in many foreign economies and resulting financial turmoil both abroad and at home seemed, at times, to raise the risk of an excessive weakening of aggregate demand."[59] Here the

---

[56] Branch (2009, 513).
[57] Meyer (2004, 110); Woodward (2000, 190–191).
[58] Greenspan (2007, 195); Woodward (2000, 211–212).
[59] Board of Governors of the Federal Reserve System (1998, 5).

subjective risk estimates of Greenspan and his colleagues would play a major role in shaping the decision to err in the direction of stimulus – "mopping up" in a way that saw the financial stability ultimately stop short of endangering the wider economy.

In terms of lessons learned, in looking back on the preemptive March 1997 rate increase, Greenspan later conceded that the Fed "never tried to rein in stock prices again."[60] Instead, Greenspan argued that identifying a bubble in advance "requires a judgment that hundreds of thousands of informed investors have it all wrong," while also suggesting that "bubbles that burst are scarcely benign, [but] the consequences need not be catastrophic for the economy." Continuing, he argued that "monetary policy is best primarily focused on stability of the general level of prices of goods and services."[61] With respect to the aftermath of crises, Greenspan argued that the proper approach would be to "mitigate the fallout when it occurs and, hopefully, ease the transition to the next expansion."[62] In this way, leaning against the market had yielded to cleaning after the crash.

## Deregulation: Monetary Policy Displaces Financial Regulation

Moving to a third stage of debate, the policy rethinking pertained not only to monetary policy and lender of last resort accommodation, but also the scope for regulation. Although Clinton had briefly stressed the need for a "New International Financial Architecture" as a foundation for a new post-Asian crisis framework, the postcrisis recovery broke any reformist momentum. Instead, within the Clinton administration, the end of the 1990s saw movement toward a near-groupthink-styled overconfidence in liberalization. Indeed, the pressure was so great that even where leading figures such as Treasury Secretary Rubin and Securities and Exchange Commission (SEC) Chair Arthur Levitt had marginal doubts regarding newer financial trends – e.g., with respect to derivatives – they would yield to the conventional wisdom. Ironically, prior to entering government, Rubin's experiences at Goldman Sachs had left him wary of the potential for derivatives as

[60] Greenspan (2007, 179).
[61] Greenspan (1999a).
[62] Greenspan (1999b).

a source of unmanageable liabilities. Yet, within the administration, Rubin's wariness was seen as reflecting a certain stodginess, leading Deputy Treasury Secretary Larry Summers to compare Rubin to a tennis player who kept playing with a wooden racket. Rubin later recalled that Summers "thought I was overly concerned with the risks of derivatives [on grounds that] ... derivatives serve an important purpose in allocating risk." Nevertheless, given Rubin's past experiences in seeing private agents take risks they did not fully understand, he would concede that even as Summers' position "held together under normal circumstances" it seemed to overlook "what might happen under extraordinary circumstances."[63] In this light, even as Rubin would seem to have been at the height of his influence, he was as constrained as anyone by the prevailing conventional wisdom – and acceded to Summers' views.

Given these pressures to unanimity, what opponents there were – most notably Commodity Futures Trading Commission (CFTC) Chair Brooksley Born – would often be dismissed as ill-informed. Taking office in August 1996, Born confronted the antiregulatory consensus at a meeting with Greenspan, at which she claimed that he had voiced opposition to regulation to prevent fraud, on the grounds that "if a floor broker was committing fraud, the customer would figure it out and stop doing business with him." When Born – as a lawyer – sought to counter this view, Greenspan allegedly countered that "I guess you and I will never agree about fraud."[64] In this context, Born increasingly came to question whether derivatives should enjoy their continued exemption from regulatory oversight. Although a key justification for their exemption had been their ostensibly customized nature, Born noted that "swaps had become so commonplace that many of them were practically standardized and used off-the-shelf contract language" in ways that would seem to justify the establishment of exchanges and efforts to promote transparency.[65] In December 1997, the Securities and Exchange Commission (SEC) floated a proposal for

---

[63] Reflecting later on his failure to express his concerns more forcefully, Rubin argued that "[a]ll of the forces in the system were arrayed against it" and as the financial industry "certainly didn't want any increase in these requirements. There was no potential for mobilizing public opinion." Goodman (2008); quote in text from Rubin and Weisberg (2003, 288).
[64] Roig-Franzia (2009).
[65] McLean and Nocera (2010, 100).

a "Broker Dealer Lite" regime, which would entail voluntary disclosure by investment banks. However, in Born's view, the CFTC had exclusive jurisdiction over such matters, and she directed her deputy Michael Greenberger to draft a "concept release" response, posing "a series of open-ended questions aimed at 'reexamining' the agency's approach to derivatives."[66]

In March 1998 – only a few months before the Russian default and LTCM crash – Born distributed this draft throughout the executive branch, inciting a broad backlash. In one early confrontation, Summers told her that he had just met with "a group of bankers who said that if the CFTC insisted on pursuing their concept release, they would move their derivatives business to London."[67] Soon thereafter, in late April 1998, the President's Working Group – made up of key advisers, including Greenspan, Rubin, and Levitt – met, with Rubin taking the lead in opposing the release.[68] Highlighting tendencies to groupthink, Levitt recalled that the rest of the Working Group "tended to follow the leadership of those all-powerful financial officers." Reflecting on his own failure to speak, he recalled that "I got caught up in the argument and ... could have made a difference."[69] Following two weeks of runaround from Treasury, the CFTC published the release – prompting Rubin, Greenspan, and Levitt to request that Congress block the CFTC's efforts. In August 1998, these attitudes would briefly soften, as the Russian and LTCM crises spurred broader reflection on the regulation of derivatives. Indeed, at an October 1998 Senate banking committee hearing, Republican Chairman Leach said to Born, "We owe you an apology."[70] Nevertheless, Congress froze the CFTC's regulatory authority for six months, and stripped the SEC and CFTC of any authority to regulate derivatives. Combined with the Gramm-Leach-Bliley Act of 1999, which had removed Glass-Steagall-era barriers between investment and commercial banking, the Commodity Futures Modernization Act of 2000 can be seen as manifesting a deregulatory consensus in full legislative form.

While it may appear puzzling that a decade of recurring crises had failed to force a reconsideration of the Neoliberal stress on

[66] McLean and Nocera (2010, 104).
[67] McLean and Nocera (2010, 104).
[68] McLean and Nocera (2010, 104–105).
[69] Levitt (2009).
[70] McLean and Nocera (2010, 107).

deregulation, this is less surprising to the extent that Federal Reserve fine-tuning was seen as enabling their recurring resolution. For example, in November 1997, Summers would cite the Peso crisis as a success story, arguing that it had "worked out very well. Mexico grew at 8 percent in the last year." Foreshadowing later arguments regarding public support for private banks in the Global Financial Crisis, Summers would argue that US tax payers had "gotten paid back early" and "actually turned a $500 million profit," concluding that with the prompt provision of immediate assistance, "you can rebuild confidence and you can get that psychology back on your side."[71] Similarly, Rubin argued in a January 1998 address at Georgetown University that bailout-styled responses were justified given the utilitarian costs to the economy of failing to take such steps. Rubin would assert that he "would not give one nickel to help any creditor or investor," but then suggested that those who urged "that we must ensure that all creditors take a loss" overlook the "reality of the situation" in which a "byproduct of programs designed to restore stability and growth may be that some creditors will be protected from the full consequences of their actions."[72] Such claims that the imperatives of economic recovery precluded reform would in this way delay institutional change, while ensuing recovery would ironically deprive reform advocates of political support.

By the end of the decade, a degree of confidence in the scope for fine-tuning would be widely shared – as John Kenneth Galbraith argued that Keynes himself "would have found much to admire in Alan Greenspan's policies" and his longtime rival Milton Friedman would ask whether Greenspan has "an insight into the economy and the shocks that other people don't have?'"[73] By February 1999, *Time* magazine would put Greenspan, Rubin, and Summers on its cover as the "Committee to Save the World." Giving voice to this intellectual confidence, Greenspan would later argue that by the 1980s, "a rejuvenated but somewhat chastened Keynesianism, with a stagflation fix to reflect the importance of inflation expectations, re-emerged." Greenspan specifically lauded "[t]he model constructed by Federal Reserve staff, combining the elements of Keynesianism, monetarism,

---

[71] Summers (1997).
[72] Rubin (1998).
[73] Frankel and Orzag (2002, 19); Parker (2005, 583–584).

and other more recent contributions to economic theory" as "particularly helpful to the Fed's Board of Governors over the years of my tenure."[74] Over the next decade, this overconfidence would provide a key source of policy accommodation, as the aftermath of the technology bubble collapse spurred fiscal, monetary, and regulatory easing – at the cost of setting the stage for the subprime bubble and Global Financial Crisis.

## 7.5 Conclusions

Over the 1980s, the Reagan-era construction of the principled foundations of the Neoliberal order would see the market power of labor broken and the market power of finance established. In this setting, Clinton would seek less to challenge the prevailing Neoliberal order than to work within its premises, enabling its intellectual conversion as a commitment to budgetary restraint would be combined with acceptance of the Federal Reserve's discretionary fine-tuning. However, Clinton did not merely acquiesce to the Neoliberal order. Instead, he would help to refine it in key ways, not simply in a rapid response to the 1994–1995 Mexican peso crisis and embrace of a balanced budget, but also via New Keynesian appointments to the Federal Reserve. In this light, while Greenspan had commenced a tightening in 1994, appointees such as Alan Blinder and Janet Yellen would urge a more balanced, Taylor rule-styled approach to reconciling concerns for limiting inflation and boosting employment. These moves mattered not only for the Clinton administration, but also for the stability of the Neoliberal order – as the New Classical frameworks that had justified the early 1980s renunciation of fine-tuning of wage-price spirals were increasingly inadequate to a mid-1990s context requiring the fine-tuning of asset-price trends. Where the Clinton administration advanced the conversion of the Neoliberal order in a more New Keynesian direction, it played a key role in keeping the order on an even keel.

Moving forward, intellectual debates over discretionary macroeconomic policy and regulatory initiatives evolved across efforts to promote a mid-1990s soft-landing, fears regarding "irrational exuberance," and concerns for the cost of regulation. First, as the Federal

[74] Greenspan (2013, 7).

Reserve gradually eased into 1996, Greenspan stressed the importance of technological change and a "traumatized worker" phenomenon in expanding the room for monetary easing. Second, however, even as the Federal Reserve saw concerns for wage-price spirals reduced, this would be undercut by concerns for asset-price bubbles and irrational exuberance. These concerns justified a brief attempt at tightening in early 1997, but this in turn came into conflict with the need to promote recovery from the Asian Financial Crisis – leading to an eventual renunciation of monetary restraint as a means to forestall crises. Third and finally, the perceived successful handling of the late 1990s Asian, Russian, and LTCM crises prompted a relaxation of concerns for regulation. Instead, the Greenspan Federal Reserve would come to favor an approach of accommodating bubbles, mitigating the fallout, and easing the transition to a revived growth. Yet, even as this policy mix of fine-tuning and deregulation had merit, it would prove destabilizing where it engendered misplaced certainty in what Ben Bernanke later termed a "Great Moderation" of economic performance – obscuring concentrations of market power and speculative pressures that would mount into the 2000s.

# 8 Constructing the Global Financial Crisis: From Accommodation to Iteration

"You never want a serious crisis to go to waste."
          Obama chief of staff designate Rahm Emanuel, November 2008[1]

"Governments should practice the same principle as doctors: First, do no harm."
          Barack Obama, April 14, 2009, Georgetown University[2]

## 8.1 Introduction/Overview

To the extent that the crises of the 1930s and 1970s held lessons for the Global Financial Crisis, Obama Chief of Staff Rahm Emanuel argued that "You never want a serious crisis to go to waste." From this perspective, just as the crises of the 1930s and 1970s had reshaped earlier orders, so the Global Financial Crisis might enable a new great transformation, ushering in large-scale reform. Yet, such expectations of punctuated change obscured the often-iterative nature of past transformations, as what appeared sudden shifts "from a distance" often, on closer inspection, were marked by alternating periods of retreat and advance. In past crises, initial policy concerns for recovery often held back reformist advance, with pressures for more lasting change building across several moments of instability. Consider that it had taken nearly two decades – from the Great Crash of 1929 to the banking crises of 1933, across the 1937 recession, and through wartime inflation – for the final outlines of the Keynesian order to form. Likewise, the Great Stagflation of the 1970s had an iterative character, with diminishing returns from fine-tuning revealing themselves over several bouts of inflation, before Reagan and Volcker finally succeeded in employing legal and monetary measures to reshape labor

[1] Seib (2008).
[2] Obama (2009e).

expectations. From this vantage point, Emanuel's principled suggestion that one should never let a crisis "go to waste" must be situated alongside a more utilitarian contemporaneous view – voiced by Barack Obama, and shared by Treasury Secretary Geithner and National Economic Commission Chair Lawrence Summers – that policy should "do no harm" to any incipient recovery. Making sense of responses to the Global Financial Crisis requires situating these two views together, as debate was shaped by contending concerns for fast thinking reform and slow thinking recovery.

Building on these insights, I highlight in this chapter not only the role of misplaced certainty in the run-up to the Global Financial Crisis – as it obscured the emergence of new concentrations of market power and speculative dynamics – but also the tensions between Emanuel-styled principled reform and Obama-styled utilitarian recovery as these shaped responses to the crisis. In the first section of this chapter, I accordingly address the collapse of the technology bubble and concerns for post–September 11 deflation, as these not only spurred initially successful Neoliberal efforts at monetary, fiscal, and regulatory accommodation, but also reinforced misplaced certainty in a "Great Moderation" and led policymakers to overlook increases in market power and risk taking. In the second section, I focus on the Bernanke-era misplaced confidence in the policy contributions to a Great Moderation, as Bernanke would underrate the risks inherent in seeking to align market and policy expectations, overrate the dangers of revived wage-price pressures, and overlook the speculative dynamics fueling the subprime bubble. In the third section, I argue that even as the Global Financial Crisis enabled a fast-thinking principled engagement – as Obama stressed the public interest in reforms to *restrain* private risk taking – such reformist impulses would also be undercut by slow-thinking-styled utilitarian concerns that reform might threaten recovery – as policymakers undertook monetary, fiscal, and regulatory accommodation to *promote* private risk taking. To be sure, I also acknowledge important advances that followed the Global Financial Crisis – in antitrust-styled efforts to reform derivatives markets and efforts at macroprudential regulation. Yet, these would be accompanied by a continued Neoliberal commitment to accommodating asset-price bubbles via "too big to fail" arrangements. In this light, I conclude that the Global Financial Crisis is best seen as advancing iterative change, as the need for a "great accommodation" undercut any "great transformation."

## 8.2 The First Great Accommodation: Monetary, Fiscal, and Regulatory Accommodation

Where the Asian crises of 1997–1998 initially spurred a broad monetary easing, the Federal Reserve would pull back as it raised interest rates over 1999, seeking to unwind the stimulus – as rates would peak at 6.5 percent in May 2000. Looking back, Greenspan recalled that policymakers sought "first to take back the liquidity we'd added to the system to safeguard it during the international financial crisis" and then to take back a "little more" as insurance "against the tightness of the U.S. labor market." In this way, the Federal Reserve positioned its monetary policy "to try for another soft landing when the business cycle ultimately turned."[3] Yet, having succeeded in its mid-1990s efforts to accomplish a soft landing, the Federal Reserve would encounter greater difficulties in the new decade, as the early-2000 collapse of the technology stock bubble would see Nasdaq peak at over 5,000, before going on to lose more than half its value by the year's end. This crash would combine with a brief late 2000 recession – as after the unemployment rate hit its low point of 3.9 percent in October 2000, it would gradually rise to 4.5 in April 2001 and 4.9 percent in August 2001.[4]

In the absence of a repeat soft landing, monetary, fiscal, and regulatory policies would move to a broadly expansionary stance. First, monetary moves would come almost immediately with the onset of

---

[3] Greenspan (2007, 202, 211–212).
[4] The limits of monetary policy in dealing with concentrations of market power could also be seen over this period. While overall inflation rose from 1.6 percent in 1998 to 3.4 percent by 2000, this did not reflect any economy-wide trend. Instead, inflation remained contained in more perfectly competitive sectors, as the price of services inched up by only 2.6 percent in 1999 and 3.9 percent in 2000. In contrast, prices increased much more rapidly in oligopolistic sectors – most importantly, energy, where it rose by 13.4 percent in 1999 and by 14.2 percent in 2000. The FOMC had itself noted this in its June 1999 meeting, suggesting that increased consumer prices were "associated in part with a jump in energy prices" and that producer prices "also were affected by the volatility of energy prices." Federal Open Market Committee (1999); Council of Economic Advisers (2003, 319, 350).

recession, as Greenspan would convene an emergency Federal Open Market Committee (FOMC) meeting via conference call on January 3, 2001 to cut the federal funds rate by a half point, to 6 percent.[5] Over 2001, the FOMC would continue in this trend, bringing the federal funds rate down to 3.5 percent by August 2001. The September 11 terrorist attacks would subsequently lead the Federal Reserve to implement another six rate cuts into 2003 – reflecting concerns for not simply economic forces but the wider societal trauma. Given this backdrop, the December 2001 collapse of the Enron corporation amid a wave of corporate scandals would see the federal funds rate taken down further to 1.25 percent by November 2002. Yet, this was still not the end of the accommodation. With the slow recovery and 6 percent unemployment fueling fears of a self-reinforcing deflation, Greenspan would take rates down one more quarter point, to 1 percent.[6]

Second, while fiscal policy is often less flexible than monetary policy, it was "set to move" in early 2001, given both the accumulation of surpluses over the late Clinton term and the George W. Bush campaign's pledges for substantial tax cuts. Through the campaign, Bush had signaled that he would not repeat his father's "read my lips"-era heresies, affirming in a January 2000 primary debate that his pledge was "not only 'no new taxes.' [but] … 'tax cuts, so help me God.'"[7] To be sure, the Bush campaign's principled position of tax cuts was not based on any anticipation of the 2001 recession. However, the recession would reinforce arguments for fiscal easing. Moreover, Greenspan would himself provide crucial political cover for the cuts, disappointing his Clinton-era allies, who feared that he was squandering the surplus. Greenspan would counter that his goal was to seek a middle ground between restraint and stimulus, working with Treasury Secretary Paul O'Neill to argue for "triggers" that might limit tax cuts should deficits reappear. However, the Bush administration would reject such qualifications, on grounds that supply-side incentives would have to be permanent to have their full effect. In this light, Greenspan later conceded that he had been politically naïve, having "misjudged the emotions of the moment."[8] Ultimately, Bush was able to advance a

---

[5] Greenspan (2007, 213).
[6] Council of Economic Advisers (2007, 280).
[7] Woodward (2006, 16).
[8] Greenspan (2007, 222).

$1.35 trillion cut, one which combined broad cuts in marginal rates with a short-term $40 billion Keynesian stimulus, amounting to as much as $600 per household – with checks fortuitously arriving in the mail in the weeks after the September 11 attacks.

Third and finally, these two forms of macroeconomic accommodation would be supplemented by regulatory accommodation, particularly in the lax approach to the subprime and securitization bubbles. Such accommodation spurred demand by enabling new loans that drove up real estate values and, in turn, wealth. In November 2002 congressional testimony, Greenspan would note the importance of the housing bubble to recovery, casting mortgage markets as "a powerful stabilizing force over the past two years of economic distress by facilitating the extraction of some of the equity that home-owners had built up" and emphasizing the importance of "the turnover of the housing stock, home equity loans, and cash-outs associated with the refinancing of existing mortgages."[9] In February 2004, he reiterated this point, referring to "a large extraction of cash from home equity" that had in turn "supported personal consumption expenditures and home improvement."[10] Looking back, he would elaborate that "Consumer spending carried the economy through the post-9/11 malaise, and what carried consumer spending was housing."[11] (The key reform to come out of the dot-com crash would be the Sarbanes-Oxley Act of 2002, which provided a "microprudential" focus on the management of accounting firms, remaining short of later "macroprudential" reforms that might limit systemic risk taking.)

Taken as a whole, this combination of monetary, fiscal, and regulatory accommodation reflected an increasingly misplaced certainty in discretionary macroeconomic policymaking, rooted in attachments to New Keynesian heuristics like the Taylor rule, in emergent historical arguments for a Great Moderation, and in disciplinary groupthink that repressed insights from other schools of thought. First, these policies of accommodation reflected the Federal Reserve's integration of

---

[9] Greenspan (2002).
[10] Greenspan (2004b).
[11] Greenspan would later even publish a paper showing that from 2001 through 2004, "borrowing against home equity by American households generated an average of $425 billion per year in spendable cash," doubling the $177 billion "generated annually during the preceding four-year period." Quoted in Van Overtveldt (2009, 99–100); quotes in text from Greenspan (2007, 229–230).

New Keynesian frameworks like the Taylor rule with an increasing willingness to employ subjective discretion –what Greenspan termed "risk management" – in modifying their dictates. Illustrating this Federal Reserve methodology in a 2004 address, Greenspan would contrast types of "uncertainty" which plague monetary policy, contrasting Knightian uncertainty, "in which the probability distribution of outcomes is unknown," from risks that could be expressed in "a known probability distribution."[12] Given this distinction, Greenspan conceded that formal models like the Taylor rule may often work as optimal guides to the effects of policy actions of economic trends – explicitly noting that, "[a]s John Taylor has emphasized, in the face of an incipient increase in inflation, nominal interest rates must move up more than one-for-one." However, Greenspan also argued that policymakers must also be open to the possibility that "the true structure of the economy" may change in ways that require adjusting such relationships. Reflecting such concerns, Greenspan argued that Federal Reserve policymakers had moved in 2003 toward a pronounced easing, seeking to limit deflation "even though baseline forecasts from most conventional models ... did not project deflation."[13] Put differently, even as Federal Reserve officials did not believe deflation was likely, they saw its potential costs as sufficiently severe to outweigh the risks of overstimulating the economy. As Greenspan later put it, "on the basis of a balancing of risk," the FOMC was "willing to chance that by cutting rates we might foster a bubble [or] an inflationary boom."[14] Yet, even as Greenspan's approach appears prudent in recognizing the need to adjust the weighting of variables in a policy mix, it did not extend to questioning the components of policy mix. This remained locked into a backward-looking stress on labor market trends and the use of discretionary monetary policy to moderate wage-price pressures, to the neglect of the shifts in financial market power and speculative dynamics that drove asset-price pressures and which might be addressed through a wider array of regulatory and macroprudential measures.

Second, providing a historical narrative to reinforce this misplaced certainty, then Federal Reserve Board member – prior to serving as

[12] Greenspan (2004a).
[13] Greenspan (2004a).
[14] Greenspan (2007, 229).

Chair of the Bush Council of Economic Advisers and eventual Federal Reserve Board Chair – Ben Bernanke would claim that a "Great Moderation" encompassing a "remarkable decline in the variability of both output and inflation" had emerged in recent years, producing a state in which recessions had become "less frequent and less severe." From this perspective, while the poor state of economic knowledge had contributed to the economic disarray of the 1970s, the New Keynesian refinement of intervening decades had made possible this improvement. Lauding the trend to "deregulation in many industries" for having "increased macroeconomic flexibility and stability," Bernanke argued that monetary policy "played a large part in stabilizing inflation" and "helped moderate the variability of output as well."[15] In a similar elucidation of this conventional wisdom, Bernanke would, in an address in honor of Milton Friedman, stress the effectiveness of lender of last resort activism and endorse Friedman's stress on maintaining a stable monetary environment in post-crisis settings.[16] Taken as a whole, deregulation, prudent monetary fine-tuning, and post-crisis activism were all seen as key ingredients enabling a Great Moderation.

Finally, such views would embody an increasing overconfidence as key figures – including Greenspan, Summers, and New York Federal Reserve President Timothy Geithner – cultivated a groupthink-styled climate of limited debate, limiting in particular insights from behavioral economics regarding the scope for market abuses and risk taking which might justify greater regulation. For example, Greenspan would dismiss concerns for subprime abuses raised by Federal Reserve Governor Edward Gramlich – who chaired the Federal Reserve Committee on Consumer and Community Affairs – on moral hazard grounds, warning that "if we publicly announced that we were regulating these institutions," this might enable "egregious lenders" to fleece "subprime borrowers at a much higher rate."[17] Similarly, at the August 2005 Jackson Hole conference, Summers would counter regulatory arguments advanced by IMF Chief Economist Raghuram Rajan, who argued that remuneration policies providing incentives to private risk taking could justify regulatory countermeasures. Rajan argued that

---

[15] Bernanke (2004a).
[16] Bernanke (2002b).
[17] Wessel (2009, 63).

bonus-driven incentive structures could encourage agents to take "risks that generate severe adverse consequences with small probability" and "to herd with other investment managers" in ways that could "move asset prices away from fundamentals."[18] Rajan concluded that where "monetary policy alone is insufficient," pay regulation could have "a macro-prudential rationale."[19] In reply, Summers criticized Rajan's "Luddite" premise, objecting to "the tendency toward restriction that runs through the tone of the presentation" as one that might "support a wide variety of misguided policy impulses in many countries."[20] Retreating, Rajan would move to "cite Chairman Greenspan" on regulation, accepting that one should "as the medical profession is advised, do no harm."[21] Finally, at the New York Federal Reserve, newly installed President Timothy Geithner would dismiss warnings of a subprime bubble from the behavioral economist Robert Shiller, who sat on the Bank's Advisory Board. Shiller later recalled feeling like he was "violating groupthink" by raising the issue and worrying that the notion of a bubble "sounded like a newspaper term." Geithner subsequently removed Shiller from the board.[22]

Having succeeded after prolonged efforts in enabling recovery from the tech bubble, September 11 attacks, and deflation scare, the Federal Reserve would over 2003 and into 2004 set aside concerns for deflation and commence a gradual tightening. This shift would occur over two years, across seventeen quarter-point increases from June 2004 to June 2006 taking the federal funds rate up to 5.25 percent. Having set this path, Greenspan would retire in January 2006 with his reputation at something of a "market peak." On February 6, 2006, President George W. Bush visited the Federal Reserve headquarters to attend the public swearing in of incoming Chairman Ben Bernanke – though it was as much to laud his predecessor Alan Greenspan, who Bush suggested was "the only central banker ever to achieve rock-star status."[23] Yet, even as Bernanke would broadly continue with Greenspan's broad approach, he would also intensify trends that obscured new sources of market power and risk taking – in a misplaced certainty regarding

[18] Rajan (2005, 315–317).
[19] Rajan (2005, 353–354).
[20] Summers, quoted in Knight (2005, 387–389).
[21] Rajan, quoted in Knight (2005, 396).
[22] Suskind (2012, 57).
[23] Wessel (2009, 50).

the scope for Federal Reserve communication via "open mouth operations" and in a misplaced concern for wage-price pressures, paralleled by neglect of concentrations of financial market power and risk taking that would prove increasingly destabilizing.

## 8.3 From Great Accommodation to Misplaced Certainty: Market Risk and Power

In taking the reins at the Federal Reserve, Bernanke maintained broad continuity with key aspects of the Greenspan playbook. First, in terms of the conduct of monetary policy, Bernanke favored a similarly New Keynesian view of a Taylor curve depicting a "menu of possible combinations of output volatility and inflation volatility from which monetary policymakers can choose in the long run."[24] Second, speaking to the scope for risk management-styled policy judgment, Bernanke argued that such rules could not substitute for a "forecast-based alternative" to account for "the changing structure of the economy" that would then enhance or moderate the prescriptions of baseline rules.[25] New York University economist Mark Gertler summed up the approach that would characterize the Greenspan and Bernanke eras, arguing that "the Fed follows a Taylor rule but not mechanically. They deviate when financial crises hit."[26] Third, with respect to taking action to clamp down on asset prices, Bernanke had long argued against the use of monetary policy to tamp down on bubbles, urging that central banks avoid "the historically relevant risk that a bubble, once 'pricked,' can easily degenerate into a panic."[27]

Building on this foundation, Bernanke would also manifest key differences that exacerbated market risk taking and obscured new sources of market power. First, as to risk taking, Bernanke built on late-Greenspan era trends in more clearly defining inflation targets and using "forward guidance" in public communications. While Greenspan had moved in this direction since the 1990s, he had never completely

---

[24] Bernanke (2004a).
[25] Bernanke elaborated that "under the forecast-based approach ... the public will generally find inferring the likely course of policy to be a great deal more difficult," increasing the importance of clear "communication ... for central banks that employ a forecast-based approach." Bernanke (2004c).
[26] Van Overtveldt (2009, 75).
[27] Bernanke and Gertler (1999, 78–81).

abandoned a preference for what he termed a "constructive ambiguity" as a means to keeping markets more competitive. Greenspan had argued that "markets uncertain as to the direction of interest rates would create a desired large buffer of both bids and offers."[28] This accords with Jacqueline Best's arguments regarding the merits of a constructive ambiguity in preventing a hardening of expectations and misplaced certainty that might eventually collapse in crisis.[29] To be sure, by the 1990s Greenspan had increasingly come to accept that markets had become "sufficiently broad and liquid" to justify "greater transparency in our deliberations."[30] Yet, Bernanke would go even further in arguing for the benefits of clarity. In the short term, Bernanke argued that improved communications would increase the "predictability of FOMC rate decisions," stabilizing financial market expectations regarding asset values. In the middle term, it would stabilize inflation expectations, as workers would become "more restrained in their wage-setting and pricing behavior." Finally, given such stable financial and labor markets, the Federal Reserve could "exert greater influence over the longer-term interest rates that most matter for spending decisions."[31] Yet, Bernanke would later be criticized for failing to recognize the ways in which market and policy certainty could counsel less moderation than risk taking. Speaking to the housing bubble, former Federal Reserve staffer Stephen Axilrod critiqued "the virtual guarantee contained in official FOMC statements that the easy availability of cheap short-term debt would be long sustained – a guarantee that probably encouraged market participants to take on more risk."[32] In sum, misplaced policy and market certainty could together fuel excessive risk taking.

Second, lacking Greenspan's sense of technological changes and "traumatized worker" dynamics, Bernanke continued to focus on the market power of labor – in effect, still "fighting the last war" from the 1970s. Having continued a prolonged tightening when he took office, this concern for inflation would lead Bernanke to take too long to loosen. In September 2007, Federal Reserve officials finally began to respond to an erosion of financial markets with a half point

[28] Greenspan (2007, 151).
[29] Best (2005).
[30] Greenspan (2007, 151).
[31] Bernanke (2004b).
[32] Axilrod (2011, 146–147).

reduction in the federal funds rate – the first cut since June 2003.[33] Yet they would remain inhibited by fears of inflation. Only three months after the collapse of the investment bank Bear Stearns, in June 2008, Bernanke warned that "some indicators of longer-term inflation expectations have risen in recent months."[34] Even as he acknowledged the "contraction in housing activity," he warned of the potential for a wage-price spiral, arguing that "the possibility that commodity prices will continue to rise [is] ... an important risk to the inflation forecast." Bernanke elaborated that if the "currently high level of inflation" were sustained, that "might lead the public to revise up its expectations for longer-term inflation" in ways that could become "embedded in the domestic wage- and price-setting process."[35] Only ten days later, in Federal Reserve deliberations, Bernanke's colleague Janet Yellen – now on the Board as President of the San Francisco Federal Reserve Bank – would note concerns for financial weakness, but similarly suggest that wage-price pressures were more pressing than asset-price instabilities.[36] In this light, Bernanke and Yellen can be seen as highlighting the tendencies of policymakers to "fight the last war" – as conceptions of market power remained associated with labor and wage-price spirals, despite the intervening accumulation of financial power.

[33] The Bush administration also shifted to recognize the need for fiscal measures. Initially, newly installed treasury secretary Paulson was opposed – saying he "hated" the idea. However, by mid-December 2007, he recognized mounting financial instability, and in mid-January 2008, Bush would propose a $150 billion fiscal stimulus, signing it into law in mid-February. Paulson (2010, 84).
[34] Bernanke (2008a).
[35] On September 11, 2008, the head of the Bank of England, Mervyn King, was arguing that output was unlikely to drop significantly over the fall, reflecting a continued concern for inflation. See Irwin (2013, 139); quotes in text from Bernanke (2008b).
[36] In the June 24 FOMC deliberations, Yellen argued that "our next move on the funds rate is likely to be up" on grounds that "there's no doubt that a wage-price spiral could develop, and dealing with it would be a very difficult and very painful problem." Yellen's concerns, however, were exacerbated by the limits of using a single tool to address two priorities – a fear of a low growth and a fear of inflation. To reconcile these competing concerns, she would employ the Taylor rule heuristic, noting that "the federal funds rate remains well below the recommendations of most versions of the Taylor rule" and so argued that it would be "appropriate going forward to at least take out some insurance against the development of a wage–price spiral mentality, and that could take the form of gradually removing that discrepancy from what, for example, a Taylor rule recommends." Federal Open Market Committee (2008a, 111–112).

In turn, this misplaced focus on wage-price inflation further masked asset-price instability – even as housing values would peak in April 2006.[37] In his first speech as Chairman of the Council of Economic Advisers, Bernanke had argued in March 2005 that "[w]hile speculative behavior appears to be surfacing in some local markets, strong economic fundamentals are contributing importantly to the housing boom."[38] Interestingly, speculative excesses had been recognized at the Federal Reserve in an "everyday" sense. For example, Research Director David Stockton offered at the December 2005 FOMC meeting "one more piece of evidence that ... the end is near in this sector." He recalled "channel surfing the other night," coming across "a new television series on the Discovery Channel entitled 'Flip That House.' ... As far as I could tell, the gist of the show was that with some spackling, a few strategically placed azaleas, and access to a bank, you too could tap into the great real estate wealth machine. It was enough to put even the most ardent believer in market efficiency into existential crisis. [Laughter]"[39] Yet, this realization aside, the subprime bubble would not spark explicit regulatory measures until late in the game. Bernanke paralleled New York Federal Reserve President George Harrison's delayed efforts at applying "direct pressure" on margin lending in 1929 – relating in his June 2008 congressional testimony the issuance of "new rules [to] apply to all types of mortgage lenders" that would "require lenders to verify the income and assets on which they rely when making the credit decision." Such measures, like those of early 1929, might have mattered more had they been applied sooner.[40]

To his credit, Bernanke would later concede that Federal Reserve oversights had stemmed from misplaced confidence regarding earlier successes, particularly the dot-com crash. Looking back, Bernanke noted that "[policy] expectations ... were shaped by the apparent analogy to the bursting of the dot-com bubble a few years earlier ... [which] was followed by only a mild recession."[41] In sum, given misplaced

---

[37] This would foreshadow a collapse in the securitization market, as the $75 billion in subprime securitizations issued in the second quarter of 2007 fell to $12 billion in the third. Financial Crisis Inquiry Commission (2011, 214).
[38] Bernanke (2005).
[39] Federal Open Market Committee (2005, 12).
[40] Bernanke (2008b).
[41] Bernanke (2014).

intellectual beliefs in the scope for coordinating market expectations, in reemergent wage-price pressures which necessitated restraint, and in the scope for "mopping up" after crises in post-dot-com fashion, policymakers would be unprepared for the post-Lehman collapse.[42]

## 8.4 The Global Financial Crisis: Fast Recovery, Slow Reform, and Iterative Change

The Global Financial Crisis, owing to its magnitude and the need for enhanced fiscal and monetary support, would compel a broadening of debate over not only the terms of monetary and fiscal accommodation but also the tensions between regulatory accommodation and financial reform. In this light, the crisis is best seen as a mechanism of iterative advance, as Obama's fast thinking communicative appeals fed expectations of reform while administration figures such as Treasury Secretary Timothy Geithner and National Economic Council Chair Larry Summers resisted such principled appeals as undercutting a necessary slow thinking focus on utilitarian gains. In the first part of this section, I address the shift in Obama's rhetoric from advocating fast thinking, principled change to slow thinking, utilitarian financial accommodation. Speaking to the scope for such retrenchment, for example, the administration would abandon support for executive pay reform and permit large bonus payments on grounds that these were needed to enable recovery by firms receiving public assistance. Similarly, the administration would cast its "stress tests" as a means to revive the confidence and risk taking necessary to recovery. In the second section, I move to highlight the iterative character of subsequent reform, particularly in the Dodd-Frank legislation – noting that even as Dodd-Frank sustained the "too big to fail" arrangements that had enabled Neoliberal asset-price accommodation, it also promoted

---

[42] Bernanke would comment on shifting views of Lehman weekend, noting that while "the conventional wisdom now is that it was obvious that Lehman should be saved but that the Fed and the Treasury ... made the big mistake of letting it go ... The truth is actually quite the opposite. Conventional wisdom at the time was overwhelmingly in favor of letting Lehman fail, but Tim, Hank and I were very much convinced that we should do everything possible not to let it fail. But then of course we ran out of options" Sorkin (2014). The Financial Crisis Inquiry Commission (2011, 340–343) would counter that loans only needed to be "secured to the satisfaction of the Federal Reserve."

macroprudential and antitrust measures, providing a potential basis for later iterations of reform.

## Shifting Constructions: Obama's Rhetorical Advance and Regulatory Accommodation

Obama's early interpretive leadership in the crisis stressed the need for fast thinking principled reform – in ways meant to secure public support for early monetary and fiscal accommodation. On monetary grounds, the Federal Reserve would follow the September 2008 $85 billion rescue of American International Group (AIG) by cutting the federal funds rate to near-zero by the year's end, and by initiating in November 2008 a first round of "quantitative easing," or asset purchases designed to pump money into the system, followed by further rounds of "QE" in late 2010 and September 2012. On fiscal grounds, the Bush administration would likewise succeed in securing the $700 billion in Troubled Asset Relief Program (TARP), followed by the Obama administration's $787 billion stimulus. Yet, to the extent that rhetorical appeals for such monetary and fiscal easing were accompanied by Bush and Obama pledges of support for financial reforms to *limit* market risk taking, they would impede the kind of regulatory easing that had seen Federal Reserve in earlier crises *promote* financial risk taking as a further means to recovery.[43] This tension would shape early Obama administration debates, as principled reform would be at odds with utilitarian recovery, forcing Obama to backtrack from fast thinking appeals in favor of slow thinking accommodation.

Indeed, particularly from September 2008 until March 2009, Obama's interpretive leadership can be seen as having favored principled appeals to populist sentiment. For example, in an October 2008 campaign speech, Obama declared that he would put in place "common-sense regulations ... that will restore accountability and

---

[43] It is worth noting that George W. Bush (2008) had provided early interpretative leadership in justifying TARP – and did not simply argue for utilitarian measures – but he would further concede the need for a rethinking of regulatory efforts, to "take a closer look at the operations of companies across the financial spectrum and ensure that their practices do not threaten overall financial stability." Acknowledging outrage over executive pay, Bush stressed that "[a]ny rescue plan ... should make certain that failed executives do not receive a windfall from your tax dollars."

responsibility in our corporate boardrooms."[44] Following his inauguration, Obama offered reinforced principled support for pay restraints, arguing in a February address that "to restore our financial system, we've got to restore trust [and] make certain that taxpayer funds are not subsidizing excessive compensation packages on Wall Street." To discourage such "shameful" practices, Obama pledged that "top executives at firms receiving extraordinary help from U.S. taxpayers will have their compensation capped at $500,000" and asserted that these measures were "only the beginning of a long-term effort ... to examine the ways in which the means and manner of executive compensation have contributed to a reckless culture."[45] Sustaining a brewing anger over executive pay, the next several months would see new developments work to increase pressure to act on pay matters. In particular, on March 11, AIG – having received $170 billion from the US government and just declared a fourth-quarter 2008 loss of $62 billion – disclosed it would pay $165 million in bonuses.[46] Obama accordingly moved to denounce "executives ... who turned to the American people, hat in hand, when they were in trouble ... [yet] paid themselves their customary lavish bonuses."[47]

Yet, even as fast thinking principled responses attracted attention, latent slow thinking utilitarian inhibitions would reassert themselves. First, this could be seen in evolving administration rhetoric. In internal administration debates, Treasury Secretary Geithner and National Economic Chair Lawrence Summers would criticize appeals for regulatory restraints as reflecting populist excess, and urge instead a utilitarian stress on the need to "first, do no harm" in any policy initiative. Only three days into the administration, at a public appearance at which Obama publically rebuked TARP-recipient firms for paying bonuses, Geithner stayed silent, viewing such appeals as embodying populist excess that could impede recovery. When handed a set of talking points by political aide Stephanie Cutter, Geithner recalled "skim[ming] ... the outrage I was expected to express," before informing Cutter that "I'm not doing this." Instead, Geithner simply "sat uncomfortably next to the President while he expressed outrage."

[44] Obama (2008).
[45] Obama (2009c).
[46] Suskind (2012, 213).
[47] Obama (2009c).

Justifying this stance, Geithner offered the utilitarian claim that "the most important thing was to repair the banking system, not to get caught up in vilifying it."[48] Looking back on the emotional context of the time, Geithner recalled a visit to meet with Bill Clinton, who argued that "when it came to the anger about bailouts and Wall Street ... the American people were just too angry to be appeased." Clinton suggested that "You could take [Goldman CEO] Lloyd Blankfein into a dark alley and slit his throat, and it would satisfy them for about two days ... Then the bloodlust would rise again."[49]

Moreover, Obama's own rhetoric would similarly be marked by increasing restraint. Indeed, in his January 2009 inaugural address, Obama had echoed Clinton's mid-1990s balance between views of government as either the "problem" or "solution" to crisis. Striking the same sort of "truce" with Reagan that Clinton had struck, Obama argued that the question was "not whether our government is too big or too small, but whether it works."[50] Subsequently, more explicitly shifting to a coordinative rhetoric, in a mid-April 2009 speech at Georgetown University, Obama would urge a more utilitarian stress on recovery. Obama argued that his administration's regulatory restraint reflected a belief that "preemptive government takeovers are likely to end up costing taxpayers even more in the end, and because it's more likely to undermine than create confidence." Concluding in utilitarian fashion, he argued that "Governments should practice the same principle as doctors: First, do no harm."[51]

Second, such utilitarian restraints would manifest themselves in institutional settings, where the Treasury resisted imposing restrictions on pay in favor of efforts to recover TARP funds. This could be seen in the crafting of a June 2009 Treasury Interim Final Rule regarding the implementation of pay controls, and its instructions to the "Special Master for Executive Compensation" – initially Washington attorney Kenneth Feinberg, who was given authority to oversee compensation standards at TARP-recipient firms.[52] However, the Treasury

---

[48] Geithner (2014, 290–291, 330–331).
[49] Geithner (2014, 330–331).
[50] Obama (2009a).
[51] Obama (2009e).
[52] Feinberg's authority pertained to compensation at the seven TARP-recipient firms, until they had repaid the government: Bank of America, Citigroup, AIG, GM, GMAC, Chrysler, and Chrysler Financial. Moreover, his authority was

assigned Feinberg something of a dual mandate. Even as he was instructed to limit incentives "to take unnecessary or excessive risks" at TARP-recipient firms, he was also expected to preserve the competitiveness of firms, by taking into account "compensation structures and amounts for persons in similar positions or roles at similar entities that are similarly situated."[53] In balancing these contending imperatives – of restraining risk and retaining employees – Feinberg recalled that Geithner "did not talk about avenging popular anger over executive pay abuses" so much as "the need to keep the seven companies in business so that the taxpayers could eventually get their money back."[54] This need to strike a balance would lead Feinberg to position himself with firms as a protector against populist excesses. Moreover, where the firms sought high bonuses to retain employees, Treasury would push Feinberg behind the scenes to privilege retention over restraint.[55] Ultimately, however, the clearest way for banks to evade pay controls would be by repaying their TARP obligations, and so they would push to exit and escape oversight.

Similarly, regulatory easing would continue as the Geithner Treasury's major economic initiative – its "stress tests" – provided a means to revive market confidence. Introduced in his first major address as treasury secretary, Geithner would use the stress tests as a political defense mechanism to fend off pressures for what he saw as populist excesses and as a means to encourage revived market confidence. Describing the process, Geithner announced that the administration would "require banking institutions to go through a carefully designed comprehensive stress test" and would "help this process by providing a new program of capital support for those institutions which need it," albeit while imposing conditions that should discourage reliance

---

limited to compensation packages for each company's top twenty-five earners, and designing compensation structures for employees twenty-six to one hundred in those firms (Feinberg, 2011, 350–351).

[53] Feinberg (2010).
[54] Brill (2010).
[55] For example, when it came to AIG, Feinberg's push for accountability was met with resistance from Treasury and the New York Federal Reserve. Feinberg was particularly frustrated as AIG executives refused to accept their own stock as part of their bonuses. Assistant Treasury Secretary for Financial Stability Herb Allison later confirmed pressing Feinberg for a compromise in which AIG executives would receive a "phantom" salarized stock that would reflect the value of the four AIG units that had turned a profit. Brill (2010).

on public assistance.⁵⁶ When the results were announced in May 2009, ten of the nineteen institutions were required to raise capital by a combined amount of $75 billion – a not-too-onerous amount.⁵⁷ Moreover, from the administration's perspective, the tests had served to buy time in the context of calls for stronger regulatory measures – and so would ease the immediacy of populist pressures.

## *From Recovery to Iterative Transformation: Reinforcing and Reforming Neoliberalism*

Given the success of fiscal, monetary, and regulatory easing in putting a floor under the crisis, the Obama administration would in late April 2009 begin shifting its attention to financial reform in earnest. To the extent that it had at first deferred financial reform, Obama would later note that the administration had been concerned that "the markets were very fragile and us trying to move forward massive legislation around banks and the financial marketplace at a time when they were still healing would have been policy malpractice."⁵⁸ Likewise, Geithner would argue that during the transition, the administration had been concerned that there were "some near-term tensions between financial reform, which would ultimately require banks to take less risk, and economic recovery, which would depend on banks getting out of their defensive crouches and taking risks again."⁵⁹ Nevertheless, the administration also faced a statutory deadline under TARP legislation of April 30 that would prompt Rahm Emanuel to call a May 2009 meeting with Geithner, Summers, and Council of Economic Advisers Chair Christina Romer to pull together an agenda. Following an hour of debate, Emanuel asked the treasury secretary to sum up "what … you need here?" prompting Geithner to argue for "systemic risk regulator, resolution authority and leverage." Emanuel added "let's throw in the consumer financial agency, and everything else can be flushed."⁶⁰ In terms of characterizing the ultimate package, Emanuel's colloquial description is not far off.

---

[56] Geithner (2009).
[57] For a broadly positive evaluation of the stress tests, see Blinder (2013, 257–260).
[58] Wolffe (2010, 172).
[59] Geithner (2014, 397–398).
[60] Suskind (2012, 282).

Formalizing its position, the Treasury Department's blueprint for reform would come out in mid-June 2009, in an eighty-nine page document *Financial Regulatory Reform*. This provided a broad foundation for the Dodd-Frank financial reform legislation passed in July 2010. Structuring its priorities, the Treasury offered a four-point domestic agenda, stressing the need to: (1) establish a systemic regulator in a Financial Stability Oversight Council, which could address macroprudential-styled concerns for systemic risk – encompassing "stronger capital and other prudential standards for all financial firms, and even higher standards for large, interconnected firms"; (2) establish a Consumer Financial Protection Bureau (CFPB) to promote transparency and simplicity in financial products; (3) enable the regulation of all segments of the financial system, particularly the "shadow banking system" where derivatives markets had concentrated risk "in opaque and complex ways"; and (4) provide new tools for liquidating failed firms and managing crises, "so that we are not left with untenable choices between bailouts and financial collapse."[61]

Taking the first broad item on the Treasury agenda, the Federal Reserve would assume the lead in developing a macroprudential regulatory agenda – defined as focused on employing regulatory measures for macroeconomic ends. For example, this could entail efforts to motivate restraint in risk taking by systemically important financial institutions through measures like countercyclical capital buffers or liquidity requirements. Moreover, where macroprudential instruments could be used to enable financial stability, they would offer the Federal Reserve an "alibi," as it could demonstrate a concern for financial stability while remaining free to keep monetary policy purely focused on its dual mandate of promoting full employment and price stability. In June 2014, Federal Reserve Chair Janet Yellen would highlight the merit of a "macroprudential approach to supervision and regulation" advancing "the construction of 'countercyclical macroprudential tools'" in a way that would limit demands on conventional monetary policy.[62] Similarly, Federal Reserve Vice Chairman Stanley Fischer would argue that "when the central bank for macroeconomic reasons

---

[61] On these points, see Department of the Treasury (2009, 3–6).
[62] Yellen (2014).

does not want to raise the interest rate," it can "use macroprudential policies" to reconcile financial stability and overall growth.[63]

Second, overlapping with consumer protection concerns on the Treasury agenda, Federal Reserve Board member Lael Brainard noted that the CFPB could itself have a macroprudential component where it "has authority to adjust the definition of qualifying mortgages, which affects mortgage credit at all lenders." While Brainard stressed that the CFPB "operates primarily under a consumer protection mandate," her analysis speaks to the institutional ambiguities that can enable ongoing policy repurposing.[64]

Third, "Hamiltonian" macroprudential efforts at restraining competitive excesses should not distract from "Jeffersonian" antitrust stresses on breaking market power. In particular, Dodd-Frank can be seen as enabling antitrust-styled efforts to promote competition rather than direct regulation, not least as Commodity Futures Trading Commission (CFTC) Chair Gary Gensler played a key role in shaping Dodd-Frank legislation. Prior to the crisis, derivatives dealers had enjoyed a high degree of market power by virtue of the opaque nature of their markets, where deals were often executed in one-to-one settings. In this light, CFTC Chair Gensler set as his main agenda the breaking of the "derivatives cartel," to force derivatives into the sunlight where they could be standardized and traded openly.[65] Of particular importance would be the more than sixty rules that the CFTC would write on matters ranging from the global reach of US regulators to the number of bids on swap purchases. For example, more bids could expose swap purchases to competitive forces and so Gensler favored a rule requiring five bids prior to any sale. In response, the industry would appeal to Barney Frank in Congress, to Securities and Exchange Commission Chair Mary Schapiro – who cast Gensler's proposal as "arbitrary" – and other CFTC commission members who pressed Gensler to cut the number to two, rising to three after a year. Nevertheless, even requiring two bids was a change over the status quo, exemplifying the CFTC's efforts to promote market competition and counter potential abuses of market power.[66]

---

[63] Fischer (2014).
[64] Brainard (2014).
[65] Suskind (2012, 173).
[66] Brush and Schmidt (2013).

Finally, even as such reforms had the potential to contain abuses of market power, utilitarian arguments to limit reform would retain force. Perhaps most strikingly in this way – given the early appeal of calls to address the "too big to fail" problem – the Dodd-Frank framework would sustain potential provisions of emergency aid to large "too big to fail" firms. This resistance speaks in large part to the ambiguity of the "too big to fail" problem – which could be seen as justifying shifting emphases on the regulation of market power, antitrust efforts to break such power, or some degree of utilitarian acceptance of the importance of such power to the economy. Anticipating the ultimate regulatory-utilitarian synthesis, Obama himself would at a late 2009 "town hall" appearance urge "reforms that involve making sure that if you've got these really big companies – the JP Morgans or the Goldman Sachses or these companies that have been called 'too big to fail' – well, you know what? If you're that big, then you better have a whole bunch of safeguards so that we don't have to bail you out if you make bad mistakes."[67] Given Obama's own unwillingness to break the power of "big" firms – and to the extent that the Neoliberal order depended on the accommodation of asset-price bubbles – the Dodd-Frank reform left in place lender of last resort supports for such large firms. While no longer able to lend to individual firms, the Federal Reserve could still lend to "classes" of institutions. Geithner would later concede that the Federal Reserve remained able to lend to "too big to fail" firms – asking "Does it still exist? … Yeah, of course it does." Geithner cast ending "too big to fail" as "like Moby Dick for economists or regulators. It's not just quixotic, it's misguided," elaborating that "there are constellations of storms, of panics, of fires that are so bad that it's very hard to imagine that you could be indifferent to the failure of the financial system"[68] In this light, Dodd-Frank would formalize the process of bailouts, rather than end them, sustaining the potential for the Neoliberal accommodation of asset-price increases.

However, with a gradual recovery, a greater rhetorical space would reemerge for reformist advocacy – as Obama's own rhetoric eventually departed again from purely utilitarian appeals. Indeed, Obama argued in his 2015 State of the Union address that "we need to set our sights higher than just making sure government doesn't screw things up …

[67] Obama (2009f).
[68] Sorkin (2014).

We need to do more than just do no harm."[69] Taken as a whole, this suggests the merit of an iterative approach to the crises that over time can surmount the ratchets against reform – with the final iteration only in retrospect appearing as a punctuated shock.

## 8.5 Conclusion: From Accommodations to an Incomplete Transformation

In this chapter, I have argued that overconfidence in a Great Moderation spurred two successive accommodations in response to the collapse of the technology bubble and the Global Financial Crisis. In the earlier case, the technology bubble's collapse would spark a rapid shift toward macroeconomic easing: on the monetary front, the Greenspan Federal Reserve commenced three years of sustained rate reductions; on the fiscal front, the Bush administration combined broad reductions in marginal tax rates with a short-term rebate that would hit soon in the aftermath of the September 11 terrorist attacks; on the regulatory front, the Greenspan Federal Reserve resisted pressures to clamp down on subprime abuses, being fully aware of the importance of rising asset values to consumption and demand. To the extent that policymakers might have had concerns for the accumulation of market power and risk taking, these were limited by an ideational consensus on a Great Moderation and the operational merits of a "risk management" approach to monetary policy. These trends would be reinforced as Greenspan's successor Ben Bernanke employed a "forward guidance" approach to monetary policy meant to enhance policy certainty while placing a revived stress on the need to contain wage-price pressures. These measures both worked to increase market confidence and led policymakers to overrate the scope for wage-price instability and overlook the dangers of financial instability, even as the collapse of Bear Stearns in early 2008 foreshadowed the excesses that culminated in the fall of Lehman Brothers.

In a second accommodation, even as the Global Financial Crisis witnessed an initial repudiation of consensus on the Great Moderation, the scope for reform would eventually be limited by utilitarian arguments that policy should "do no harm" to recovery – leading policymakers to replicate key accommodative aspects of the

[69] Obama (2015).

macroeconomic playbook from the earlier part of the decade. On the monetary front, the Federal Reserve moved not only to reduce interest rates but also shifted to promote a range of more unconventional monetary measures that included FDIC guarantees, asset purchases in a range of financial markets, rounds of quantitative easing, and – in support of Paulson's Treasury – the TARP program. On the fiscal front, the Obama administration would initiate a more decisive fiscal stimulus – in a $787 billion combination of tax cuts and spending increases. Finally, in terms of immediate regulatory efforts, the administration would be wary of undermining business confidence and so adopted a utilitarian approach that saw promises of action on executive pay and risk taking yield to a more market-friendly support for administration "stress tests." To the extent that this accommodation forestalled pressures for reform, early suggestions of a great transformation or Keynesian revival would be limited, as the ultimate Dodd-Frank reforms sustained core Neoliberal precepts, while also foreshadowing avenues for reformist advance. In terms of sustaining Neoliberal features, Dodd-Frank provided for the continued use of "too big to fail"-styled bailouts as a means to sustain asset values. However, in terms of reformist possibilities, Dodd-Frank also offered two potential avenues of change, in CFTC-styled efforts at promoting financial competition and in the Federal Reserve's concessions to the need for macroprudential measures.

Given these fast and slow thinking tensions between reform and recovery, the shift from Emanuel's November 2008 assertion that you "never want a serious crisis to go to waste" to Obama's April 2009 argument that governments should "do no harm" appears less puzzling, if no less frustrating to critics. Indeed, such tensions would be recognized by Paul Volcker himself, who lamented the unwillingness of Obama officials to recognize that reform often must "do some harm, short term ... to create the larger good." Elaborating, Volcker argued that "do no harm ... always sounds reasonable ... where there'll be consensus that we need to act in a forceful way. But you never get that consensus, because many of the actors, the institutions and so forth, will follow their own self-interest right off a cliff."[70] To be sure, one might argue that Volcker underrates the iterative challenge of achieving consensus. In 1979, Volcker had disregarded calls to "do no harm"

---

[70] Suskind (2012, 289).

in setting out to break the market power of labor – but he had been abetted by the advanced nature of Stagflationary crises, which had enabled consensus for his significant restraint. In contrast, similar support for "doing some harm" was not yet sufficiently developed in 2009. In this light, to the extent that transformative change often shifts between concerns for reform and recovery, the Global Financial Crisis may represent less a failed "great transformation" than a moment in an ongoing "iterative transformation" – in which intellectual stability inhibits adjustment to economic instability.

# PART IV
# *Conclusions*

# 9 Theoretical, Historical, and Policy Implications

You are engaged on a double task, Recovery and Reform ... even wise and necessary Reform may, in some respects, impede and complicate Recovery. For it will upset the confidence of the business world and weaken their existing motives to action, before you have had time to put other motives in their place.

John Maynard Keynes, Open Letter to President Roosevelt, 1933[1]

In a crisis, you have to choose ... Are you going to solve the problem, or are you going to teach people a lesson? They're in direct conflict.

Timothy Geithner, April 2010[2]

## 9.1 Overview – Construction, Conversion, and Crisis

Stability causes instability. Drawing on constructivist and discursive institutionalist insights, this social psychological analysis suggests that even as ideas initially play a key role in stabilizing self-reinforcing expectations, such stability can yield to self-reinforcing instability, as agents repress information in ways that cause renewed crisis.[3] Developing these insights, I have specifically offered a theoretical framework positing three stages of order development – of construction, conversion, and misplaced certainty, which fuels crises. First, economic policy orders are constructed on principled foundations, as interpretive leadership facilitates the principled construction of social, regulatory, or legal restraints on market power and speculative excess. Second, these principled beliefs over time undergo an intellectual conversion into more cognitive frameworks, as Neoclassical Synthesis or New Keynesian-styled heuristics guide macroeconomic fine-tuning.[4]

---

[1] Keynes (1936a); Minsky (1986); Shiller (2000).
[2] Green (2010).
[3] Best (2005; 2008); Blyth (2002); Schmidt (2008; 2010; 2013).
[4] Samuelson and Solow (1960); Taylor (1993).

205

To be sure, such heuristics have benefits. Yet, their strengths can also become weaknesses where they obscure new sources of market power and speculative excess. In this light, a third stage of order decline sees misplaced confidence in outmoded practices culminate in crises that spur iterations of debate over order reconstruction.

Having developed this framework, I applied it to trace the development of the Progressive, Keynesian, and Neoliberal orders – as each passed through stages of order construction, conversion, and misplaced certainty and crisis. First, Theodore Roosevelt's construction of the Progressive order – premised on a degree of balance between the interests of capital and labor – yielded to Wilson's intellectual conversion of Progressivism in the emergence of modern fiscal and monetary policy, which in turn enabled the misplaced monetary confidence of the 1920s that led to the Great Crash and Great Depression. Second, Franklin Roosevelt's construction of the Keynesian order – premised on the restraint of finance and the regulation of wage-driven demand – yielded to intellectual conversion as the Neoclassical Synthesis of the 1960s saw overconfidence in fiscal fine-tuning facilitate the unsustainable accommodation of wage-price pressures, culminating in the Great Stagflation of the 1970s. Finally, the Reagan-Volcker construction of the Neoliberal order – premised on the renewed containment of labor and accommodation of finance – would be refined via an intellectual conversion at the Federal Reserve, which fueled New Keynesian overconfidence in a Great Moderation and culminated in the Global Financial Crisis.[5]

In this conclusion, I highlight theoretical, historical, and policy implications of this analysis. First, I stress the contributions of social psychological institutionalist insights and concerns for time in enabling a more "general theory" of the construction and collapse of institutional orders – one which recognizes that self-reinforcing stability can cause self-reinforcing instability. Second, on historical grounds,

---

[5] By highlighting this recurrence of similar tendencies to institutional overconfidence – as the Council of Economic Advisers eclipsed the Federal Reserve in the 1960s and the Federal Reserve reemerged to eclipse the Council in the 1990s – this analysis demonstrates that while there always exists a need for elite expertise, the rise of any specific intellectual consensus (e.g., in the Neoclassical Synthesis or New Keynesianism) or institutional influence (e.g., of the Council of Economic Advisers or Federal Reserve) should never be taken as enduring or as given.

I suggest that insights from this argument could also be extended to other policy contexts, and so offer a parallel account of the development of *international* economic policy orders, as the Keynesian and Neoliberal orders developed and declined in parallel international settings. Finally, I address notions of pragmatic or technocratic views of ideas, highlighting a "pragmatic paradox" where efforts to limit populist ideological excesses can fuel intellectual and technocratic excesses.

## 9.2 Toward a General Theory: Stabilizing and Destabilzing Ideas in Time

This analysis speaks to the need for a more general theory of ideational stability and instability across time – as current Political Economy debates occupy two "universes" in which ideas can be either a source of stability *or* instability. Indeed, contending views of the role of ideas in promoting stability or instability often coexist in the same analyses, reflecting divergent views of the efficiency with which agents use information. Such theoretical pluralism can admittedly be useful, but scope remains for a more integrated analysis of the conditions under which ideas might promote stability *or* instability. To this end, the framework in this effort encompasses not simply a sociological sense of ideational structures, but more broadly a social psychological sense of agent inefficiencies, thereby enabling a more general theory of order development *and* decline.

First, from what might be cast as a more sociological vantage point, this analysis builds on accounts that stress the ways in which ideas *stabilize* institutions and interests in enduring fashions. As John Maynard Keynes argued, ideas enable agents to surmount a pervasive uncertainty and construct "conventions" that shape state and market interests over time.[6] In this view, ideas themselves *are* interests – or, as Alexander

---

[6] Uncertainty can be defined as a qualitative function of interpretive ambiguity – reflecting the absence of shared interpretations of reality – or as a quantitative function of limits to knowledge – reflecting the inability to form subjective probability estimates. In the latter – more rationalist –"Knightian" view, uncertainty can be managed through the construction of shared conventions that enable the better management of risks – as Greenspan (2004a) argued in the run-up to the Global Financial Crisis. In the former – more psychological – "Keynesian" view, uncertainty can pertain even to the conventions used in efforts at risk management, to the point that these conventions can either reduce uncertainty or exacerbate it in ways that generate new risks – as

Wendt defined them, "beliefs about how to meet needs."[7] Moreover, where institutionalized and internalized by agents, such ideas can take on self-stabilizing lives of their own, in ways that persist over the long run. In terms of theories of political development, for example, such insights have found expression in the work of scholars such as Martha Finnemore and Kathryn Sikkink, who model a "norm life cycle" in which norm entrepreneurs shape standards of behavior, norm leaders persuade publics of their merit, and these ideas finally assume lives of their own.[8] These insights have more broadly shaped a range of institutionalist perspectives, as scholars such as Paul Pierson and Giovanni Capoccia and R. Daniel Kelemen have sought to explain how ideas are reinforced by norms, incentives, or organizational settings in ways that take on a self-reinforcing momentum.

Yet, such frameworks often suffer from blind spots which are in turn better recognized as more social psychological perspectives stress the ways in which ideas can lead agents to repress unwanted information and fuel increasing inefficiencies. In these lights, ideas can over time play a more destabilizing role – rendering ostensibly self-reinforcing institutions prone to rapid collapse. For example, in such contexts, Keynesian insights regarding "conventions" that ostensibly promote stability can be said to "flip" and yield to Keynesian insights regarding "animal spirits" that fuel market manias. Where animal spirits become destabilized, as Keynes put it, the "practice of calmness and immobility, of certainty and security, suddenly breaks down," and all the "pretty, polite techniques, made for a well-paneled board room and a nicely regulated market, are liable to collapse."[9] In more recent Political Economy debates, such insights have found expression in the works of figures such as Michael Barnett and Martha Finnemore, who argue that institutional "pathologies" can build over time, as organizational agents may grow "insulated" from the values that they are meant to espouse, giving rise to dysfunction and inefficiencies that can potentially fuel collapse.[10]

---

Greenspan's risk management itself reinforced market confidence in destabilizing fashion. On these Knightian and Keynesian distinctions, see Best (2008).

[7] Wendt (1999, 130).
[8] Finnemore and Sikkink (1998).
[9] Keynes (1937, 115–116).
[10] Barnett and Finnemore (1999; 2004).

*Theoretical, Historical, and Policy Implications* 209

Placed side-by-side, these approaches reflect unintegrated alternative views of social reality. Like relativity and quantum mechanics, these approaches cannot be reconciled in one model. Taking his "sociological" and "social psychological" insights together, for example, Keynes writes in two ways – as the former stresses the stabilizing weight of conventions and the latter stresses the destabilizing effects of animal spirits. Likewise, Finnemore – with her coauthors – writes of sociological path-dependent dynamics that sustain norm life cycles *and* social psychological dynamics that have the potential to engender not only organizational but also order pathologies. While each perspective offers insights, the challenge is to link together such analyses to show how stable conventions can be undermined by destabilizing animal spirits, or how path-dependencies yield to pathologies.

To redress these oversights, drawing on Kahneman, the analysis offered in this volume suggests that a more explicit stress on time across stages of "fast" and "slow" thinking can be useful, as social structures *initially* shape self-reinforcing orders, but agents *subsequently* repress aspects of those orders in ways that destabilize them. In this way, by placing social *and* social psychological interactions "in time," it is possible to develop a better sense of the efficiencies enabling the construction of orders, and the inefficiencies that can endogenously fuel crises – as endogenous dynamics cause ostensibly exogenous shocks.

## 9.3 Systemic Implications: Hegemonic Stability Causes Hegemonic Instability

While this analysis has concentrated on Comparative Political Economy concerns for domestic policy orders, it also has implications for International Political Economy debates over the rise and fall of systemic orders, as misplaced certainty in systemic interventions and macroeconomic fine-tuning can also engender global instability. Consider first the collapse of the interwar international economic order. In broad terms, the mercantilist principled ethos that emerged in the aftermath of the 1919 Versailles settlement fueled a systemic culture of noncooperation that left monetary policy as the only means of stabilizing the international economic order. Yet, just as domestic monetary policy was overburdened in its challenge of reconciling growth with price stability, technocratic hubris obscured the magnitude of the global challenge of reconciling growth and currency stability. Indeed, even as the United States acted "responsibly" in cutting interest rates in late 1927 to provide the British with a comparative advantage in international financial markets, this move would help ignite the speculative boom that culminated in the Great Crash.[11] While not denying legal differences across the international and domestic realms, the same tendencies to monetary policy hubris – absent regulatory or legal tools – set the stage for international and domestic collapse.

The shift from stability to overconfidence is even more striking across the Bretton Woods order, as wage-price stability initially provided a transnational "purchasing power parity" foundation for currency stability.[12] To maintain such stabilities, incomes policies were accordingly used during the Bretton Woods era to stabilize fixed exchange rates, as the 1959–1960 US steel strike was seen by the Eisenhower administration through a systemic lens, and as Kennedy issued appeals to domestic wage-price interests that stressed the importance of low inflation to the Bretton Woods order. Likewise, the same Keynesian-Neoclassical cleavage that shaped 1960s debates over incomes policies also marked debate over multilateral arrangements, which increasingly comprised "technical" fixes favored by the Neoclassical Keynesians over more administrative measures.[13] Paralleling its silence on the wage-price guideposts, the Johnson Council would in its final *Economic Report* recast exchange rates as market-driven prices, urging greater exchange rate flexibility to facilitate international adjustment. In January 1973, the Nixon administration's dismantling of wage and price guidelines was widely interpreted as a renunciation of hegemonic responsibility in stabilizing exchange rates.[14] Market agents would subsequently – as John Odell put it – lose confidence "that central banks would back them if they held against the tide," a pessimism that eventually assumed a self-reinforcing status.[15] Over the remainder of the decade, US policy efforts at stabilizing the interplay of inflation and unemployment would be paralleled by efforts at stabilizing the dollar while promoting growth. In neither case could macroeconomic policy

---

[11] Eichengreen (1992, 218–220).
[12] Keynes (1936b).
[13] Best (2004; 2005) develops these insights in more explicit fashion.
[14] Matusow (1998, 236); Odell (1982, 321, 323); Volcker and Gyohten (1992), 112–113.
[15] Odell (1982, 302).

reconcile these dual dilemmas. It was therefore not an exogenous shift in hegemonic resources that undermined the Bretton Woods order so much as the intellectual conversion of a Keynesian global order into a Neoclassical alternative that came to rely uneasily on fine-tuning.

Finally, into the early twenty-first century, misplaced certainty in the ability of monetary policy to engineer "soft landings" would accompany a similar overconfidence in the ability of policymakers to "mop up" after recurring debt and currency crises. Over the 1990s – across the Mexican Peso Crisis and Asian Financial Crises – success in managing each round of crisis would breed policy confidence in the scope for increasing deregulation *and* fine-tuning. Such hubris culminated in the response of Federal Reserve officials to the post–September 11 deflation scare, as faith in "risk management" led to overlapping fiscal, monetary, and regulatory policy accommodation of the subprime bubble and "global savings glut" – which fed back on the global economy and, for a time, the hegemonic standing of the United States itself.

## 9.4 Policy Implications: Pragmatic Reform and Technocratic Expertise

To what degree must economic policymakers be engaged with broader public values, or – on the other hand – be insulated from inconsistent public preferences? This analysis finally has key implications for such debates over the "social distribution of knowledge" and tensions between democratic or expert authority. In addressing the construction of economic policy orders, I have argued that where interpretive leadership sustains principled consent to regulatory mechanisms, such regulatory legitimacy can ease efforts at fiscal or monetary fine-tuning. However, the subsequent atrophying of communicative connections – often, ironically, in the context of efforts to promote intellectual refinement – can leave policymakers with a diminished set of institutional and policy options. This can in turn lead to the deterioration of policy correlations and blind officials to new sources of market power or speculative excess – as stabilizing conventions yield to destabilizing animal spirits.

Put differently, this analysis suggests that initially pragmatic policymaking can blind policymakers to the need to adjust in ways that fuel excesses of technocratic certitude. Where economists and policy elites construct cognitive heuristics like the Phillips curve and Taylor rule to aid in communication with decision makers and in implementation of policy goals, such heuristics may acquire an ideological weight of their own, in ways that obscure not only changes in institutional environments, market structure, and speculative psychology – but eventually blind officials to new sources of instability and crises.[16] In this sense, a key policy challenge lies in recognizing the point at which pragmatic heuristics can become pathological blinders – as ideas which initially enhance policy effectiveness can later limit policy efficiency. Put differently, this analysis offers insights into a "pragmatic paradox": while pragmatic policymaking may require a degree of intellectual refinement, intellectual refinement may fuel later technocratic pathologies. Taken as a whole, this reinforces the larger insight of this effort – that stability can impede efficiency, in ways that cause instability and crisis.

---

[16] On pragmatism as emphasizing both this need for policy relevance and an aversion to ideological rigidities, see Rorty (1987).

# Bibliography

Abdelal, Rawi. 2007. *Capital Rules: The Construction of Global Finance.* Cambridge, MA: Harvard University Press.

Ackley, Gardner. 1965. "Memorandum for the President from Gardner Ackley, December 28, 1965, subject 'Wage Guideposts for 1966'," *Volume II, Document Supplement, Administrative History of the CEA.* [Lyndon B. Johnson Presidential Library].

——— 1966. "The Contribution of the Guidelines." In *Guidelines, Informal Controls, and the Market Place,* edited by George P. Shultz and Robert Z. Aliber, 67–78. Chicago: University of Chicago Press.

——— 1967. "Memo, Ackley to Califano, 'Wage-Price Policy,'" December 28, 1967, CEA Microfilm, Roll 64, Johnson Library.

——— 1973. "Transcript, Gardner Ackley Oral History Interview I, 04/13/73, by Joe B. Frantz." http://digital.lbjlibrary.org/files/original/d7f87950886 b4afa59a5156576fcd8b9.pdf

——— 1974. "Transcript, Gardner Ackley Oral History Interview II, 03/07/74, by Joe B. Frantz." [Lyndon B. Johnson Library].

Ackley, Gardner, Arthur Okun, and James Duesenberry. 1966. "Statement by Gardner Ackley, Chairman, Arthur M. Okun, and James S. Duesenberry, Members, Council of Economic Advisers Before the Executive and Legislative Reorganization Subcommittee of the House Committee on Government Operations on HR 11916, A Bill to Amend the Employment Act of 1946." (September 12).

Adler, Emanuel and Peter M. Haas. 1992. "Conclusion: Epistemic Communities, World Order, and the Creation of a Reflective Research Program." *International Organization* 46(1): 367–390.

Ahamed, Liaquat. 2009 *Lords of Finance: The Bankers Who Broke the World.* New York, NY: Penguin.

Akerlof, George A. and Robert J. Shiller. 2010. *Animal Spirits: How Human Psychology Drives the Economy, and Why It Matters for Global Capitalism.* Princeton, NJ: Princeton University Press.

Allen, Frederick Lewis. 1931. *Only Yesterday: An Informal History of the Nineteen Twenties.* New York, NY: Harper Perennial Modern Classics.

Alter, Jonathan. 2010. *The Promise: President Obama, Year One*. New York, NY: Simon and Schuster.

Andrews, David M. 1994. "Capital Mobility and State Autonomy: Toward a Structural Theory of International Monetary Relations." *International Studies Quarterly* 38(2): 193–218.

Appelbaum, Binyamin. 2012. "Cautious Moves on Foreclosures Haunting Obama." *New York Times* (August 19). www.nytimes.com/2012/08/20/business/economy/slow-response-to-housing-crisis-now-weighs-on-obama.html

Axilrod. Stephen. 2011. *Inside the Fed: Monetary Policy and Its Management, Martin through Greenspan to Bernanke*. Cambridge, MA: MIT Press.

Baker, Andrew (2013) "The New Political Economy of the Macroprudential Ideational Shift." *New Political Economy* 18(1):112–139.

Baker, Andrew and Wesley Widmaier (2014) "The Institutionalist Roots of Macroprudential Ideas: Veblen and Galbraith on Regulation, Policy Success and Overconfidence." *New Political Economy* 19(4): 487–506.

Baker, Peter. 2009. "The Mellowing of William Jefferson Clinton." *New York Times Magazine* (May 31). www.nytimes.com/2009/05/31/magazine/31clinton-t.html?pagewanted=all

Barber, William J. 1975. The Kennedy Years: Purposeful Pedagogy. In *Exhortation and Controls: The Search for a Wage-Price Policy 1945–1971*, edited by Craufurd D. Goodwin, 135–193. Washington, DC: The Brookings Institution.

Barnett, Michael and Martha Finnemore. 1999. "The Politics, Power, and Pathologies of International Organizations." *International Organization* 53(4): 699–732.

2004. *Rules for the World*. Ithaca, NY: Cornell University Press.

Barnett, Michael and Raymond Duvall. 2005. *Power in Global Governance*. Ithaca, NY: Cornell University Press.

Barofsky, Neil. 2012. *Bailout*. New York: Simon and Schuster.

Bell, Daniel. 1960. *The End of Ideology: On the Exhaustion of Political Ideas in the Fifties*. Cambridge, MA: Harvard University Press.

Berg, A. Scott. 2013. *Wilson*. New York, NY: Simon and Schuster.

Berger, Peter and Thomas Luckmann. 1966. *The Social Construction of Reality*. New York, NY: Anchor Books.

Berle, Adolf A. and Gardiner C. Means. 1936. *The Modern Corporation and Private Property*. New York, NY: Transaction.

Berman, Sheri. 2006. *The Primacy of Politics: Social Democracy and the Making of Europe's Twentieth Century*. New York, NY: Cambridge University Press.

Bernanke, Ben S. 2002a. "Asset-Price 'Bubbles' and Monetary Policy." Remarks Before the New York Chapter of the National Association for

Business Economics (October 15). www.federalreserve.gov/boarddocs/speeches/2002/20021015/default.htm

2002b. "Remarks at the Conference to Honor Milton Friedman." University of Chicago (November 8). www.federalreserve.gov/BOARDDOCS/SPEECHES/2002/20021108/default.htm

2002c. "Deflation: Making Sure 'It' Doesn't Happen Here." Remarks before the National Economists Club, Washington, DC (November 21). www.federalreserve.gov/boarddocs/speeches/2002/20021121/default.htm

2004a. "The Great Moderation." Remarks at the meetings of the Eastern Economic Association, Washington, DC (February 20). www.federalreserve.gov/BOARDDOCS/SPEECHES/2004/20040220/default.htm

2004b. "Central Bank Talk and Monetary Policy." Remarks at the Japan Society Corporate Luncheon, New York (October 7). www.federalreserve.gov/Boarddocs/speeches/2004/200410072/default.htm

2004c. "The Logic of Monetary Policy." Remarks Before the National Economists Club, Washington, DC (December 2). www.federalreserve.gov/boarddocs/speeches/2004/20041202/default.htm

2005. "Skills, Ownership and Economic Security." Address given at the American Enterprise Institute (July 12). http://georgewbush-whitehouse.archives.gov/cea/20050712.html

2008a. "Remarks on Class Day at Harvard University." (June 4). www.federalreserve.gov/newsevents/speech/bernanke20080604a.htm

2008b. "Semiannual Monetary Policy Report to the Congress before the Committee on Banking, Housing, and Urban Affairs." US Senate (July 15). www.federalreserve.gov/newsevents/testimony/bernanke20080715a.htm

2008c. "Federal Reserve Policies in the Financial Crisis." Remarks at the Greater Austin Chamber of Commerce, Austin, Texas (December 1). www.federalreserve.gov/newsevents/speech/bernanke20081201a.htm

2010a. "Monetary Policy and the Housing Bubble." Remarks at the Annual Meeting of the American Economic Association, Atlanta, Georgia, January 3, 2010. www.federalreserve.gov/newsevents/speech/bernanke20100103a.htm

2010b. "The Economic Outlook and Monetary Policy: Remarks at the Federal Reserve Bank of Kansas City Economic Symposium, Jackson Hole, Wyoming." (August 27). www.federalreserve.gov/newsevents/speech/bernanke20100827a.htm

2010c. "Implications of the Financial Crisis for Economics." Remarks at the Conference Co-sponsored by the Center for Economic Policy Studies and the Bendheim Center for Finance, Princeton University,

Princeton, New Jersey (September 24). www.federalreserve.gov/newsevents/speech/bernanke20100924a.htm

2013. "Transcript of Chairman Bernanke's Press Conference." (December 12). www.federalreserve.gov/mediacenter/files/FOMCpresconf20121212.pdf

2014. "The Federal Reserve: Looking Back, Looking Forward." Remarks at the Annual Meeting of the American Economic Association, Philadelphia, Pennsylvania (January 3). www.federalreserve.gov/newsevents/speech/bernanke20140103a.htm

2015. "The Taylor Rule: A Benchmark for Monetary Policy?" *Ben Bernanke's Blog*. www.brookings.edu/blogs/ben-bernanke/posts/2015/04/28-taylor-rule-monetary-policy

Bernanke, Ben and Mark Gertler. 1999. "Monetary Policy and Asset Price Volatility." In Federal Reserve Bank of Kansas City, *New Challenges for Monetary Policy*, 77–128. www.kc.frb.org/publicat/sympos/1999/S99gert.pdf

Berns, Gregory. 2008. *Iconoclast: A Neuroscientist Reveals How to Think Differently*. Cambridge, MA: Harvard Business School Press.

Bernstein, Irving. 1996. *Guns or Butter: The Presidency of Lyndon Johnson*. New York, NY: Oxford University Press.

Best, Jacqueline. 2004. "Hollowing Out Keynesian Norms: How the Search for a Technical Fix Undermined the Bretton Woods Regime." *Review of International Studies* 30(3): 383–404.

2005. *The Limits of Transparency: Ambiguity and the History of International Finance*. Ithaca, NY: Cornell University Press.

2008. "Ambiguity, Uncertainty, and Risk: Rethinking Indeterminacy." *International Political Sociology* 2:355–374.

2010. "The Limits of Financial Risk Management: Or What we Didn't Learn from the Asian Crisis." *New Political Economy* 15(1): 29–49.

Best, Jacqueline and Wesley W. Widmaier. 2006. "Micro- or Macro-Moralities? Economic Discourses and Policy Possibilities." *Review of International Political Economy* 13(4): 609–631.

Biven, W. Carl. 2002. *Jimmy Carter's Economy: Policy in an Age of Limits*. Chapel Hill, NC: University of North Carolina Press.

Blanchard, Olivier, Giovanni Dell'Ariccia, and Paolo Mauro. 2010. "Rethinking Macroeconomic Policy." *IMF Staff Position Note* (February 12), SPN/10/03. www.imf.org/external/pubs/ft/spn/2010/spn1003.pdf

Blinder, Alan. 1998. "The Fall and Rise of Keynesian Economics." *Economic Record* 64(4): 278–294.

Blinder, Alan and Ricardo Reis. 2005a. "Understanding the Greenspan Standard." Paper prepared for the Federal Reserve Bank of Kansas City symposium, "The Greenspan Era: Lessons for the Future," Jackson Hole,

Wyoming. www.kc.frb.org/PUBLICAT/SYMPOS/2005/pdf/BlinderReis.paper.0804.pdf

Blinder, Alan and Ricardo Reis, 2005b. "Understanding the Greenspan Standard," Proceedings, Federal Reserve Bank of Kansas City, (August), 11–96. www.kansascityfed.org/Publicat/sympos/2005/PDF/Blinder-Reis2005.pdf

Blinder, Alan. 2013. *After the Music Stopped: The Financial Crisis, the Response, and the Work Ahead*. New York, NY: Penguin Press HC, Kindle Edition.

Blyth, Mark. 2001. "The Transformation of the Swedish Model: Economic Ideas, Distributional Conflict, and Institutional Change." *World Politics* 54(1): 1–26.

　2002. *Great Transformations: Economic Ideas and Institutional Change in the Twentieth Century*. Cambridge: Cambridge University Press.

　2003. "Structures Do Not Come with an Instruction Sheet: Interests, Ideas and Progress in Political Science." *Perspectives on Politics* 1: 695–706.

　2013. "Paradigms and Paradox: The Politics of Economic Ideas in Two Moments of Crisis." *Governance* 26(2): 197–215.

Brainard, Lael. 2014. "Financial Stability: A Conversation with Lael Brainard (Uncorrected Transcript)." *The Brookings Institution*, Washington, DC (December 3). www.brookings.edu/~/media/events/2014/12/03-financial-stability/20141203_financial_stability_brainard_transcript.pdf

Branch, Taylor. 2009. *The Clinton Tapes: Wrestling History with the President*. New York, NY: Simon and Schuster.

Brecher, Jeremy. 1997. *Strike!* Cambridge, MA: South End Press.

Bremmer, Robert P. 2004. *Chairman of the Fed: William McChesney Martin Jr. and the Creation of the American Financial System*. New Haven, CT: Yale University Press.

Brill, Steven. 2010. "What's a Bailed-Out Banker Really Worth?" *New York Times Magazine* (January 3). www.nytimes.com/2010/01/03/magazine/03Compensation-t.html?pagewanted=all

Bruner, Robert F. and Sean Carr. 2007. *The Panic of 1907: Lessons Learned from the Market's Perfect Storm*, Hoboken, NJ: John Wiley and Sons.

Brush, Silla and Robert Schmidt. 2013. "How the Bank Lobby Loosened U.S. Reins on Derivatives." Bloomberg.Com (September 4). www.bloomberg.com/news/2013-09-04/how-the-bank-lobby-loosened-u-s-reins-on-derivatives.html

Burns, Arthur. 1957. *Prosperity without Inflation*. New York, NY: Fordham University Press.

　1978. *Reflections of an Economic Policy Maker: Speeches and Congressional Statements: 1969–1978*. Washington, DC: American Enterprise Institute.

Burns, Arthur. "The Anguish of Central Banking." *The 1979 Per Jacobsson Lecture* (September 30). www.perjacobsson.org/lectures/1979.pdf

Burns, Arthur and Paul Samuelson. 1967. *Full Employment, Guideposts, and Economic Stability*. Washington, DC: The AEI Press.

Bush, George H. W., and Brent Scowcroft. 1998. *A World Transformed*. New York, NY: Alfred A. Knopf.

Bush, George W. 2008. "Address to the Nation on the National Economy." (September 24). www.presidency.ucsb.edu/ws/?pid=84355

Bush, George. W. 2010. *Decision Points*. New York, NY: Crown Publishers.

Califano, Joseph A. 1991. *The Triumph and Tragedy of Lyndon Johnson*. New York, NY: Simon and Schuster.

Cannon, Lou. 1991. *President Reagan: The Role of a Lifetime*. New York, NY: Perseus/Public Affairs.

Capoccia, Giovanni and R. Daniel Kelemen. 2007. "The Study of Critical Junctures: Theory, Narrative, and Counterfactuals in Historical Institutionalism." *World Politics* 59(3):341–369.

Carpenter, David. 2014. *The Consumer Financial Protection Bureau (CFPB): A Legal Analysis*. Washington, DC: Congressional Research Service. http://fas.org/sgp/crs/misc/R42572.pdf

Carstensen, Martin B. 2011. "Paradigm man vs. the Bricoleur: Bricolage as an Alternative Vision of Agency in Ideational Change." *European Political Science Review* 3:147–167.

Carstensen, Martin B. and Vivien A. Schmidt. 2016. "Power Through, Over and In Ideas: Conceptualizing Ideational Power in Discursive Institutionalism," *Journal of European Public Policy*, forthcoming.

Carter, Jimmy. 1978. "Anti-Inflation Program Address to the Nation." (October 24). www.presidency.ucsb.edu/ws/?pid=30040

 1979. "Address to the Nation on Energy and National Goals." (July 15). www.presidency.ucsb.edu/ws/?pid=32596

 1982 *Keeping Faith: Memoirs of a President*. New York, NY: Bantam Books.

Chernow, Ron. 2011. *Confidence Men: Wall Street, Washington, and the Education of a President*. New York, NY: Harper Collins.

Chwieroth, Jeffrey. 2010. *Capital Ideas: The IMF and the Rise of Financial Liberalization*. Princeton: Princeton University Press.

Clifford, Clark with Richard Holbrooke 1991. *Counsel to the President: A Memoir*, New York, NY: Doubleday.

Clinton, William J. 1993a. "Address to the Nation on the Economic Program." (February 15). www.presidency.ucsb.edu/ws/?pid=47155

 1993b. "Address Before a Joint Session of Congress on Administration Goals." (February 17). www.presidency.ucsb.edu/ws/?pid=47232

1995. "Interview With Peter Malof of New Hampshire Public Radio." (May 19). www.presidency.ucsb.edu/ws/?pid=87512

1996. "Address Before a Joint Session of the Congress on the State of the Union." (January 23). www.presidency.ucsb.edu/ws/?pid=53091

1997. "Inaugural Address," (January 20). www.presidency.ucsb.edu/ws/?pid=54183

1998. "Remarks to the Council on Foreign Relations in New York City." (September 14). www.presidency.ucsb.edu/ws/?pid=54898

2004. *My Life*. New York, NY: Random House.

Cochrane, James L. 1975. "The Johnson Years: Moral Suasion Goes to War." In *Exhortation and Controls: The Search for a Wage-Price Policy 1945–1971*, edited by Craufurd D. Goodwin, 193–294. Washington, DC: The Brookings Institution.

Committee For Economic Development. 1945. *International Trade, Foreign Investment, and Domestic Employment*. New York, NY: Committee For Economic Development.

1958. *Defense against inflation: Policies for Price Stability in a Growing Economy*. New York, NY: Committee For Economic Development.

1970. *Further Weapons Against Inflation: Measures to Supplement General Fiscal and Monetary Policies*, New York, NY: Committee For Economic Development.

The Conference on Inflation (September 27–28, 1974). 1974. Washington, DC: US Government Printing Office.

Cooper, John Milton. 2009. *Woodrow Wilson: A Biography*. New York, NY: Vintage.

Council of Economic Advisers. 1955. *The Economic Report of the President*. Washington, DC: US Government Printing Office.

1957. *The Economic Report of the President*. Washington, DC: US Government Printing Office.

1961. "A Second Look at Policy in 1961." (March 17) POF CEA Box 73 (1/1961-12/1961), John F. Kennedy Library.

1964. *Council of Economic Advisers Oral History Interview –JFK#1, 8/1/1964*. www.jfklibrary.org/Asset-Viewer/Archives/JFKOH-CEA-01.aspx

1969. *The Council of Economic Advisers During the Administration of President Lyndon B. Johnson, November 1963-January 1969*. Okun Papers (176: CEA Papers, 1963–1969).

Cuff, Robert D. 1969. "Woodrow Wilson and Business-Government Relations during World War I." *The Review of Politics* 31(3): 385–407.

Dallek, Robert. 1998. *Flawed Giant: Lyndon Johnson and his Times 1961–1973*. New York, NY: Oxford University Press.

Darman, Richard. 1996. *Who's in Control? Polar Politics and the Sensible Center*. New York, NY: Simon and Schuster.
De Marchi, Neil. 1975. "The First Nixon Administration: Prelude to Controls." In *Exhortation and controls: The search for a wage-price policy 1945–1971*, edited by Craufurd D. Goodwin, 295–353. Washington, DC: The Brookings Institution.
Department of the Treasury. 2009. *Financial Regulatory Reform: A New Foundation: Rebuilding Financial Supervision and Regulation*. http://online.wsj.com/public/resources/documents/finregfinal06172009.pdf
DiMaggio P. J., and W. W. Powell (eds.) 1991. *The New Institutionalism in Organizational Analysis*. Chicago: University of Chicago Press.
Dobbin, F. 1994. *Forging Industrial Policy: The United States, Britain and France in the Railway Age*. New York, NY: Cambridge University Press.
Donald, Aida D. 2008. *Lion in the White House: A Life of Theodore Roosevelt*. New York: Basic Books.
Donovan, Robert J. 1977. *Conflict and Crisis: The Presidency of Harry S Truman*. New York: W.W. Norton.
Drew, Elizabeth. 1996. *Showdown*. New York: Touchstone Books.
Ebenstein, Lanny. 2007. *Milton Friedman: A Biography*. New York, NY: Palgrave Macmillan.
Eckstein, Harold. 1975. "Case Study and Theory in Political Science." In *Handbook of Political Science*, edited by F. I. Greenstein and N. W. Polsby, 79–138. Reading, MA: Addison-Wesley.
Economic Commission for Europe. 1967. *Incomes Policies in Postwar Europe: A Study of Policies, Growth and Distribution*. Geneva: Economic Commission for Europe.
Eichengreen, Barry. 1992. *Golden Fetters: The Gold Standard and the Great Depression*. New York, NY: Oxford University Press.
  1996. *Globalizing Capital*. Princeton, NJ: Princeton University Press.
Eisenhower, Dwight D. 1957. "Annual Message to the Congress on the State of the Union." (January 10). www.presidency.ucsb.edu/ws/?pid=11029
  1959a. "Letter to the President of the United Steelworkers and to Representatives of the Steel Industry." www.presidency.ucsb.edu/ws/?pid=11503
  1959b. "The President's News Conference." (September 28). www.presidency.ucsb.edu/ws/?pid=11538
  1959c. "Remarks at the Economic Conference Breakfast." (November 2). www.presidency.ucsb.edu/ws/?pid=11572
  1965. *Waging Peace: 1956–1961*. New York: Doubleday and Company.
Ellsberg, Daniel. 1961. "Risk, Ambiguity, and the Savage Axioms." *Quarterly Journal of Economics* 75(4): 643–669.

Elster, Jon. 1999. *Alchemies of the Mind: Rationality and the Emotions*. New York, NY: Cambridge University Press.

Fearon, James and Alexander Wendt. 2002. "Rationalism v. Constructivism: A Skeptical View." In *Handbook of International Relations*, edited by Walter Carlsnaes, Thomas Risse, and Beth A. Simmons, 52–73. London: Sage Publications.

Federal Open Market Committee. 1979. "Meeting of the Federal Open Market Committee." (October 6). www.federalreserve.gov/monetary-policy/files/FOMC19791006meeting.pdf

1994. "Meeting of the Federal Open Market Committee." (February 3–4). www.federalreserve.gov/monetarypolicy/files/FOMC19940204 meeting.pdf

1995. "Meeting of the Federal Open Market Committee." (December 19). www.federalreserve.gov/monetarypolicy/files/FOMC19951219 meeting.pdf

1996. "Meeting of the Federal Open Market Committee." (September 24). www.federalreserve.gov/monetarypolicy/files/FOMC19960924 meeting.pdf

1999. "Minutes of the Federal Open Market Committee." (June 29). www.federalreserve.gov/fomc/minutes/19990629.htm

2005. "Minutes of the Federal Open Market Committee." (December 13). www.federalreserve.gov/monetarypolicy/files/FOMC20051213 meeting.pdf

2008a. "Meeting of the Federal Open Market Committee." (June 24–25). www.federalreserve.gov/monetarypolicy/files/FOMC20080625 meeting.pdf

2008b. "Meeting of the Federal Open Market Committee." (December 15–16). www.federalreserve.gov/monetarypolicy/files/FOMC20081216 meeting.pdf

Federal Reserve Board of Governors. 1943. *Annual Report of the Federal Reserve Board of Governors*. Washington, DC: Federal Reserve System.

1998. *Annual Report of the Federal Reserve Board of Governors*. Washington, DC: Federal Reserve System.

Feinberg, Kenneth R. 2010. "Special Master for TARP Executive Compensation Written Testimony before the House Financial Services Committee." (February 25). www.treasury.gov/press-center/press-releases/Pages/tg565.aspx

Feinberg, Kenneth R. 2011. "Symposium on Executive Compensation Keynote Address." *Vanderbilt Law Review* 64(2): 349–358.

Feis, Herbert. 1966. *1933: Characters in Crisis*. Boston, MA: Little, Brown.

Financial Crisis Inquiry Commission. 2011. The Financial Crisis Inquiry Commission Report U.S. Government Printing Office. http://c0182732.cdn1.cloudfiles.rackspacecloud.com/fcic_final_report_full.pdf

Finnemore, Martha. 1996. *National Interests in International Society*. Ithaca, NY: Cornell University Press.

Finnemore, Martha and Kathryn Sikkink. 1998. "International Norm Dynamics and Political Change." *International Organization* 52: 887–917.

Fioretos, Orfeo. 2011. "Historical Institutionalism in International Relations." *International Organization* 65(2): 367–399.

Fischer, Stanley. 2014. "Financial Sector Reform: How Far Are We?" Remarks at the Martin Feldstein Lecture, National Bureau of Economic Research, Cambridge, Massachusetts (July 10). www.federalreserve.gov/newsevents/speech/fischer20140710a.htm

Ford, Gerald R. 1974. "The President's News Conference of August 28, 1974." www.presidency.ucsb.edu/ws/index.php?pid=4671&st=&st1=

1979. *A Time to Heal: The Autobiography of Gerald R. Ford*. New York, NY: Harper and Row.

Frank, Robert, Thomas Gilovich, and Dennis T. Regan. 1993. "Does Studying Economics Inhibit Cooperation?" *Journal of Economic Perspectives* 7(2):159–171.

Frankel, Jeffrey and Peter Orzag (eds.) 2002. *American Economic Policy in the 1990s*. Cambridge, MA: MIT Press.

Friedman, Milton. 1962. *Capitalism and Freedom*. University of Chicago Press.

1966. "What Price Guideposts?" In *Guidelines, informal controls, and the market place*, edited by George P. Shultz and Robert Z. Aliber, 17–40. Chicago: University of Chicago Press.

1968. "The Role of Monetary Policy." *American Economic Review* 58:1–17.

1970. "The Social Responsibility of Business is to Increase Its Profits." *New York Times Magazine*. September 13.

1974. "Inflation, Taxation, Indexation." In *Inflation: Causes, Consequences, Cures*, IEA Readings No. 14. London: The Institute of Economic Affairs.

1987. "Good Ends, Bad Means." In *The Catholic Challenge to the American Economy*, edited by Thomas M. Gannon, 99–106. New York, NY: Macmillan.

Friedman, Milton and Anna J. Schwartz. 1963. *A Monetary History of the United States*. Princeton, NJ: Princeton University Press.

Friedman, Milton and Walter Heller. 1969. *Monetary vs. Fiscal Policy*. New York, NY: W. W. Norton.

Fukuyama, Francis. 1991. *The End of History and the Last Man*. New York, NY: Free Press, 1991.

Galbraith, John Kenneth. 1936. "Monopoly Power and Price Rigidities." *Quarterly Journal of Economics* 50:456–475.
  1941. "Financing and Inflation: Some Comments on Professor Hansen's Article: 'The Selection and Timing of Price Controls.'" *Review of Economics and Statistics* 23(2): 82–85.
  1946. "Reflections on Price Control." *The Quarterly Journal of Economics* 60:475–489.
  1952. *Theory of Price Control*. Cambridge: Harvard University Press.
  1954. *The Great Crash, 1929*. Boston, MA: Houghton-Mifflin.
  1958. *The Affluent Society*. Boston, MA: Houghton-Mifflin.
  1967a. *The New Industrial State*. Boston, MA: Houghton-Mifflin.
  1967b. "A Review of a Review." *The Public Interest* (Fall):109–118.
  1971. "How Keynes Came to America." In *A Contemporary Guide to Economics, Peace, and Laughter*, edited by Andrea D. Williams, 44–56. Boston, MA: Houghton-Mifflin.
  1975. *Money*. Boston, MA: Houghton-Mifflin.
  1981. *A Life in Our Times*. New York, NY: Ballantine Books.
Gallup, George, 1978. "The Gallup Poll Release: Americans Say Government, Not Business or Labor, Is Most Responsible For Inflation." (October 15).
Geisst, Charles R. 2000. *Monopolies in America*. Oxford: Oxford University Press.
Geithner, Timothy. 2009. "Remarks by Treasury Secretary Timothy Geithner Introducing the Financial Stability Plan." (February 10). www.treasury.gov/press-center/press-releases/Pages/tg18.aspx
  2014. *Stress Test: Reflection on Financial Crises*. New York, NY: Crown.
George, Alexander and Andrew Bennett. 2005. *Case Studies and Theory Development in the Social Sciences*. Cambridge, MA: MIT Press.
Gilpin, Robert. 1981. *War and Change in International Politics*. New York, NY: Cambridge University Press.
Goodhart, Charles. 1975. "Monetary Relationships: A View from Threadneedle Street." *Papers in Monetary Economics*, Reserve Bank of Australia, Vol. 1.
Goodman, James (ed.). 1998. *John Kenneth Galbraith: Letters to Kennedy*. Cambridge, MA: Harvard University Press.
Goodman, Peter S. 2008. "The Reckoning: Taking Hard New Look at a Greenspan Legacy." *New York Times*. (October 9). www.nytimes.com/2008/10/09/business/economy/09greenspan.html?pagewanted=all&_r=0
Goodwin, Craufurd D. 1975. *Exhortation and Controls: The Search for a Wage-Price Policy 1945–1971*. Washington, DC: The Brookings Institution.
Goodwin, Craufurd D. and R. Stanley Herren. 1975. "The Truman Administration: Problems and Policies Unfold." In *Exhortation and*

Controls: *The Search for a Wage-Price Policy 1945–1971*, edited by Craufurd D. Goodwin, 9–94. Washington, DC: The Brookings Institution.
Gordon, H. Scott. 1975. "The Eisenhower Administration: The Doctrine of Shared Responsibility." In *Exhortation and Controls: The Search for a Wage-Price Policy 1945–1971*, edited by Craufurd D. Goodwin, 95–134. Washington, DC: The Brookings Institution.
Gordon, Robert J. 1990. "What is New Keynesian Economics?" *Journal of Economic Literature* 28:1115–1171.
Gourevitch, Peter. 1986. *Politics in Hard Times: Comparative Responses to International Economic Crises*. Ithaca, NY: Cornell University Press.
Green, Joshua. 2010. "Inside Man." *The Atlantic*. www.theatlantic.com/magazine/archive/2010/03/inside-man/7992/
Greene, John Robert. 2000. *The Presidency of George Bush*. Lawrence: University of Kansas Press.
Greenspan, Alan. 1996. "The Challenge of Central Banking in a Democratic Society." Remarks at the Annual Dinner and Francis Boyer Lecture of The American Enterprise Institute for Public Policy Research, Washington, DC (December 5). www.federalreserve.gov/boarddocs/speeches/1996/19961205.htm
　1997a. "Testimony of Chairman Alan Greenspan Before the Committee on Banking, Housing, and Urban Affairs, U.S. Senate (February 26). www.federalreserve.gov/boarddocs/hh/1997/february/testimony.htm
　1997b. "Remarks at the Economic Club of New York." (December 2). www.bis.org/review/r971208d.pdf
　1999a. Statement before the Joint Economic Committee, United States Congress (June 17, 1999). www.federalreserve.gov/boarddocs/testimony/1999/19990617.htm
　1999b. "The Federal Reserve's Semiannual Report on Monetary Policy." Testimony before the Committee on Banking and Financial Services, U.S. House of Representatives, July 22, 1999. www.federalreserve.gov/boarddocs/hh/1999/july/testimony.htm
　1999c. "Do Efficient Financial Markets Mitigate Financial Crises?" remarks before the 1999 Financial Markets Conference of the Federal Reserve Bank of Atlanta. (October 19). www.federalreserve.gov/boarddocs/speeches/1999/19991019.htm
　2002. "The Economic Outlook: Testimony Before the Joint Economic Committee, U.S. Congress." (November 13). www.federalreserve.gov/BoardDocs/Testimony/2002/20021113/default.htm
　2003. "The Reagan Legacy." Remarks at the Ronald Reagan Library, Simi Valley, California (April 9) www.federalreserve.gov/BoardDocs/speeches/2003/200304092/default.htm

    2004a. "Risk and Uncertainty in Monetary Policy." Remarks at the Meetings of the American Economic Association, San Diego, California (January 3). www.federalreserve.gov/boarddocs/speeches/2004/20040103/default.htm

    2004b. "Understanding Household Debt Obligations." Remarks at the Credit Union National Association 2004 Governmental Affairs Conference, Washington, DC (February 23). www.federalreserve.gov/boardDocs/speeches/2004/20040223/default.htm

    2005. "Opening Remarks: The Greenspan era: Lessons for the Future." Proceedings, Federal Reserve Bank of Kansas City (August 2005), 1–10. www.kansascityfed.org/Publicat/sympos/2005/PDF/Green-opening2005.pdf

    2007. *The Age of Turbulence*. New York, NY: Penguin.

    2008. "Markets and the Judiciary." Address to the Sandra Day O'Connor Project Conference (October 2). www.law.georgetown.edu/news/documents/Greenspan.pdf

    2009. "We Need a Better Cushion Against Risk." *Financial Times* (March 26).

    2013. *The Map and the Territory*. New York, NY: Penguin.

Greenwald, Bruce and Joseph Stiglitz. 1993. New and old Keynesians. *Journal of Economic Perspectives* 7:23–44.

Greider, William. 1987. *Secrets of The Temple*. New York, NY: Simon and Schuster.

Gross, Daniel. 2009. "We'll Be Judged on How We Dealt with the Things That Were Broken." *Slate.Com* (December 23) www.slate.com/articles/news_and_politics/newsmakers/2009/12/well_be_judged_on_how_we_dealt_with_the_things_that_were_broken.html

Grossman, Jonathan. 1975. "The Coal Strike of 1902 – Turning Point in U.S. Policy." *Monthly Labor Review* 98: 21. www.dol.gov/oasam/programs/history/coalstrike.htm#15

Gysler, Matthias, Jamie Brown Kruse and Renate Schubert. 2002. "Ambiguity and Gender Differences in Financial Decision Making: An Experimental Examination of Competence and Confidence Effects." Working paper (May 2002). www.cer.ethz.ch/research/wp_02_23_paper.pdf

Haas, Garland A. 1992. *Jimmy Carter and the Politics of Frustration*. Jefferson, NC: McFarland and Company.

Haas, Peter M. 1992. "Epistemic Communities and International Policy Coordination." *International Organization* 46:1–35.

Halberstam, David. 1972. *The Best and The Brightest*. New York, NY: Random House.

Hall, Christopher G. L. 1997. *Steel Phoenix: The Fall and Rise of the U.S. Defense Industry*. New York, NY: St. Martin's Press.

Hall, Peter. 1989. *The Political Power of Economic Ideas: Keynesianism Across Nations*. Princeton, NJ: Princeton University Press.
  1993. "Policy Paradigms, Social Learning and the State: The Case of Economic Policy-Making in Britain." *Comparative Politics* 25: 275–296.
  2010. "Historical Institutionalism In Rationalist and Sociological Perspective." In *Explaining Institutional Change: Ambiguity, Agency and Power*, edited by James Mahoney and Kathleen Thelen, 204–224. Cambridge: Cambridge University Press.
Hall, P. and R. R. Taylor. 1996. "Political Science and the Three New Institutionalisms." *Political Studies* 44(5): 936–957.
Hall, Peter, A. and David Soskice (eds.) 2001. *Varieties of Capitalism: The Institutional Foundations of Comparative Advantage*. Oxford: Oxford University Press.
Hall, Rodney Bruce. 2009. *Central Banking as Global Governance: Constructing Financial Credibility*. Cambridge: Cambridge University Press.
Harbaugh, William Henry. 1961. *Power And Responsibility: The Life And Times Of Theodore Roosevelt*. New York, NY: Farrar, Straus and Cudahy.
Hargrove, Erwin C. and Samuel A. Morley (eds.) 1984. *The President and the Council of Economic Advisers*. Boulder, CO: Westview.
Harris, John. 2006. *The Survivor: Bill Clinton in the White House*. New York, NY: Random House.
Hartz, Louis. 1955. *The Liberal Tradition in America*. New York, NY: Harcourt, Brace.
Hay, Colin. 1996. "Narrating Crisis: The Discursive Construction of the Winter of Discontent," *Sociology* 30(2): 253–277.
Hayek, Friedrich. 1944. *The Road to Serfdom*. New York: Routledge.
  1945. "The Use of Knowledge in Society." *American Economic Review* 35(4): 519–530.
Helleiner, Eric. 1994. *States and the Reemergence of Global Finance: From Bretton Woods to the 1990s*. Ithaca, NY: Cornell University Press.
  2003. "Economic Liberalism and Its Critics: The Past as Prologue?" *Review of International Political Economy* 10(4): 685–696.
  2010. "A Bretton Woods Moment? The 2007–2008 Crisis and the Future of Global Finance." *International Affairs* 86(3): 619–636.
Heller, Walter. 1966. *New Dimensions of Political Economy*. New York, NY: W. W. Norton.
  1971. "Transcript, Walter Heller Oral History Interview II, 12/21/71, by David G. McComb." (Internet Copy, LBJ Library) https://fraser.stlouisfed.org/docs/meltzer/heller_interviewII_19711221.pdf
Hetzel, Robert L. 1998. "Arthur Burns and Inflation." *Federal Reserve Bank of Richmond Economic Quarterly* 84(1):21–44.

Hetzel, Robert L. 2008. *The Monetary Policy of the Federal Reserve: A History*. Cambridge: Cambridge University Press.

Himmelberg, Robert. 1968. "Business, Antitrust Policy, and the Industrial Board of the Department of Commerce, 1919." *Business History Review* 42(1):1–23.

Hirsh, Michael. 2010. *Capital Offense*. Hoboken, NJ: John Wiley and Sons.

Hoerr, John. 1988. *And the Wolf Finally Came: The Decline of the American Steel Industry*. Pittsburgh: University of Pittsburgh Press.

Hofstadter, Richard. 1962. *Anti-Intellectualism in American Life*. New York, NY: Vintage.

1965. *The Paranoid Style in American Politics and Other Essays*. New York, NY: Alfred A. Knopf.

Hopf, Ted. 2010. "The Logic of Habit in International Relations." *European Journal of International Relations* 16(4):539–561.

Holmes, Marcus and David Traven. 2015. "Acting Rationally Without Really Thinking: The Logic of Rational Intuitionism for International Relations Theory." *International Studies Review* 17: 414–440.

Hoover, Herbert. 1952. *Memoirs, The Great Depression, 1929–1941*. New York, NY: Macmillan.

Ikenberry, G. John. 1993. "Creating Yesterday's New World Order: Keynesian 'New Thinking' and the Anglo-American Postwar Settlement." In *Ideas and Foreign Policy: Beliefs, Institutions and Political Change*, edited by Judith Goldstein and Robert O. Keohane, 57–86. Ithaca, NY: Cornell University Press.

Irwin, Neil. 2013. *The Alchemists: Three Central Bankers and a World on Fire*. New York, NY: Penguin.

Jacobs, Meg. 2005. *Pocketbook Politics: Economic Citizenship in Twentieth-Century America*. Princeton, NJ: Princeton University Press.

Jackson, P. T. and D. Nexon. 2013. "International Theory in a Post-paradigmatic Era: From Substantive Wagers to Scientific Ontologies." *European Journal of International Relations* 19(3): 543–565.

James, Harold. 1996. *International Monetary Cooperation Since Bretton Woods*. New York, NY: Oxford University Press.

Janis, Irving. 1972. *Victims of Groupthink*. Boston, MA: Houghton-Mifflin.

Johnson, Lyndon B. 1965. "Televised Statement by the President Announcing Settlement of the Steel Dispute." (September 3). www.presidency.ucsb.edu/ws/index.php?pid=27222&st=&st1=

1968a. "The President's News Conference at the LBJ Ranch." (January 1). www.presidency.ucsb.edu/site/docs/pppus.php?admin=036&year=1968&id=1

1968b. "Statement by the President Upon Signing the Tax Bill." Public Papers of the President (June 28). www.presidency.ucsb.edu/ws/index.php?pid=28964&st=&st1=

Johnson, Simon and James Kwak. 2010. *Thirteen Bankers: The Wall Street Takeover and the Next Financial Meltdown*. New York, NY: Pantheon.

Kahn, Alfred. [Miller Center] (2003). "Interview with Alfred E. Kahn." Charlottesville, VA: University of Virginia. http://millercenter.org-/president/carter/oralhistory/alfred-e-kahn

Kahneman, Daniel. 2011. *Thinking, Fast and Slow*. New York, NY: Penguin

Kaplan, Morton. 1957. *System and Process in International Relations*. New York, NY: John Wiley.

Kennedy, John F. 1961a. "Annual Message to Congress on the State of the Union." (January 30) www.presidency.ucsb.edu/ws/index.php?pid=8045&st=&st1=

1961b. "Special Message to the Congress: Program for Economic Recovery and Growth." (February 2). www.presidency.ucsb.edu/ws/?pid=8111

1962a. "Commencement Address at Yale University." (June 11). www.presidency.ucsb.edu/ws/index.php?pid=29661&st=Ideology&st1

1962b. "Address and Question and Answer Period at the Economic Club of New York." (December 14). Public Papers of the President. www.presidency.ucsb.edu/ws/?pid=9057

Keohane, Robert. 1984. *After Hegemony*. Princeton, NJ: Princeton University Press.

Keynes, John Maynard. 1920. *The Economic Consequences of the Peace*. New York, NY: Harcourt Brace.

1931. *Essays in Persuasion*. London: Macmillan.

1933. "An Open Letter to President Roosevelt." *New York Times* (December 31, 1933). http://economistsview.typepad.com/economistsview/2008/11/keynes-open-let.html

1936a. *The General Theory of Employment, Interest, and Money*. New York, NY: Harcourt Brace Jovanovich.

1936b. Letter to W. Luck. In *The Collected Writings of John Maynard Keynes: Volume XII*, edited by Donald Moggridge, 500–502. London: Macmillan.

1937. "The General Theory of Employment." *The Quarterly Journal of Economics* 51(2): 209–223.

1940a. *How to Pay for the War*. London: Macmillan.

1940b. "Notes on the Budget II: Price and Wage Policy." In *The Collected Writings of John Maynard Keynes: Volume XXII: Activities 1939–1945: Internal War Finance*, edited by Donald Moggridge, 222–230. London: Macmillan.

Kim, H. J. and J. C. Sharman. 2014. "Accounts and Accountability: Corruption, Human Rights and Individual Accountability Norms." *International Organization* 68: 417–448.

Kindleberger, Charles P. 1973. *The World in Depression 1929–1939*. Berkeley: University of California Press.

1989. *Manias, Panics, and Crashes: A History of Financial Crises*. New York, NY: Basic Books.

Knight, Malcolm D. 2005. "General Discussion: Has Financial Development made the World Riskier?" Proceedings, Federal Reserve Bank of Kansas City (August), 387–397. www.kansascityfed.org/Publicat/sympos/2005/PDF/GD5_2005.pdf

Koenig, E. F., Leeson, R., and Kahn, G. (2012). "Introduction." In *The Taylor Rule and the Transformation of Monetary Policy*, edited by Koenig, Leeson, and Kahn, ix–xix. Stanford, CA: Hoover Institution Press.

Krugman, Paul. 1994. *Peddling Prosperity*. New York, NY: W. W. Norton.

2000. "Reckonings; Cheney Gets Vulgar." *New York Times* (December 6). www.nytimes.com/2000/12/06/opinion/reckonings-cheney-gets-vulgar.html

2015. "The MIT Gang." *New York Times* (July 24). www.nytimes.com/2015/07/24/opinion/paul-krugman-the-mit-gang.html?rref=collection%2Fcolumn%2Fpaul-krugman&action=click&contentCollection=opinion&region=stream&module=stream_unit&contentPlacement=3&pgtype=collection

Lekachman, Robert. 1966. *The Age of Keynes*. New York: Random House.

Levitt, Arthur. 2009. "*Frontline* Interview." www.pbs.org/wgbh/pages/frontline/warning/interviews/levitt.html

Lucas, Robert. 1980. "The Death of Keynesian Economics." *Issues and Ideas*. University of Chicago: Graduate School of Business.

2003. "Macroeconomic Priorities." *American Economic Review*. 93(1): 1–14.

Lucas, Robert E. and Thomas Sargent. 1978. "After Keynesian Macroeconomics." In *After the Phillips curve: Persistence of High inflation and High Unemployment*, 49–82. Boston, MA: Federal Reserve Bank of Boston.

MacKay, Charles. 1841. [1980] *Extraordinary Popular Delusions and the Madness of Crowds*. New York, NY: Harmony.

Mahoney, James and Kathleen Thelen. 2010. "A Theory of Gradual Institutional Change." In *Explaining Institutional Change: Ambiguity, Agency and Power*, edited by James Mahoney and Kathleen Thelen, 1–37. Cambridge: Cambridge University Press.

Mankiw, N. Gregory. 1992. "The Reincarnation of Keynesian Economics." *European Economic Review* 36:559–65; Reprinted in *A Macroeconomics Reader*, edited by Brian Snowdon and Howard R. Vane (1997), 445–451. New York, NY: Routledge.

1997. *Principles of Economics*. New York, NY: Dryden Press.

Mankiw, N. Gregory and David Romer (eds.) 1991. *New Keynesian Economics, Vols. 1 and 2*. Cambridge, MA: MIT Press.

Mansfield, Harvey C. 1947. *A Short History of OPA*. Washington, DC: Office of Price Administration.
Matusow, Allen J. 1984. *The Unraveling of America*. New York, NY: Harper and Row.
  1998. *Nixon's Economy*. Lawrence, KS: University Press of Kansas.
Maxfield, Sylvia. 1998. *Gatekeepers of Growth: The International Political Economy of Central Banking in Developing Countries*. Princeton, NJ: Princeton University Press.
McCartin, Joseph. 2013. *Collision Course*. Oxford: Oxford University Press.
McLean, Bethany and Joe Nocera. 2010. *All the Devils are Here: The Hidden History of the Global Financial Crisis*. New York, NY: Portfolio/Penguin.
McNamara, Kathleen. 1998. *The Currency of Ideas: Monetary Politics in the European Union*. Ithaca, NY: Cornell University Press.
Means, Gardiner C. 1962. *Pricing Power and the Public Interest, A Study Based on Steel*. New York, NY: Harper and Row.
Mehrling, Perry. 2007. "An Interview with Paul A. Volcker." In *Inside the Economist's Mind: Conversations with Eminent Economists*, edited by Paul A. Samuelson and William A. Barnett, 168–191. Malden, MA: Blackwell.
Meltzer, Allan H. 2009. *A History of the Federal Reserve, Volume 2, Book 2, 1970–1986*. Chicago: University of Chicago Press.
Meyer, Laurence H. 2004. *A Term at the Fed*. New York, NY: Harper Collins.
Mieczkowski, Yanek. 2005. *Gerald Ford and the Challenges of the 1970s*. Lexington: University Press of Kentucky.
Miller, Rich and Ryan, Jennifer. 2012. "Europe Crisis Rescue Begins With MIT Men as a Matter of Trust." *Bloomberg.Com* (January 13). www.bloomberg.com/news/articles/2012-01-12/rescuing-europe-from-debt-crisis-begins-with-men-of-mit-as-matter-of-trust
Minsky, Hyman P. 1986. *Stabilizing an Unstable Economy*. New Haven, CT: Yale University Press.
  1992. "The Financial Instability Hypothesis." The Jerome Levy Economics Institute Working Paper No. 74 (May 1992). www.levy.org/pubs/wp74.pdf
Mitzen, Jennifer and Randall Schweller. 2011. "Knowing the Unknown Unknowns: Misplaced Certainty and the Onset of War." *Security Studies* 20(1):2–35(34).
Morgan, Iwan. 2004. "Jimmy Carter, Bill Clinton and the New Democratic Economics." *The Historical Journal* 47(4): 1015–1039.
Moschella, Manuela and Eleni Tsingou. 2013. *Great Expectations, Slow Transformations: Incremental Change in Financial Governance*. Colchester, UK: ECPR Press.

Muth, John. 1961. "Rational Expectations and the Theory of Price Movements." *Econometrica* 29:315–360.
Navasky, V. S. 1967. "Galbraith on Galbraith." *The New York Times Book Review* (June 25).
Nelson, Edward. 2007. "Milton Friedman and U.S. Monetary History: 1961–2006." *Federal Reserve Bank of St. Louis Review* (May/June): 153–182.
Nixon, Richard. 1962. *Six Crises*. New York, NY: Doubleday.
  1969. "The President's News Conference of January 27, 1969." (January 27). www.presidency.ucsb.edu/ws/?pid=1942
  1970. "Address to the Nation on Economic Policy and Productivity." (June 17). www.presidency.ucsb.edu/ws/?pid=2549
  1971. "Address to the Nation on the Post-Freeze Economic Stabilization Program: The Continuing Fight Against Inflation." (October 7). www.presidency.ucsb.edu/ws/?pid=3183
  1973. "Special Message to the Congress Announcing Phase III of the Economic Stabilization Program and Requesting Extension of Authorizing Legislation." (January 11). www.presidency.ucsb.edu/ws/?pid=4119
  1974. "Message to the Congress Transmitting the Cost of Living Council's Quarterly Report on the Economic Stabilization Program." (January 22). www.presidency.ucsb.edu/ws/?pid=4230
  1978. *RN: The Memoirs of Richard Nixon*. New York, NY: Touchstone.
Nocera, Joe. 2011. "Sheila Bair's Bank Shot." *New York Times Magazine* (July 9).
Neumann, Iver B. and Pouliot, Vincent. 2011. "Untimely Russia: Hysteresis in Russian-Western Relations over the Past Millennium." *Security Studies*, 20(1): 105–137..
Obama, Barack. 2008. "Campaign Stop in Indianapolis, Indiana." (October 8). www.presidentialrhetoric.com/campaign2008/obama/10.08.08.html
  2009a. "Inaugural Address." (January 20). www.presidency.ucsb.edu/ws/?pid=44
  2009b. "Remarks Following a Meeting With Economic Advisers and an Exchange With Reporters."(January 29). www.presidency.ucsb.edu/ws/?pid=85709
  2009c. "Remarks by President Barack Obama on Executive Compensation with Secretary Geithner." February 4, 2009. www.whitehouse.gov/the_press_office/RemarksbyPresidentBarackObamaOnExecutiveCompensationSecretaryGeithner/
  2009d. "Remarks by the President upon Departure." (March 18). www.whitehouse.gov/the_press_office/Remarks-of-the-President-Upon-Departure

2009e. "Remarks by the President on the Economy." Georgetown University, Washington, DC. April 14, 2009. www.whitehouse.gov/the_press_office/Remarks-by-the-President-on-the-Economy-at-Georgetown-University/

2009f. "Remarks at Lehigh Carbon Community College and a Question-and-Answer Session in Allentown, Pennsylvania." (December 4). www.presidency.ucsb.edu/ws/?pid=86971

2010. "Remarks on Signing the Dodd-Frank Wall Street Reform and Consumer Protection Act." (July 21). www.presidency.ucsb.edu/ws/?pid=88213

2011. "Address to the Nation on the Federal Budget." (July 25). www.presidency.ucsb.edu/ws/?pid=90657

2015. "State of the Union Address." (January 20). www.whitehouse.gov/the-press-office/2015/01/20/remarks-president-state-union-address-january-20-2015

Odell, John S. 1982. *U.S. International Monetary Policy: Markets, Power and Ideas as Sources of Social Change*. Princeton, NJ: Princeton University Press.

Okun, Arthur. 1968. "Memo, Okun to the President, 'Explanation of Possible World Financial Crisis.'" May 21, 1968; EX FG 11–3 Box 61 (4/12/68–6/1/68).

Parker, Richard. 2005. *John Kenneth Galbraith: His Life, His Politics, His Economics*. New York, NY: Farrar, Strauss and Giroux.

Paulson, Henry M. 2010. *On the Brink: Inside the Race to Stop the Collapse of the Global Financial System*. New York, NY: Business Plus.

Perry, George L. 1967. "Wages and the Guideposts." *American Economic Review* 57 (4): 897–904.

Phillips, Kevin, 1991. *The Politics of Rich and Poor*. New York, NY: Harper Collins.

Pierson, Paul 2000. "Increasing Returns, Path Dependence, and the Study of Politics." *American Political Science Review* 94(2): 251–267.

Pierson, Paul. 2004. *Politics in Time. History, Institutions and Social Analysis*. Princeton, NJ: Princeton University Press.

Polanyi, Karl. 1944. *The Great Transformation*. Boston: Beacon Press.

Pouliot, Vincent. 2010. *International Security in Practice*. Cambridge: Cambridge University Press.

Rajan, Raghuram G. 2005. "Has Financial Development Made the World Riskier?" *Proceedings, Federal Reserve Bank of Kansas City* (August), 313–369. www.kansascityfed.org/Publicat/sympos/2005/PDF/Rajan2005.pdf

Reagan, Ronald. 1981a. "First Inaugural Address." (January 20). http://millercenter.org/president/speeches/detail/3407

1981b. "The President's News Conference." (January 29). www.presidency.ucsb.edu/ws/?pid=44101

1981c. "Address Before a Joint Session of the Congress on the Program for Economic Recovery." (February 18). www.presidency.ucsb.edu/ws/?pid=43425.

1981d. "Remarks and a Question-and-Answer Session With Reporters on the Air Traffic Controllers Strike." (August 3). www.presidency.ucsb.edu/ws/?pid=44138

1981e. "Remarks in Chicago, Illinois, at the Annual Convention and Centennial Observance of the United Brotherhood of Carpenters and Joiners." (September 3). www.presidency.ucsb.edu/ws/?pid=44193

1981f. "The President's News Conference." (October 1). www.presidency.ucsb.edu/ws/?pid=44327

1981g. "Interview with the President." (December 23). www.presidency.ucsb.edu/ws/?pid=43386

1982. "The President's News Conference." (February 18). www.presidency.ucsb.edu/ws/?pid=42183

Redfield William C. 1919. "The Industrial Board of the Department of Commerce." *Federal Reserve Bulletin* (March 1, 1919): 246–248. http://fraser.stlouisfed.org/download-page/page.pdf?pid=62&id=282947

Reeves, Richard. 1993. *President Kennedy: Profile of Power*. New York, NY: Touchstone.

2005. *President Reagan: The Triumph of Imagination*. New York: Simon and Schuster.

Reinhart, Carmen and Kenneth Rogoff. 2009. *This Time is Different: Eight Centuries of Financial Folly*. Princeton, NJ: Princeton University Press.

Robinson, Archie. 1981. *George Meany and His Times*. New York, NY: Simon and Schuster, 1981.

Rockoff, Hugh. 1984. *Drastic Measures: A History of Wage and Price Controls in the United States*. Cambridge: Cambridge University Press.

1990. "The 'Wizard of Oz' as a Monetary Allegory." *Journal of Political Economy* 98 (1990): 739–760.

Roig-Franzia, Manuel. 2009. "Credit Crisis Cassandra: Brooksley Born's Unheeded Warning Is a Rueful Echo 10 Years On." *Washington Post* (May 26). www.washingtonpost.com/wp-dyn/content/article/2009/05/25/AR2009052502108.html

Romer, Christina. 1986. "Spurious Volatility in Historical Unemployment Data." *Journal of Political Economy* 94 (1):1–37.

1992. "What Ended the Great Depression?" *The Journal of Economic History* 52(4):757–784.

Romer, Christina and David H. Romer. 2002. "The Evolution of Postwar Understanding and Stabilization Policy." In *Rethinking Stabilization Policy*, Federal Reserve Bank of Kansas City, 11–78.

Roosa, Robert V. 1967. *The Dollar and World Liquidity*. New York, NY: Random House.

Roosevelt, Franklin. 1933a. "First Inaugural Address." (March 4). http://millercenter.org/president/speeches/detail/3280

1933b. "Fireside Chat on Banking." (March 12). www.presidency.ucsb.edu/ws/?pid=14540

1942a. "Message to Congress on an Economic Stabilization Program." (April 27). www.presidency.ucsb.edu/ws/?pid=16251.

1942b. "Fireside Chat." April 28, 1942, *Public Papers of the President* www.presidency.ucsb.edu/site/docs/pppus.php?admin=032&year=1942&id=49

Roosevelt, Theodore, 1901. "First Annual Message." (December 3). www.presidency.ucsb.edu/ws/?pid=29542

1912. "Theodore Roosevelt, Address at the Coliseum, San Francisco." (September 14). http://ehistory.osu.edu/osu/mmh/1912/1912documents/LimitationofGovernment.cfm

Rorty, Richard. 1987. "Method, Social Science, and Social Hope." In *Interpreting Politics*, edited by Michael T. Gibbons, 241–259. New York, NY: New York University Press.

Ross, Andrew. 2006. "Coming in from the Cold: Constructivism and Emotions." *European Journal of International Relations* 12(2): 197–222.

Ross, Arthur M. 1966. "Guideline Policy – Where We are and How We Got There." In *Guidelines, Informal Controls, and the Market Place*, edited by George P. Shultz and Robert Z. Aliber, 97–142. Chicago: University of Chicago Press.

Rostow, Walt. W. 1960. "Economics for the Nuclear Age." *Harvard Business Review* 38(1):41–49.

1972. *The Diffusion of Power: An Essay in Recent History*. New York, NY: Macmillan.

Rowen, Hobart. 1994. *Self-Inflicted Wounds*. New York, NY: Times Books.

Rubin, Robert. 1998. "Address on the Asian Financial Situation to Georgetown University," Washington, DC (January 21).

Rubin, Robert with Jacob Weisberg. 2004. *In an Uncertain World: Tough Choices from Wall Street to Washington*. New York, NY: Random House.

Rubin, Robert. 2005. "Luncheon address: The Greenspan era: Lessons for the Future." Proceedings, Federal Reserve Bank of Kansas City (August), 301–310. www.kansascityfed.org/Publicat/sympos/2005/PDF/Rubin2005.pdf

Ruggie, John Gerard. 1982. "International Regimes, Transactions, and Change: Embedded Liberalism in the Postwar Economic Order." *International Organization* 36(2):379–415.

Samuelson, Paul. 1948. *Economics: An Introductory Analysis*. New York, NY: McGraw-Hill.

1955. *Economics: An Introductory Analysis*. New York, NY: McGraw-Hill.

1997. "Credo of a Lucky Textbook Author." *Journal of Economic Perspectives* 11:153–160.
Samuelson, Paul and Robert Solow. 1960. "Analytical Aspects of Anti-Inflationary Policy." *American Economic Review* 50:177–194.
Samuelson, Paul and William A. Barnett. 2007. *Inside the Economist's Mind: Conversations with Eminent Economists*. Malden, MA: Blackwell.
Samuelson, Paul A. 1979. "Myths and Realities about the Crash and Depression." *Journal of Portfolio Management* 6 (1): 9–12.
Scheiber, Noam. 2011. *The Escape Artists: How Obama's Team Fumbled The Recovery*. New York, NY: Simon and Schuster.
2012. "The Memo that Larry Summers Didn't Want Obama to See." *The New Republic* (February 22). www.newrepublic.com/article/politics/100961/memo-Larry-Summers-Obama
Schlesinger, Jr., Arthur. 1949. *The Vital Center: The Politics of Freedom*. Boston, MA: Houghton Mifflin.
1957. *The Crisis of the Old Order, 1919–1933*. Boston, MA: Houghton Mifflin.
Schmidt, Vivien A. 2008. "Discursive Institutionalism: The Explanatory Power of Ideas and Discourse." *Annual Review of Political Science* 11: 303–326.
2010. "Taking Ideas and Discourse Seriously: Explaining Change through Discursive Institutionalism as the Fourth 'New Institutionalism.'" *European Political Science Review* 2(1): 1–25.
2013. "Speaking to the Markets or to the People? A Discursive Institutionalist Analysis of the EU's Sovereign Debt Crisis." *The British Journal of Politics and International Relations* 16(1): 188–209.
Schultze, Charles [Miller Center] (2003). "Interview with Charles Schultze." Charlottesville, VA: University of Virginia. http://millercenter.org/president/carter/oralhistory/charles-schultze
Seabrooke, Leonard. 2006. *The Social Sources of Financial Power: Domestic Legitimacy and International Financial Orders*. Ithaca, NY: Cornell University Press.
Seib, Gerald. 2008. "In Crisis, Opportunity for Obama." *Wall Street Journal* (November 21). www.wsj.com/articles/SB122721278056345271
Shabecoff, Philip. 1979. "Hope Springs Eternal for Inflation Fighters." *New York Times* (3 June), 4E.
Shales, Amity. 2014. *Coolidge*. New York, NY: Harper Collins.
Sheahan, John. 1967. *The Wage-Price Guideposts*. Washington, DC: The Brookings Institution.
Shepsle, K. A. 2006. "Rational Choice Institutionalism." In *Oxford Handbook of Political Institutions*, edited by S. Binder, R. Rhodes, and B. Rockman, 23–38. Oxford: Oxford University Press.

Shiller, Robert. 2000. *Irrational Exuberance*. Princeton, NJ: Princeton University Press.

Shultz, George P. and Kenneth W. Dam. 1977. *Economic policy beyond the Headlines*. New York, NY: W. W. Norton and Company.

Shultz, George P. and Robert Z. Aliber (eds). 1966. *Guidelines, Informal Controls, and the Marketplace*. Chicago: University of Chicago Press.

Silber, William L. 2013. *Volcker: The Triumph of Persistence*. New York, NY: Bloomsbury Press.

Silk, Leonard. 1984. *Economics in the Real World*. New York, NY: Simon and Schuster.

1974. *The Economists*. New York, NY: Basic Books.

Skidelsky, Robert. 2001. *John Maynard Keynes: Fighting for Freedom, 1937–1946*. New York, NY: Viking.

Skowronek, Stephen. 1993. *The Politics Presidents Make: Leadership from John Adams to Bill Clinton*. Cambridge, MA: Harvard University Press.

2011. *Presidential Leadership in Political Time: Reprise and Reappraisal*. Lawrence: University Press of Kansas.

Smith, Jean Edward. 2007. *FDR*. New York, NY: Random House.

Snowdon, Brian, and Howard Vane. 1995. "New-Keynesian Economics Today: The Empire Strikes Back." *American Economist* 39(1):48–65.

Sobel, Robert. 1980. *The Worldly Economists*. New York, NY: The Free Press.

Solomon, Robert. 1982. *The International Monetary System, 1945–1981*. New York, NY: Harper and Row.

Solomon, Steven. 1995. *The Confidence Game*. New York, NY: Simon and Schuster.

Solow, Robert. 1966. "The Case Against the Case against the Guideposts. In *Guidelines, Informal Controls, and the Market Place*, edited by George P. Shultz and Robert Z. Aliber, 41–54. Chicago: University of Chicago Press.

1967. "The New Industrial State or Son of Affluence." *The Public Interest* (Fall 1967), 100–108. www.nationalaffairs.com/doclib/20080522_196 700909thenewindustrialstateorsonofaffluencerobertmsolow.pdf

Sorensen, Theodore. 1965. *Kennedy*. New York, NY: Harper and Row.

Sorkin, Andrew Ross. 2009. *Too Big To Fail: Inside the Battle to Save Wall Street*. New York, NY: Penguin Press.

2014, "What Timothy Geithner Really Thinks." *The New York Times Magazine* (May 8). www.nytimes.com/2014/05/11/magazine/what-timothy-geithner-really-thinks.html?_r=1

Sproul, Allan, Roy Blough and Paul McCracken, "The Economic Situation and the Balance of Payments" (January 18, 1961); Reprinted in Robert Roosa, 1967. *The Dollar and World Liquidity*. New York, NY: Random House, pp. 265–271.

Stein, Herbert. 1996. *The Fiscal Revolution in America*. Washington, DC: AEI Press.
Stiglitz, Joseph. 2003. *The Roaring Nineties*. New York, NY: Norton.
Stockman, David A. 1986. *The Triumph of Politics: Why the Reagan Revolution Failed*. New York, NY: Harper and Row.
Summers, Lawrence H. 1997. "Protecting the System: APEC Conference." (Interview with Lawrence Summers)." *Newshour with Jim Lehrer* (November 26).
Suskind, Ron. 2012. *Confidence Men: Wall Street, Washington and the Education of a President*. New York, NY: Harper.
Szenberg, Michale, Aron Gottesman, and Lall Ramrattan. 2005. *Paul A. Samuelson: On Being an Economist*. New York, NY: Jorge Pinto Books.
Taussig, Frank W. 1919. "Price-Fixing as Seen by a Price-Fixer." *The Quarterly Journal of Economics* 33(2):205–241.
Taylor, John B. 1993. "Discretion versus Policy Rules in Practice." *Carnegie-Rochester Conference Series on Public Policy* 39, 195–214. www.stanford.edu/~johntayl/Onlinepaperscombinedbyyear/1993/Discretion_versus_Policy_Rules_in_Practice.pdf
  2005. "Lessons Learned from the Greenspan Era." Written version of comments on a paper by Alan Blinder and Ricardo Reis for the Federal Reserve Bank of Kansas City Conference. *The Greenspan Era: Lessons for the Future*, held in Jackson Hole, Wyoming, August 25–27. www.stanford.edu/~johntayl/JacksonHole2005.pdf
  2007. "An Interview with Milton Friedman." In *Inside the Economist's Mind: Conversations with Eminent Economists, edited by* Paul Samuelson and William A. Barnett, 110–142. Malden, MA: Blackwell.
  2009. *Getting off Track: How Government Actions and Interventions Caused, Prolonged, and Worsened the Financial Crisis* Stanford, CA: Hoover Institution Press.
Tempalski, Jerry. 2006. "Revenue Effects of Major Tax Bills." U.S. Treasury Department, Office of Tax Analysis. Office of Tax Analysis Working Paper 81 (September). www.treasury.gov/resource-center/tax-policy/tax-analysis/Documents/ota81.pdf
Tiffany, Paul A. 1988. *The Decline of American Steel: How Management, Labor and Government Went Wrong*. New York, NY: Oxford University Press.
Tobin, James. 1966. *The Intellectual Revolution in U.S. Economic Policy-Making*. London: Longmans, Green.
Triffin, Robert. 1961. *Gold and the Dollar crisis: The future of convertibility*. New Haven, CT: Yale University Press.
Truman, Harry S. 1946a. "Radio Address to the American People on the Railroad Strike Emergency." (May 24). www.presidency.ucsb.edu/ws/index.php?pid=12406&st=&st1=

1946b. "Special Message to Congress Urging Legislation for Industrial Peace."(May25).www.presidency.ucsb.edu/ws/index.php?pid=12407&st=&st1=

Truman, Harry S. 1952. "Radio and Television Address to the American People on the Need for Government Operation of the Steel Mills." (April 8). www.presidency.ucsb.edu/ws/?pid=14454

Tsingou, Eleni. 2014. 'The Club Rules in Global Financial Governance." *The Political Quarterly* 85(4): 417–419.

Tulis, Jeffrey. 1987. *The Rhetorical Presidency*. Princeton, NJ: Pricenton University Press.

US Congress. Joint Economic Committee. 1966. *Twentieth Anniversary of the Employment Act of 1946: An Economic Symposium, Hearing Before the Joint Economic Committee, Congress of the United States*. 89th Cong., 2nd Sess., February 23, 1966. Washington, DC: US Government Printing Press.

US Congress. Joint Economic Committee. 1971. *Hearings on the President's New Economic Policy*. 92nd Cong., 1st sess., August 31, 1971.

US Congress. Joint Economic Committee. 1972. *Review of Phase II of the New Economic Program*. 92nd Cong., 2nd sess., April 14–24, 1972.

1979. *Hearings Before the Joint Economic Committee*. 96th Cong., 1st sess., January 29, 1979. Washington, DC: US Government Printing Office,1979.

1982. *The 1982 Economic Report of the President*, 97th Cong., 1st. sess., January 26, 1982.

US House of Representatives. 1966. "A Bill to Amend the Employment Act of 1946 To Bring to Bear an Informed Public Opinion upon Price and Wage Behavior Which Threatens National Economic Stability." H.R. HR1196, 89 Cong. (1966).

Van Overtveldt, Johan. 2009. *Bernanke's Test*. Chicago: Agate.

Volcker, Paul. 1978. "The Role of Monetary Targets in an Age of Inflation." *Journal Of Monetary Economics* 4(2): 329–339.

2000. "Interview with Paul Volcker, 'From Carter to Reagan.'" *The Commanding Heights*. www.pbs.org/wgbh/commandingheights/shared/minitextlo/int_paulvolcker.html#6

Volcker, Paul and Toyoo Gyohten. 1992. *Changing Fortunes*. New York, NY: Times Books.

Waltz, Kenneth. 1979. *Theory of International Politics*. New York, NY: McGraw-Hill.

Ward, Jon. 2008. "He Found the Flaw?" *Washington Times* (October 24). http://washingtontimes.com/weblogs/potus-notes/2008/Oct/24/he-found-flaw/

Weber, Arnold. 1973. *In Pursuit of Price Stability*. Washington, DC: Brookings.

Wendt, Alexander. 1987. "The Agent-Structure Problem in International Relations Theory." *International Organization* 41(3): 335–370.
   1992. "Anarchy is What States Make of It: The Social Construction of Power Politics." *International Organization* 46(2):391–425.
   1999. *Social Theory of International Politics*. Cambridge: Cambridge University Press.
Wessel, David. 2009. *In Fed We Trust*. New York, NY: Crown.
Widmaier, Wesley W. 2003a. "Constructing Monetary Crises: Monetary Understandings and State Interests in Cooperation." *Review of International Studies* 29:61–77.
   2003b. "Keynesianism as a Constructivist Theory of the International Political Economy." *Millennium: Journal of International Studies* 32: 87–107.
   2004. "The Social Construction of the 'Impossible Trinity': The Intersubjective Bases of Monetary Cooperation." *International Studies Quarterly* 48: 433–453.
   2005. "The Meaning of an Inflation Crisis: Steel, Enron and Macroeconomic Policy." *Journal of Post-Keynesian Economics* 27(4): 553–571.
   2007. "Where You Stand Depends on How You Think: Economic Ideas, the Decline of the Council of Economic Advisers, and the Rise of the Federal Reserve." *New Political Economy* 12(1): 43–59.
Widmaier, Wesley W., Mark Blyth, and Leonard Seabrooke. 2007. "The Social Construction of Wars and Crises as Openings for Change." *International Studies Quarterly* 51(4):747–759.
Willentz, Sean. 2008. *The Age of Reagan*. New York, NY: Harper Collins.
Wilson, Woodrow. 1913a. "Address to a Joint Session of Congress on Tariff Reform." (April 8). www.presidency.ucsb.edu/ws/?pid=65368
   1913b. "Address to a Joint Session of Congress on the Banking System." (June 23). www.presidency.ucsb.edu/ws/?pid=65369
Woodward, Bob. 1994. *The Agenda*. New York, NY: Simon and Schuster.
   2000. *Maestro: Greenspan's Fed and the American Boom*. New York: Simon and Schuster.
   2006. *State of Denial*. New York, NY: Simon and Schuster.
Wolffe, Richard. 2010. *Revival: The Struggle for Survival Inside the Obama White House*. New York, NY: Broadway.
Woolley, John T. 1984. *Monetary Politics: The Federal Reserve and the Politics of Monetary Policy*. Cambridge: Cambridge University Press.
Yellen, Janet. 1996. "Monetary Policy: Goals and Strategy." Remarks at the National Association of Business Economists, Washington, DC (March 13). https://fraser.stlouisfed.org/docs/historical/federal%20reserve%20history/bog_members_statements/yellen_19960313.pdf
   2009. "Presentation to the 18th Annual Hyman P. Minsky Conference on the State of the U.S. and World Economies – 'Meeting the

Challenges of the Financial Crisis'." Organized by the Levy Economics Institute of Bard College New York City (April 16). www.frbsf.org/our-district/press/presidents-speeches/yellen-speeches/2009/april/yellen-minsky-meltdown-central-bankers/04161.pdf

2012. "The View from Inside the Fed." In *The Taylor Rule and the Transformation of Monetary Policy*, edited by Evan F., Koenig, Robert Leeson, and George A. Kahn, 281–289. Stanford, CA: Hoover Institution Press.

2014. "Monetary Policy and Financial Stability." Remarks at the 2014 Michel Camdessus Central Banking Lecture, International Monetary Fund, Washington, DC (July 2). www.federalreserve.gov/newsevents/speech/yellen20140702a.htm

# Index

Abel, I.W., 95
Ackley, Gardner
  on defense expenditures, 103n94
  on economic stimulation, 94
  on failure of CEA to garner public/business support, 106–107
  on inflation, 96, 97
  on tax increase, 101–102
  on wage-price guideposts, 98, 99
  on wage-price policy, 102
Advisory Commission, 37
Advisory Committee on Labor Management Policy, 85
affective heuristics, 17–18
*The Affluent Society* (Galbraith), 80–81
agriculture
  emergence from depression in, 31
  and Jefferson, 51
  policy under T. Roosevelt, 30, 32–33
  and Populist movement, 30
airline industry
  and International Association of Machinists, 96, 105
  and PATCO strike, 136, 140–141
Akerlof, George, 4
Allison, Herb, 195n55
ambiguity aversion, 20n49
American International Group (AIG)
  and accountability, 195n55
  compensation of executives at, 193
  rescue of, 192, 193
American Nickel Company, 37–38
anti-intellectualism, 78–79
antitrust issues
  under F.D. Roosevelt, 55
  under J.F. Kennedy, 90
  under Obama, 26, 198, 199
  under Reagan, 19
  Sherman Anti-trust law, 38, 38n31
  under Wilson, 25, 30, 34, 38–40
  *See also* Dodd-Frank Act (2010); steel industry
Asian Financial Crises, 23, 162–163, 178, 181
asset-price issues
  bubbles, 41, 170–171, 173
  containment, 170–173
  masking of instability, 190
  stability, 41–42
austerity
  under Carter, 123, 126, 127
  under Johnson, 102
  Stein on, 119–120
automobile industry
  and New Inflation, 69–70
  United Auto Workers, 69, 86–87, 140–141
  and wage-price restraint, 86–87
Axilrod, Stephen, 188

Baker, Howard, 153
Baker, Jim, 148, 151
Baker Plan (1985), 151, 156
banking
  domestic banking crisis, 149–150
  shadow banking system, 197, 198
  stemming of crisis under F.D. Roosevelt, 53–54
Banking Act (1933), 54
Banking Act (1935), 54
Banking Crises of 1939, 179
Barnett, Michael, 11, 11n25, 208
Barr, Shelia, 149
Baruch, Bernard, 37, 57
Bear Stearns, collapse of, 189, 200
beliefs, causal *vs.* principled, 15
Bell, Daniel, 20, 79

Bell, Stephen, 13, 14
Bentsen, Lloyd, 158–159, 160
Berger, Peter, 15
Berlin crisis, 87
Bernanke, Ben, 22
  becomes Chairman of Federal Reserve, 186–187
  on bubbles, 22, 187
  on dot.com crash, 190
  on forecast-based approach, 187n25
  on Great Moderation, 184–185
  on Lehman, 191n42
  and wage-price spirals, 189
Best, Jacqueline, 11n25, 22, 188
Bethlehem Steel, 95–96, 104, 105, 114
Big government view of Hamilton, 51
Black Monday (1987) crash, 153
Blankfein, Lloyd, 194
Blinder, Alan
  appointment to Federal Reserve Board, 157, 166
  on interest rate levels, 167–168
  on New Classicism in academia, 165
  on Taylor rule approach to inflation-unemployment balance, 177
Blough, Roger, 69, 89, 90, 95
Blumenthal, W. Michael, 126, 127
Blyth, Mark, 11n25, 10–11
Born, Brooksley, 174–175
Bowles, Chester, 59, 62
Brady Bonds, 151
Brady Plan (1989), 151, 156
Brainard, Lael, 198
Bretton Woods, 210, 211
  fixed rate, 52, 61, 68, 210
  fixed rate collapse under Nixon, 118
Broker Dealer Lite regime, 174–175
Brown, Prentiss, 58
Bryan, William Jennings, 31
Bull Moose Party, 34
Burns, Arthur
  on central banking, 110, 130, 144–145
  on cost-push inflation, 113
  on credit, 69
  on direct controls, 68
  on economic downturn, 74
  on incomes policies, 68
  on restraint, 130
  and wage-price regulation, 114

Bush, George H. W., and Greenspan, 154–155
Bush, George W./administration
  deficit under, 158
  on executive compensation, 192n43
  and fiscal stimulus, 183, 189n33
  marginal tax cuts by, 182–183
  on TARP, 192, 192n43
Business Council, 112–113

Califano, Joseph, 96, 99–100
capital gains
  under Carter, 139
  under Reagan, 138–139, 156
Capoccia, Giovanni, 12–13, 208
Carter, Jimmy/administration
  anti-inflation policies of, 125–127
  austerity under, 123
  capital gains under, 139
  conclusions of, 131
  cost-of-living adjustment under, 128–129
  crisis of confidence address/malaise speech by, 126–127
  dollar under, 125–126
  Federal Reserve under, 126, 127, 170–171
  macroeconomic stimulus under, 124n66, 124–125
  overview of, 110, 123
  promotion of recovery under, 124–125
  resignations/dismissals of cabinet members of, 127
  stagflation under, 110, 123–127
  steel industry under, 128–129
  tax-based income policies under, 125, 131
  Trigger Price Mechanism under, 129n86
  trust in government during, 128
  and Vietnam War, 126–127
  and wage-price spirals, 123, 124n69, 124–125
causal models, conversion of principled understandings into, 20
causal *vs.* principled beliefs, 15, 16
Central banking, A. Burns on, 110, 130, 144–145
*Chicago Tribune*, 141
Citicorp, 152

Index                                                                 243

Civil Works Administration, 55
classical liberalism of Jefferson, 29
Cleveland, Grover, 31
Clifford, Clark, 64
Clinton, Bill/administration
  on bailouts and Wall Street, 194,
    194n48
  on big government, 157
  derivatives under, 174–175
  and Federal Open Market
    Committee, 164
  and Greenspan, 155, 158–159,
    159n6, 160–161
  and intellectual conversion of
    Neoliberal order, 158–164
    abandonment of communicative
      engagement, 161–162
    deficit, 159–160
    Mexican crisis, 162
    public credibility, 160
    Putting People First agenda, 158
    third way between statist/
      freemarket excesses, 163–164
    tightening by Greenspan and,
      160–161
    triangulation approach to
      congressional extremes, 162
  surplus under, 182
Clinton, Hillary, 160
coal strike, 1902, 25, 30, 32
Colm, Gerhard, 65
Commerce Department Industrial
  Board, 38–39
Committee for Economic Development
  (CED), 74, 113
Commodity Futures Modernization
  Act (2000), 175
Commodity Futures Trading
  Commission (CFTC),
  174–175, 198
communicative vs. coordinative
  discourse, 15–16
Connally, John, 114, 115, 116–117
Construction Industry Stabilization
  Committee, 114
constructivism
  on inefficiencies, 11–12
  on interests as variable/instability as
    unexplained, 10–12
  on macroeconomic trade-offs, 10n20
  on power and interests, 8

consumer credit, and Neoliberalism of
  Volcker, 146
Consumer Financial Protection Bureau
  (CFPB), 197, 198
consumer groups, during Johnson
  administration, 105
Continental Airlines, 141
Continental Illinois bank,
  149–150, 156
Contract with America, 162
Coolidge, Calvin, 39
cooperative currency interventions,
  150–151
coordinative vs. communicative
  discourse, 15–16
Corrigan, Gerry, 153
Cortelyou, George B., 33
cost-of-living adjustment (COLA)
  under Carter, 128–129
  under Nixon, 115
Cost-push inflation, A. Burns
  on, 113
Council of Economic Advisors
  (CEA)
  under Carter, 123
  under Eisenhower, 69, 70, 73
  and gradualism, 14
  guidepost figure/standard of, 89n39
  on guideposts as neutral, 88n36
  under J.F. Kennedy, 88, 89, 94
  under Johnson, 102, 104
    abandonment of
      guideposts, 97–99
    exchange rates, 210
    failure to garner public/business
      support, 106–107
    and fiscal fine tuning, 100–105
    guidepost figure of, 97n70
    and incomes policies, 94, 96
    on mandatory controls, 89n37
  under Nixon, 114–115
  and overconfidence, 14, 206n5
Council of National Defense, 37
Council on Wage and Price Stability
  (COWPS), 120, 129, 139–140
crash of 1907, 25, 30, 33–34
Cronkite, Walter, 90
Cutter, Stephanie, 193

Daniels, Josephus, 37
Darman, Richard, 154

deficit
    under B. Clinton, 159–160
    under Eisenhower, 68n65
    under F.D. Roosevelt, 56
    under G.W. Bush, 158
deflation, 186
    post-September 11 scare, 211
Department of Agriculture, and Hold the Line order, 59
Depository Institutions Deregulation and Monetary Control Act (1980), 139
derivatives
    exemption from regulatory oversight, 174
    proposal of voluntary disclosure by investment banks, 174–175
    and regulation of shadow banking system, 197, 198
    and Securities and Exchange Commission, 173, 174–175
    and transparency, 198
discourse, communicative vs. coordinative, 15–16
disinflation, 112
Dodd-Frank Act (2010), 23, 197, 198, 199, 201
dollar
    and Bretton Woods, 68, 75
    under Carter, 125–126
    devaluation under F.D. Roosevelt, 54
    devaluation under Nixon, 111, 118, 129–130
    international tensions and, 116
    under J.F. Kennedy, 84–85, 90
    under Johnson, 96, 102
    under Nixon, 115–116
    and Plaza Accord, 1985, 125–126
    Stein on depreciation of, 130
    Volcker on superdollar, 151
Dot-com crisis, 23, 183, 190

economic policy paradox, 3
Economic Recovery Tax Act (1981), 147n50
*Economic Report of the President*
    under Eisenhower, 69, 70, 73
    under J.F. Kennedy, 88, 89, 94
    under Johnson, 102, 104, 210
    under Nixon, 114–115

Eichengreen, Barry, 9, 43–44
Eisenhower, Dwight D./administration
    communicative rhetoric of, 70, 75
    deficit under, 68n65
    *Economic Reports* under, 69, 70, 73
    incomes policies under, 68
    and New Inflation, 52, 68–73
    and auto industry, 69–70
    congressional view on administrative pricing, 70–71
    construction of, 68–71
    overview of, 68
    and steel industry, 69–71
    and steel strike, 1959, 71–73
    unemployment under, 74
Elliot, Harriet, 59–60
Ellsberg, Daniel, 20n49
Emanuel, Rahm
    on principled reform, 179, 180, 201
    and TARP deadline, 196
England. *See* Great Britain
Enron, collapse of, 182
exchange rate
    and Bank of England, 42
    and Bretton Woods fixed rate, 52, 61, 68, 210
    collapse of fixed, 110, 111, 129–130
    under Johnson, 210
    Keynes on stability of, 41
    under Nixon, 118
    Progressive movement and stability, 41, 42
Exchange Stabilization Fund, 54–55, 162
executive compensation
    at AIG, 193
    G.W. Bush on, 192n43
    Obama on, 193
    and TARP, 194–195
Experimental Negotiating Agreement (ENA), 128–129

Fairless, Benjamin, 62, 69
fallacy of composition, 52–53
"fast thinking" rhetoric, 17, 51–52, 155, 192–193
Federal Deposit Insurance Corporation (FDIC), 54, 201

# Index

Federal Open Market Committee (FOMC)
  and B. Clinton, 164
  and foreign economic crises, 172
  increase in power of, 54
  monetarist approach of, 145
  and steel strike, 1959, 74
  and technological change, 169
Federal Reserve, 29, 206n5
  and AIG rescue, 192
  and asset-price bubbles, 170–171, 173
  and asset-price stability, 41–42
  under Carter, 126, 127, 170–171
  criticism by Shultz, 112
  direct pressure policy of, 43, 44
  disaggregation of power in initial, 36
  and exchange rate stability, 41–44
  and gradualism, 112
  and incomes policies strengthening, 111
  initial Neoliberalism of Volcker, 142–148
    consumer credit, 146
    incomes policies, 143–144
    monetarist approach, 144–146, 147
    reaction of Reagan to, 148
    and restraint of abuses of labor power, 143–144
  and institutional agenda of Greenspan, 152–155
    Black Monday crash, 153
    financial restraint, 154
    monetary policy, 152–153
  and iterative Neoliberalism of Volcker, 148–152
    cooperative currency interventions, 150–151
    domestic banking crisis, 149–150
    end of monetarism, 148–149
    near-default of Mexico, 149–150
  under Johnson, 102
  as lender of last resort, 149, 173
  monetary austerity policy of, 126, 127
  under Nixon, 111, 112, 113, 114
  and post-September 11 deflation scare, 211
  and Progressive movement, 41–44
  and reduction in discount rate, 102
  and reduction in federal funds rate, 2007, 188–189
  and regulation/speculative credit, 42–44
  reorganization under F.D. Roosevelt, 54
  switch from wage to asset-price accommodation, 137, 142–152
  unwillingness to impose restraint, 130
  Volcker succeeds Miller at, 123, 127
  and wage-price regulation, 113, 114
  *See also* Bernanke, Ben; Federal Open Market Committee (FOMC); Federal Reserve Board; Global Financial Crisis; Greenspan, Alan; Volcker, Paul
Federal Reserve Act (1913), 25
Federal Reserve Bank of Chicago, 150
Federal Reserve Bank of New York, 85
Federal Reserve Bank of San Francisco, 189
Federal Reserve Board of Governors
  *Annual Report*, 1998, 172
  increased power of, 54
  and monetary policy, 60n33
  use of moral suasion to limit speculative loans, 42–44
  *See also* Blinder, Alan; Yellen, Janet
Feinberg, Kenneth R.
  and accountability of AIG, 195n55
  and compensation standards at TARP-recipient firms, 194–195
  and compensation to TARP-recipient firms, 194n52
financial crises
  Asian, 23, 178, 181
  crash of 1907, 25, 30, 33–34
  Great Crash of 1929, 44–45, 210
  Russian, 172, 178
  *See also* Global Financial Crisis
*Financial Regulatory Reform*, 197
Financial Stability Oversight Council, 205
Finnemore, Martha, 10, 11, 11n25, 208, 209
Fioretos, Orfeo, 12

fiscal crisis, 1965/66, 100–105
fiscal stimulus
　under Carter, 124n66, 124–125
　under Ford, 122–123
　under G.W. Bush, 183, 189n33
　under Johnson, 94
　under Obama, 192, 201
Fischer, Stanley, 197–198
Fisher, Irving, quantity theory of money of, 44–45
Flanders, Ralph, 66
Ford, Gerald/administration, and stagflation, 119–123
　anti-inflation policies of, 119–121
　and Council on Wage and Price Stability, 120
　incomes policies as unacceptable, 120
　wage-price controls as unacceptable, 120
　Whip Inflation Now program, 120–121, 131
　Greenspan on, 119, 120–121, 122–123
　overview of, 110, 119
　and recovery promotion, 121–123
　　fiscal stimulus, 122–123
　　tax cuts, 121–122
　　unemployment rates, 121, 122
forecast-based approach, 187n25
Fortas, Abe, 99
forward guidance approach, 187–188, 200
Fowler, Henry H., 102
France, and Tripartite Agreement, 54–55
Fraser, Douglas, 126, 140–141
fraud prevention, 174
Friedman, Milton, 42n43, 83n19
　on compromise, 138n7
　on Crash of 1929, 44
　on direct pressure policy of Federal Reserve, 43, 44
　on guideposts, 91
　on hide tide of monetary policy, 40
　micro-morality viewpoint of, 137–138
　on Philips curve, 82–83
　on recession, 39–40
　on second freeze under Nixon, 118
Fukuyama, Francis, 20

G7 Bonn summit, 125
Galbraith, John Kenneth, 4, 18
　on confidence in fine tuning, 176
　forced out of OPA, 58
　on incomes policies, 61, 78, 86
　as Institutionally oriented Keynesian, 80–81
　on market structures and Office of Price Administration, 60–61
　on moral suasion by Federal Reserve, 43
　on piecemeal approach to economic controls, 57–61
Geithner, Timothy
　on bailouts and Wall Street, 194n48
　on financial reform/economic recovery, 196
　on financial crises in Mexico and Asia, 162–163
　on Global Financial Crisis, 4, 205
　and overconfidence, 185, 186
　on populist excess, 162, 193–194
　on utilitarian recovery, 180, 193–194
General Electric, 66
General Maximum Price Regulation (General Max), 19–20, 57–58
General Motors, 105
The General Theory (Keynes), 56–57
Gensler, Gary, 198
Gertler, Mark, 187
Gingrich, Newt, 161–162, 163
Glass, Carter, 36, 38, 39, 43
Glass-Steagall, 151–152
Global Financial Crisis, 23
　conclusions of, 200–202
　construction of, 179–202
　first great accommodation, 181–187
　　deflation, 186
　　fiscal policy, 182–183, 200
　　forward guidance approach, 200
　　Great Moderation, 184–185
　　initial successful efforts, 181–183
　　misplaced certainty in macroeconomics, 183–187
　　monetary policy, 181–182, 183–184, 200
　　overconfidence, 185–186
　　overview of, 180
　　regulatory accommodation, 183, 200

# Index

risk management, 184, 200
  Taylor rule, 183–184
  technology bubble collapse, 181
Geithner on, 4
and misplaced certainty, 187–191
  Bernanke-era and Great Moderation, 180
  bubbles, 187
  market risk-taking, 187–188
  masking of asset-price instability, 190
  misplaced focus on wage-price inflation, 188–189
  monetary policy, 187
  overview of, 180
  risk-management policy, 187
  Taylor curve, 187
overview of, 179–181
recovery, reform, iterative change, 191–200
  administration stress tests, 201
  derivatives markets, 201
  fast thinking principled reform, 192–193
  fiscal grounds/policy, 192
  fiscal stimulus, 192, 201
  four-point domestic agenda, 197–199
  iterative transformation, 196–200
  Obama's rhetorical/regulatory accommodation, 192–196
  overview of, 180–181, 191–192
  slow thinking utilitarian inhibitions, 193–195, 200–202
  utilitarian restraints, 194–195
and subprime bubble, 9
TARP support for, 176
and utilitarian concerns, 23
Goldberg, Arthur
  as labor management chair, 85, 86
  Labor-Management Committee of, 85, 86
  and steel industry, 88n36
Gold Reserve Act (1934), 54–55
gold standard, 8
  and F.D. Roosevelt, 54–55, 75
  and Morgan, 54
  and Nixon, 115–116
  support by Cleveland, 31
Goodhart, Charles, 22
Gordon, Kermit, 68n66, 87, 100, 117

Gourevitch, Peter, 9
gradualism
  Connally on, 115
  and Council of Economic Advisors, 14
  McCracken on, 114
  and Nixon, 111–116
Gramlich, Edward, 185
Gramm-Leach-Bliley Act (1999), 175
Great Britain
  and gold standard, 8, 116
  and Tripartite Agreement, 54–55
Great Crash of 1929, 44–45, 210
Great Depression, 179
  and deflation, 44–45
  interest rate cut effect of, 210
  liberalist perspectives on, 9
  onset of, 44
  *See also* recessions
Great Moderation, 22–23, 153, 184–185, 200–201, 206
Great Society, 100, 104
Great Stagflation of 1970s, 206
  iterative character of, 179–180
  liberalist perspectives on, 9
  *See also* stagflation
Greenberger, Michael, 175
Greenspan, Alan
  on asset-price bubbles, 170–171, 173
  and Clinton, 155, 158–159, 159n6, 160–161
  and concept release, 175
  on Ford policy, 119, 120–121, 122–123
  and G.H.W. Bush, 154–155
  on home equity borrowing, 183n11
  on intellectual confidence, 176
  and Korean Crisis, 172
  limits on moral suasion of, 171n55
  on liquidity and international financial crises, 181
  on market bubbles, 4
  overconfidence of, 185
  on PATCO strike, 141
  on prices and wages, 169
  on regulation to prevent fraud, 174
  retirement from Federal Reserve, 186
  succeeds Volcker at Federal Reserve, 152
  on "traumatized workers," 169–170

Greider, William, 144
groupthink, 185, 186
guideposts, wage-price
  Ackley on, 98, 99
  congressional bill on responsibility for, 98
  and Council of Economic Advisors, 88n36, 89n39
  Friedman on, 91
  under J.F. Kennedy, 84–87
  under Johnson, 97–100, 97n70
  Solow on, 97n70, 98
  and steel industry, 88, 88n36, 91–92

Halberstam, Dave, 103n94
Hamilton, Alexander, 24, 29, 51, 198
Hamilton-Jeffersonian divide, 135
Harding, Warren, 40
Harriman, E.H., 32–33
Harrison, George, 41–42, 54n8, 190
Hayek, Friedrich, 18, 20
hedge fund collapse, 172, 178
Heller, Walter, 78
  definition of New Economics of, 81, 81n12
  on guideposts and steel industry, 88, 88n36, 91–92
  on inflation, 85
  on tax cuts, 87n31
  on trade-offs, 21n51
Henderson, Leon, 58, 58n24
Hepburn Act (1906), 25, 30, 32–33
Herzog, Jesús Silva, 150
heuristic, defining, 18n43
historical implications, 27
Hofstadter, Richard, 79
Hold the Line order, 59
home equity borrowing, Greenspan on, 183n11
Home Front Pledge campaign of OPA, 60
Hoover, Herbert
  and collapse of Progressive order, 45–46
  and direct aid to lenders after Great Crash of 1929, 45–46
  and election 1932, 46
  and Great Crash of 1929, 45
Hopkins, Harry, 55

housing bubble, 9, 188, 190
*How to Pay for the War* (Keynes), 56–57
Humphrey, George M., 69–70
Humphrey, William, 40

Ickes, Harold, 55
ideological politics, D. Bell on, 79
IMF/World Bank, 130
incomes policies, 83n19
  under Carter, 125, 131
  under Eisenhower, 68
  under Ford, 120
  Galbraith on, 61, 78, 86
  under J.F. Kennedy, 84–93
  under Johnson, 94, 96
  Rostow on, 86
  under Truman, 65
  and Volcker, 143–144
Indonesia, financial crisis in, 171–172
Industrial Board, 38–39
inefficiencies, constructivists on, 11–12
inflation
  during 1946/47, 64
  from 1979 to 1982, 148
  anti-inflation policies of Ford, 119–121
  under F.D. Roosevelt, 54–55
  under Ford, 119–121
  Heller on, 85
  under Johnson, 103–104
  during Korean War, 103
  and Neoliberal order, 165, 168, 169–170
  during World War II, 59, 103
  *See also* New Inflation; Philips curve
Inflation Czar, 125–126
instability, paradox of, ix, 3, 6–7, 205
institutionalism
  debates, overview of, 6, 7
  discursive, 12, 14–16
    power- *vs.* value-distributional tensions, 15
    principled *vs.* causal beliefs, 15, 16
  Galbraith on, 78
  historical, 16
    agent-centered, 13
    and dysfunctions, 14

# Index 249

and inefficiencies, 13–14
long processes/incremental adaptation, 12
power-distributional, 12, 13
turn toward continuous processes of development, 12
Institutional Keynesianism, 20–21, 80–81
intellectual anti-populism, 78–79
intellectual confidence, Greenspan on, 176
intellectual conversion, 5, 16–17, 20–22, 25
historical development of, 5–6
and macroeconomics, 5, 21–22
and Philips curve, 5, 21
in political time/economic policy mix, 17t1.1
of Progressive order, 30, 35–40, 206
and Taylor rule, 5, 21
*See also* Keynesian order, intellectual conversion of; Neoliberal order, intellectual conversion of
interest rates
cuts by Strong, 41
and Great Crash of 1929, 210
under J.F. Kennedy, 161
under Johnson, 101
and Neoliberal order, 167–168
Regulation Q interest rate controls, 139
and Taylor rule, 5, 16–17, 19, 20, 157
International Association of Machinists (IAM), 96, 105
interpretive biases, tensions among, 23
interwar international economic order, collapse of, 209–210
Isaac, William, 149
iterative crises. *See* misplaced certainty

Jacoby, Neil, 117
Jefferson, Thomas, 24, 198
agricultural/labor viewpoint of, 51
classical liberalism of, 29
Hamilton-Jeffersonian divide, 135
Johnson, Lyndon B./administration
and airline dispute, 96
austerity under, 102
communicative rhetoric of, 96

consumer groups during, 105
and conversion of Keynesian order, 93–105
and break from incomes policies, 94–96
conclusions, 108
and displacement of guideposts, 97–100
and fiscal crisis, 1965/66, 100–105
and fiscal stimulus, 94
and mandatory wage-price controls, 99–100
overview of, 93–94
and steel industry, 94–96
Council of Economic Advisors under
failure to garner public/business support, 106–107
and fiscal fine tuning, 100–105
guidepost figure of, 97n70
guideposts abandoned by, 97–99
on replacing incomes policies with fiscal policy, 94, 96
*Economic Reports* under, 102, 104, 210
exchange rates under, 210
and Great Society, 100, 104
inflation during, 103–104
interest rates during, 101
reduction in discount rate during, 102
tax increase under, 101–102
trust in government during, 105
and Vietnam War, 94, 100–101, 105n104

Kahn, Alfred, 125–126, 126n75, 143, 146n43
Kahneman, Daniel, 7, 16, 16n41, 17, 18n43, 23
Kaplan, Morton, 16n40
Katzenbach, Nicholas, 99, 99n78
Kefauver, Estes, 70–71
Kelemen, R. Daniel, 12–13, 208
Kennedy, J.F./administration, 77, 85n26
antitrust issues under, 90
auto industry wage-price restraint under, 86–87
avoidance of recession under, 90–93

Kennedy, J.F./administration (*cont.*)
  communicative rhetoric of, 90, 92–93
  conclusions, 107–108
  on controlling inflation, 84n22
  dollar under, 84–85, 90
  *Economic Report* under, 88, 89, 94
  GDP under, 161
  growth under, 85–86
  incomes policies under, 86–88
  incomes policy displacement under, 84–93
  interest rates under, 161
  overview of, 84
  and steel crisis, 1962, 87–90
  tax cuts under, 87–88, 92–93
  unemployment under, 161
  wage-price guideposts under, 84–87
  wage-price spirals under, 89, 90
Kennedy, Robert, 91n49
Keynes, John Maynard, 4, 18, 20
  on conventions/animal spirits, 208, 209
  on economic reform, 23–24
  on exchange rate stability, 41
  on fallacy of composition, 52–53
  on ideas as stabilizing institutions/ interests over time, 207
  on postwar monetary stability, 61
  on recovery and reform, 205
  on unemployment, 56
  on wage policy, 51
Keynesian order
  conclusions, 206
  rise and fall of, 3, 25–26, 27t1.2
  wage-price pressures leading to collapse of, 9
  *See also* Keynesian order, construction of; Keynesian order, intellectual conversion of; Keynesian order, misplaced certainty
Keynesian order, construction of, 51–76
  and communicative rhetoric, 75
  conclusions, 75–76
  context of, 73–75
    institutional, 74
    political, 73–74
    public, 75

Eisenhower and New Inflation, 52, 68–73, 75
  administrative pricing, 70–71
  auto industry, 69–70
  and communicative rhetoric, 70
  overview of, 68
  recognition of New Inflation, 68–71
  steel industry, 69–71
  steel strike, 1959, 71–73
F.D. Roosevelt,
  regulatory-macroeconomic mix, 52–61, 75, 206
  Consumer Protection Division of OPA, 59–60
  containing financial power abuse, 54–55
  containing upwards spiral, 1940, 56–61
  Galbraith on spirals, 57–61
  General Maximum Price Regulation, 57–58
  Hold the Line order, 59
  Office of Price Administration, 57–61
  reversal of downward spiral, 53–56
  stemming of banking crisis, 53–54
  wage and price fixing, 55–56
  overview of, 51–52
Truman's confrontations/rhetorical restraints, 52, 61–67
  early form of stagflation, 64–65
  overview of, 61–62
  rail workers' union, 63
  steel industry, 66, 67
  transition from wartime controls, 62–64
  undermining of wage-price stability, 65–66
  United Mine Workers, 64
  United Steelworkers Union, 62–63
  wartime challenges and judicial limits, 67
Keynesian order, intellectual conversion of, 77–108
  conclusions, 107–108
  context of, 105–107
    ideational/institutional, 106–107
    public opinion, 105–106
    social, 105

Index 251

Johnson administration, wage-price guideline displacement, 93–105
  abandonment of guideposts, 97–99
  airline dispute, 96
  break from incomes policies toward fiscal policy, 94–96
  communicative rhetoric, 96
  conclusions, 108
  fiscal crisis, 1965/66, 100–105
  fiscal stimulus, 94
  and mandatory wage-price controls, 99–100
  Neoclassical displacement of guideposts, 97–100
  overview of, 93–94
  and steel industry, 94–96
Kennedy administration, incomes policy displacement, 84–93
  auto industry wage-price restraint, 86–87
  avoidance of recession, 90–93
  communicative rhetoric, 83–84, 90, 92–93, 107
  conclusions, 107–108
  devaluation of dollar, 84–85
  growth, 85–86
  incomes policies, 86–88
  overview of, 84
  steel crisis, 1962, 87–90
  tax cuts, 87–88, 92–93
  wage-price guideposts, 84–87
Neoclassical synthesis and fiscal fine tuning, 78–84
  and Institutional Keynesianism, 78, 80–81
  and Neoclassical Keynesianism, 80, 81–84
  and Samuelson-Solow analysis, 81–82
  overview of, 77–78
  Red Scare influence on, 78–79
Keynesian order, misplaced certainty, 109–132, 207n6
  Carter administration stagflation, 110, 123–127
  anti-inflation policies, 125–127
  conclusions of, 131
  overview of, 110, 123
  promoting recovery, 124–125
  conclusions, 131–132
  context of, 110, 128–131
  institutional, 128–129
  public influence on, 128
  societal, 129–131
  Ford administration stagflation, 119–123
  anti-inflation policies, 119–121
  establishment of Council on Wage and Price Stability, 120
  fiscal stimulus, 122–123
  incomes policies as unacceptable, 120
  overview of, 110, 119
  recovery promotion, 121–123
  tax cuts, 121–122
  unemployment rates, 121, 122
  wage-price controls as unacceptable, 120
  Whip Inflation Now program, 120–121, 131
  Nixon administration stagflation, 110–119
  aversion to fiscal guidelines, 111
  business/institutional call for wage-price restraint, 112–113
  gradualism, 111–116
  move toward incomes policies, 113–116
  overview of, 110–111
  steel industry, 114, 115
  Nixon administration stagflation, New Economic Policy, 116–119, 131
  inception of New Economic Policy, 116–117
  opposition to freezing by labor, 117–118
  overview of, 110, 111
  and Pay Board, 117–118
  and Phase II guidelines, 117–118, 129–130
  and Phase III guidelines, 118
  and Phase IV gradual decontrol, 118–119
  and Price Commission, 117, 118
  overview of, 109–110
Kirkland, Lane, 143
Knightian view, 207n6
Knox, Philander, 32–33

Korean War
  inflation during, 103
  overdetermination of price stability during, 67n64
Krug, Julius A., 64
Krugman, Paul, on narrowing economic visions, 157n4

labor policy
  coal strike, 1902, 25, 30, 32
  Kahn on, 143
  and limits on market power, 139–142
  under Nixon, 117–118
  and PATCO strike, 136, 140–141
  under Reagan, 136, 139–142, 141n19
  steel industry (see steel industry)
  and T. Jefferson, 51
  under T. Roosevelt, 30, 32
  under Truman, 65–66
  and Volcker, 142–148
  Volcker on restraint of abuses of labor power, 143–144
Lamont, Thomas, 44
Lance, Bert, 127
Latin American debt crisis, 149–150, 156, 162
Lehman Brothers, 150, 200
Lever Act, 37–38, 39
Levitt, Arthur, 173, 175
Lewis, John, 64
Lewis, John L., 39
liberalism
  classical, of Jefferson, 29
  and domestic overconfidence, 9
  on effects of market power on interests, 8
libertarianism, 135
Long Term Capital Management, 172, 178
Louvre Accord (1987), 151, 156
Lucas, Robert, 83, 165
Luckmann, Thomas, 15

macroeconomics
  under Carter, 124n66, 124–125
  constructivists on trade-offs, 10n20
  and intellectual conversion, 5, 21–22

macro-morality, 135
macropurdential regulation, and Obama, 197–198
Mahoney, James, 11n24, 11n25, 12, 13, 14, 16
Malaysia, financial crisis in, 171–172
managed liabilities, 146
Mankiw, N. Gregory, 165, 166
markets
  bubbles, 4
  Galbraith on market expectations, 80–81
  Galbraith on market structures, 81
  Greenspan on bubbles, 4
  and Office of Price Administration, 60–61
  and risk-taking during Global Financial Crisis, 187–188
Marshall, Ray, 125
Martin, Edmund, 95
Martin, William M., 74, 112
Maxon, Lou, 58
McCracken, Paul, 112, 112n4, 114
McDonald, David, 69, 86–87, 89, 90
McDonough, Bill, 172
McKinley, William, 31
Meany, George, 91, 105, 117–118
Meese, Ed, 137
Mellon, Andrew W., 40, 45
mercantilist, Hamilton as, 29
Mexican Peso Crisis, 23, 162, 172, 176
Meyer, Lawrence, 171n55
micro-morality, 137–138
Miller, Adolph, 41
Miller, G. William, 126, 127, 130
mining industry, 39–40
Minsky, Hyman, 4
misplaced certainty, 5, 17, 22–24, 25
  and Global Financial Crisis, 187–191
  historical development of, 6
  and iterative character of crisis-driven change, 23–24
  and restraint, 23
  and risk taking, 22–23
  See also Keynesian order, misplaced certainty
Mitchell, Charles E., 43
Mitchell, James, 69–70, 72

monetary policy
  and austerity of Federal Reserve, 126, 127
  and Federal Reserve Board of Governors, 60n33
  and FOMC, 145
  Friedman on hide tide of, 40
  and Global Financial Crisis, 183–184, 187
    bubbles, 187
    expansionary policy, 181–182, 200
    forward guidance approach, 200
    risk management, 184, 187, 200
    Taylor rule, 183–184, 187
  and limits of monetary power, 181n4
  and Neoliberal order, 144–146, 147, 152–153
    Asian crises, 171–172
    asset-price bubbles, 170–171, 173
    containment of asset-price pressures, 170–173
    deregulation, 173–177
    end of monetarism, 148–149
    foreign economic crises, 171–173
    inflation-employment balance, 169–170
    overview of, 168–169
  postwar monetary stability, 61
  Stein on monetary tightening, 112
  See also Taylor rule
money
  quantity theory of, 44–45
  velocity of, 144n33
Morgan, J.P., 30, 32–34, 54
Mullins, David, 166

Nader, Ralph, 105
National Association of Manufacturers (NAM), 65–66
National Commission on Productivity, 113–114
National Credit Corporation, 45
National Recovery Administration (NRA), 55, 75
Neoclassical Keynesianism, 21
  and fine tuning acumen, 22–23
  redefinition of, 79

Neoclassical Synthesis (1960s), 11, 20–21, 205–206
Neoliberal order
  conclusions of, 206
  construction of, 135–156
    Black Monday (1987) crash, 153
    conclusions of, 155–156
    and consumer credit, 146
    and cooperative currency interventions, 150–151
    and domestic banking crisis, 149–150
    end of monetarism, 148–149
    and financial restraint policy, 154
    and incomes policies, 143–144
    and initial Neoliberalism of Volcker, 142–148
    and institutional agenda of Greenspan, 152–155
    and iterative neoliberalism of Volcker, 148–152
    and monetarist policy, 144–146, 147, 152–153
    and near-default of Mexico, 149–150
    overview of, 135–137, 142
    and Reagan, 137–142, 148, 206
    and restraint of labor power abuses, 143–144
    and wage-/asset-price accommodation, 142–152
  intellectual conversion of, 157–178
    abandonment of communicative engagement, 161–162
    and Asian crises, 171–172
    and asset-price containment, 170–173
    and asset-price bubbles, 170–171, 173
    and balancing of congressional extremes, 162
    and Clinton, 158–164
    conclusions, 177–178
    and deficit, 159–160
    and deregulation, 169, 173–177
    and dismantling of wage/price guidelines, 210
    and displacement and fine-tuning, 164–168

Neoliberal order (*cont.*)
   and exemption of derivatives from regulation, 174
   and foreign economic crises, 171–173
   and fraud prevention, 174
   and inflation-unemployment trade-off, 165, 168, 169–170
   and Mexican crisis, 162
   and New Classicalism, 164–165
   overview of, 157–158, 168–169
   and public credibility, 160
   and Putting People First agenda, 158
   and statist/freemarket excesses, 163–164
   and Taylor rule, 166, 167
   three debates on, 168–177
   and tightening by Greenspan, 160–161
   and voluntary disclosure by investment banks, 175
   and wage-price setting, 166
  rise and fall of, 3, 26, 27t1.2
New Classical economists, 20–21
New Classicalism, 164–165
New Economic Policy (NEP), 110
  inception of New Economic Policy, 116–117
  Nixon's stagflation, 116–119, 131
  opposition to freezing by labor, 117–118
  overview of, 110, 111
  and Pay Board, 117–118
  and Phase II guidelines, 117–118, 129–130
  and Phase III guidelines, 118
  and Phase IV gradual decontrol, 118–119
  and Price Commission, 117, 118
New Economics, 22–23
  defining, 81n12
New Freedom, 25
*The New Industrial State* (Galbraith), 81, 83
New Inflation, and Eisenhower, 52, 68–73, 75
  and auto industry, 69–70
  and communicative rhetoric of Eisenhower, 70
  congressional view on administrative pricing, 70–71
  construction of, 68–71
  overview of, 68
  and steel industry, 69–71
  and steel strike, 1959, 71–73
New Keynesianism, 20–21
  overrating of acumen in find tuning of, 22–23
  and Taylor rule, 21, 157
  *See also* Blinder, Alan; Yellen, Janet
New Nationalism, 30
Nixon, Richard (as vice president)
  and dismantling of wage and price guidelines, 210
  and economic downturn, 1960, 73–74
Nixon, Richard/administration
  *Economic Report* under, 114–115
  and stagflation, 116–119, 131
  *See also* New Economic Policy (NEP)
Norman, Montagu, 42, 54n8
North American Free Trade Agreement (NAFTA), 162

Obama, Barack/administration
  and administration stress tests, 201
  antitrust issues under, 26, 198, 199
  on executive compensation, 193
  and fast thinking principled reform, 192–193
  and fiscal grounds/policy, 192
  and fiscal stimulus, 192, 201
  four-point domestic agenda of, 197–199
    failed firm liquidation/crisis management, 197, 199
    financial product transparency/simplicity, 197, 198
    financial/shadow banking system regulation, 197, 198
    macropurdential regulation/systemic risk, 197–198
  Galbraith on market structures and OPA, 60–61
  restrained rhetoric of, 194
  rhetorical and regulatory accommodation, 192–196
  TARP under, 201

# Index

on "too big to fail," 199
and utilitarianism
  recovery, 180, 194
  restraints, 194–195
  rhetoric, 199–200
  slow thinking inhibitions, 193–195, 200–202
Odell, John, 210
Office of Economic Stabilization, 58
Office of Price Administration (OPA)
  Consumer Protection Division, 59–60
  and F.D. Roosevelt, 57–61, 136
  Home Front Pledge campaign, 60
  successes of, 60–61
  War Price and Rationing Boards, 60
Office of Price Stabilization (OPS), 62, 67
Okun, Arthur, 102–103, 104, 105
Omnibus Budget Reconciliation Act (1990), 164
O'Neill, Paul, 182
order development, stages of, 205–206
  institutional framework, 205
  intellectual framework, 205–206
  misplaced confidence, 206
Organization of Petroleum Exporting Countries (OPEC), 129, 129n87
overconfidence. *See* misplaced certainty

Palmer, A. Mitchell, 38n31, 39, 40
Panetta, Leon, 164
Panic of 1893, 31
paradigmatic debates, 7, 8
  overview of, 6, 7
PATCO, 136, 140–141, 140n14, 165
Paulson, Henry M., 189n33
Pay Board, 117–118
Penn Square bank collapse, 149
Perkins, Francis, 55
Phelps Dodge, 141
Philippines, financial crisis in, 171–172
Philips curve trade-off, 19, 20, 205–206
  constructivists on, 10n20
  Friedman on, 82–83
  and growth-inflation balance, 16–17
  and intellectual conversion, 5, 21
  misplaced certainty in, 22–23

Neoclassical Keynesians on, 21, 81–83
Pierson, Paul, 12, 208
Plaza Accord (1985), 151, 156
policy implications, 27–28
  pragmatic reform/technocratic expertise, 211–212
policy orders, staged model of
  comparisons among, 17t1.1
  historical development of model, 5–6
  overview of, 5–6
  *See also* intellectual conversion; misplaced certainty; principled construction
political development theory, 208
political time, defining, 3n2
populism
  Geithner on excess of, 162, 193–194
  intellectual anti-populism, 78–79
Populist movement, 30, 31
power- *vs.* value-distributional tensions, 15
pragmatic paradox, 27–28, 207, 212
Price Commission, 117, 118
price controls
  under F.D. Roosevelt, 18–19
  under W. Wilson, 37–38
principled construction, 5, 16, 17–20, 25
  historical development of, 5
principled reform, Emanuel on, 179, 180, 201
principled *vs.* causal beliefs, 15, 16
Professional Association of Air Traffic Controllers (PATCO), 136, 140–141, 140n14, 165
Progressive order
  and asset price stability, 41–42
  collapse of, 30, 40–46
    asset price stability, 41–42
    and election of 1932, 46
    exchange rate stability, 41, 42
    and Federal Reserve, 41–44
    and Great Crash of 1929, 44–45
    and Hoover, 45–46
    and regulation and speculative credit, 42–44
  conclusions, 47–48, 206
  construction under T. Roosevelt, 30, 31–35, 206

Progressive order (*cont.*)
  agriculture policy/railroad regulation, 30, 32–33
  capital policy, 30, 33–34
  labor policy, 30, 32
  and New Nationalism *vs.* New Freedom, 34–35
  and Panic of 1893, 31
  and Square Deal, 25, 31, 33
  intellectual conversion under W. Wilson, 25, 30, 35–40, 206
    antitrust issues, 38–40
    and disaggregation of power in initial Federal Reserve, 36
    New Nationalism-styled stress on regulation, 36–38
    tariff issues, 35–36
  rise and fall, overview, 3, 25, 27t1.2
  stages of, overview, 30
Proxmire, William, 117–118
Public Worlds Administration (PWA), 55
Putting People First, 158

quantitative easing, 192, 201
quantity theory of money, 44–45

Rabin, Yitzhak, 163
Railroad Administration, 39
railroads
  regulation under Hepburn Act, 25, 30, 32–33
  strike under Truman, 63
Rajan, Raghuram, 185–186
rationalist assumptions, and paradigmatic/institutionalist debates, 6–7
Reagan, Ronald/administration
  antitrust issues under, 19
  capital gains under, 138–139, 156
  communicative rhetoric of, 136, 140
  on compromise, 138n7
  and construction of Neoliberal order, 137–142, 206
  conclusions of, 155
  easing of restraints on capital, 139
  fiscal policy, 138–139
  labor policy, 136, 139–142, 141n19
  limits on market power of labor, 139–142
  micro-morality viewpoint of, 135, 137–138
  overview of, 135–137
  regulatory policy, 139–142
  on government as the problem, 135
  and libertarianism, 19
  reaction to Volcker's initial neoliberalism, 148
  similarities to/differences from F.D. Roosevelt, 135–137
  and system for tracking labor strikes, 141n19
  taxation under, 138–139, 147, 156
realists
  and effects of market power on interests, 8
  limitations on hegemonic perspective of, 8–9
recessions
  of 1937, 179
  of 1949, 64–65
  of 1954, 68–69
  of 1981–1982, 143
  Friedman on, 39–40
  *See also* Great Depression
Reconstruction Finance Corporation (RFC), 45
Redford, William, 38
Red Scare, 78–79
Reedy, George, 95
Reeves, Richard, 91n49
Regan, Donald, 148, 149, 150n60, 151
Regulation Q interest rate controls, 139
Regulations and Purchasing Review Board, 113–114
Reinhart, Carmen, 4
Reserve Bank of Australia (RBA), 13, 14
Reuss, Henry, 98
Reuther, Walter, 69, 86–87
Revenue Act (1913), 25, 35
risk management, during Global Financial Crisis, 184, 187, 200
Rogoff, Kenneth, 4
Romer, Christina, 196

Roosevelt, Franklin D./
    administration, 51
  banking crisis, stemming of, 53–54
  collective bargaining under, 55
  communicative rhetoric of, 51–52,
      75, 136
  and construction of Keynesian order,
      52–61, 75, 206
    and Consumer Protection Division
        of OPA, 59–60
    containing upwards spiral,
        1940, 56–61
    and containment of financial
        power abuse, 54–55
    Galbraith on, 57–61
    and General Maximum Price
        Regulation, 57–58
    and Hold the Line order, 59
    and Office of Price
        Administration, 57–61
    reversal of downward spiral, 53–56
    and stemming of banking
        crisis, 53–54
    unemployment, 56, 59
    and wage and price fixing, 55–56
  deficit under, 56
  devaluation of dollar under, 54
  and election of 1932, 46
  and gold standard, 54–55, 75
  inflation under, 54–55
  macro-morality views of, 135
  on price controls, 18–19
  similarities to/differences from
      Reagan, 135–137
Roosevelt, Theodore/
    administration, 29
  communicative rhetorical style of, 35
  construction of Progressive order
      under, 30, 31–35, 206
    agriculture policy/railroad
        regulation, 30, 32–33
    capital policy, 30, 33–34
    labor policy, 30, 32
    and New Nationalism vs. New
        Freedom, 34–35
    and Panic of 1893, 31
    and Square Deal, 25, 31, 33
  and Panic of 1893, 31
  and principled construction of a
      regulatory order, 25

Ross, Andrew, 15
Rostow, Walt W., 86
Rowen, Hobart, 105n104, 119
Rubin, Robert
  on bail-outs, 176
  and concept release, 175
  on derivatives, 11n25, 173–174
  and Korean Crisis, 172
  on Panetta, 164
  on populist excess, 162
Ruggie, John G., 10
Russia, financial crisis in, 172, 178
Ryerson, Edward L., 67

Samuelson, Paul, 21, 78, 79,
    83n19, 166
Sarbanes-Oxley Act (2002), 23
Sargent, Thomas, 83
Schapiro, Mary, 198
Schlesinger, Arthur, Jr., 37, 40, 79
Schmidt, Helmut, 122, 211
Schmidt, Vivien, 14–16
Schultze, Charles, 109
  on anti-inflation program of Carter,
      124, 126
  aversion to fiscal guidelines, 111
  on credit controls, 146n43
  on freezes, 116
  on monetarist policy, 145
  resignation attempt by, 118
Schwartz, Anna J., 39–40,
    42n43, 44
Securities and Exchange Commission
    (SEC), 173, 174–175
securitization market, 190n37
September 11 terrorist attacks on
    US, 182
shadow banking system, 197, 198
shared values, 15
Sherman Anti-trust Act, 38,
    38n31
Sherman Silver Purchase Act, 31
Shiller, Robert, 4, 186
Shultz, George, 112
Siemiller, Roy, 96
Sikkink, Kathryn, 10 11n25, 208
Silk, Leonard, 105n104
Simon, William E., 119, 121
Snyder, John, 65
Social Darwinism, 80

social psychological
    institutionalist model
  ideational stability/instability across
      time, 206, 207–209
  overview of, 4–5, 7–8
  policy implications, 207, 211–212
  systemic implications, 206–207,
      209–211
  *See also* construction; intellectual
      conversion; misplaced certainty
Solomon, Anthony, 145
Solow, Robert, 21, 83n19
  on Galbraith, 83
  on guideposts, 97n70, 98
  on setting of wages and prices, 166
Sorensen, Ted, 92
South Korea, debt crisis in, 172
Sproul, Allen, 85
Square Deal, 25, 31, 33
stability, paradox of, ix, 3, 6–7, 205
stagflation
  under Carter, 110, 123–127
  under Ford, 119–123
  under Nixon, 110–119
  and Truman, 64–65
  *See also* great Stagflation of 1970s
steel industry
  under Carter, 128–129
  under Eisenhower, 69–73
  labor policy, 88, 88n36, 91n49,
      91–92, 94–96, 128–129
  and New Inflation, 69–73
  under Truman, 66, 67
  United Steelworkers, 62–63, 69–70,
      128–129
  U.S. Steel, 95, 104, 114, 115
Stein, Herbert
  on austerity, 119–120
  on depreciation of the dollar, 130
  on freezes, 116, 118
  on gradualism, 115
  on Keynesianism, 79–80
  on monetary tightening, 112
Stigler, George, 66
stimulus. *See* fiscal stimulus
Stockman, David, 138n7, 141
Strauss, Robert, 125
Strong, Benjamin
  and asset-price bubbles, 41
  on Federal Reserve System, 29
  interest rate cut by, 41

Subcommittee on International
    Exchange and Payments,
    115–116
subprime bubble, 9, 190
subprime securitizations, 190n37
Summers, Lawrence
  on deriviatives, 173
  and overconfidence, 185–186
  on Peso crisis, 176
  and statutory deadline for
      TARP, 196
  on utilitarianism, 193
  on utilitarian recovery, 180
supply-side economics, on investment
    *vs.* consumption, 139
Supreme Court
  and National Recovery
      Administration, 55
  and steel industry, 67
  and United Mine Workers, 64
swap purchases, 198

Taft, William H., 34
Taft-Hartley, 72
tariffs, 35–36
TARP. *See* Troubled Asset Relief
    Program
Tarshis, Lorie, 79
Taussig, Frank, 37–38
taxation
  under Ford, cuts, 121–122
  under G.W. Bush, marginal cuts,
      182–183
  Heller on cuts, 87n31
  under J.F. Kennedy, cuts, 93
  under Johnson, increase, 101–102
  Keynesian preference for targeted
      cuts, 139
  progressive, 35–36
  under Reagan, cuts/increases,
      138–139, 147, 156
  and steel crisis, 1962, 87–88,
      92–93
Tax-Based Incomes Policies (TIPs), 125
Tax Equity and Fiscal Responsibility
    Act (1982), 147, 147n50
Taylor, John, 167n39
Taylor rule, 5, 19, 20, 205–206
  deviation from when financial crises
      hit, 187
  and fine-tuning of interest rates, 157

# Index

and Global Financial Crisis, 183–184
and growth-inflation balance, 16–17
misplaced certainty in, 22–23
and New Keynesianism, 21, 166
overview of, 167n39
and unemployment-inflation balance, 167
Yellen on, 167
technocratic governance, 79
Teeters, Nancy, 148
Tempalski, Jerry, 147n50
Tequila Effect, 162
Thailand, financial crisis in, 171–172
Thelen, Kathleen, 11n25, 12, 13, 16
Theobald, Thomas, 152
theoretical implications, 27
3-6-3 rule, 139
Tobin, James, 87–88
"too big to fail" problem, 199, 201
Trading with the Enemy Act (1917), 99
traumatized workers, 169–170
Trigger Price Mechanism (TPM), 129n86
Tripartite Agreement (1936), 54–55
Troubled Asset Relief Program (TARP)
  under Bush, 192, 192n43
  compensation to TARP-recipient firms, 193, 194n52
  and executive compensation, 194–195
  under Obama, 201
  statutory deadline for, 196
Truman, Harry/administration, 63n43
  communicative-styled rhetoric of, 62, 63
  confrontations/rhetorical restraints, 52, 61–67
  and early form of stagflation, 64–65
  incomes policies under, 65
  labor policy under, 65–66
  overview of, 61–62
  and railroad industry, 63
  and steel industry, 66, 67
  transition from wartime controls under, 62–64
  undermining of wage-price stability under, 65–66
  and United Mine Workers, 64
  and United Steelworkers Union, 62–63
  wage-price spirals under, 64–65
  wartime challenges/judicial limits under, 67
trust in government
  during Carter administration, 128
  during Johnson administration, 105
TWA, 141

uncertainty, defining, 207n6
Underwood Tariff, 35
unemployment
  under Eisenhower, 74
  under F.D. Roosevelt, 56, 59
  under Ford, 121, 122
  under J.F. Kennedy, 161
  Keynes on, 56
  natural rate of, 161
  and Neoliberal order, 165, 168, 169–170
  and Panic of 1893, 31
  *See also* Philips curve; Taylor rule
United Auto Workers (UAW), 69, 86–87, 140–141
United Mine Workers (UMW), 39–40, 64
United Steelworkers (USW), 62–63, 69–70, 128–129
U.S. Steel, 95, 104, 114, 115
utilitarian recovery
  Geithner on, 180, 193–194
  Obama on, 180, 194

values, shared, 15
value- *vs.* power-distributional tensions, 15
Vietnam War
  and Carter, 126–127
  duplicity of Johnson in, 105n104
  funding under Johnson, 94, 100–101
  as undermining national confidence, 136
Volcker, Paul
  appointed to Federal Reserve, 123, 127
  brief resignation from Federal Reserve, 151
  factors leading to departure from Federal Reserve, 151–152
  on incomes policies, 109

Volcker, Paul (*cont.*)
  initial Neoliberalism of, 142–148
    blowback from Reagan administration, 148
    consumer credit, 146
    incomes policies, 143–144
    monetarist approach of, 144–146, 147
    restraint of continued abuses of labor power, 143–144
  iterative Neoliberalism of, 148–152
    cooperative currency interventions, 150–151
    domestic banking crisis, 149–150
    end of monetarism, 148–149
    near-default of Mexico, 149–150
    policy shift at Federal Reserve under, 130–131
  on psychological nature of currency trends, 143n25
  on recovery/reform tension, 201–202
  tenure of, 151n62
  on velocity of money, 144n33
  and wage-price regulation, 114
  and wage-price spirals, 130–131, 142, 143–144, 149, 155

wage-price issues
  and auto industry wage-price restraint, 86–87
  codes to enable wage and price fixing, 55–56
  dismantling of guidelines, 210
  displacement of guidelines by fiscal fine tuning, 93–105
  *Economic Report* on (*see Economic Report*)
  under F.D. Roosevelt, 53–56
  under Ford, 120
  Greenspan on, 169
  guideposts (*see* guideposts, wage-price)
  under J.F. Kennedy, 84–87
  under Johnson, 99–100
  Keynes on, 51, 53
  mandatory, 89n37, 99–100
  misplaced focus on wage-price inflation, 188–189
  Neoliberal wage-price setting, 166

  under Nixon, 112–113, 114, 210
  pressures leading to collapse of Keynesian order, 9
  restraint and market expectations, 80–81
  role of labor/capital in undermining stability, 65–66
  Samuelson on setting of wages and prices, 166
  social basis for restraint, 81
  spirals (*see* wage-price spirals)
  under Truman, 65–66
  and Volcker, 114
wage-price spirals
  and Bernanke, 189
  under Carter, 123, 124n69, 124–125
  efforts to contain, 51–52, 53, 56–61
  under F.D. Roosevelt, 75
  and Global Financial Crisis, viii
  and Greenspan, 169
  under J.F. Kennedy, 89, 90
  labor power as leading to, 18, 26
  market power as leading to, 107
  overconfidence as leading to, 3, 9
  public opinion on blame for, 66
  reversal of downward, 53–56
  and rising oil prices, vii
  and steel industry, 89, 90
  under Truman, 64–65
  and Volcker, 130–131, 142, 143–144, 149, 155
  and Yellen, 189
Wage Stabilization Board (WSB), 67
Wagner, Richard, 91
Wagner Act, 55
War Labor Board (LB), 58, 59
War Price and Rationing Boards of OPA, 60
Watergate scandal, 110, 119, 126–127, 136
Weber, Arnold, 112–113
Wendt, Alexander, 10, 21, 207–208
Whip Inflation Now (WIN) program, 120–121, 131
Wilson, Charles, 66
Wilson, Woodrow, 29
  antitrust issues under, 38–40
  disaggregation of power in initial Federal Reserve under, 36

intellectual conversion of Progressive order under, 30, 35–40, 206
New Freedom of, 25, 34–35
New Nationalism-styled stress on regulation under, 36–38
price controls under, 37–38
rhetorical style of, 35
tariff issue under, 35–36
Wirtz, Willard, 96
Woodward, Bob, 170
World War II, inflation during, 59, 103

Yellen, Janet
appointment to Federal Reserve Board, 157
on federal funds rate levels, 167–168
on job security, 170
on macropurdential regulatory agenda, 197
and market power, 189
on market power, 189n36
on Taylor rule, 167, 167n39, 177, 189n36

Lightning Source UK Ltd.
Milton Keynes UK
UKHW020430250822
407747UK00008B/71